The *Doctor Who* Franchise

ALSO BY LYNNETTE PORTER

*Tarnished Heroes, Charming Villains and
Modern Monsters: Science Fiction in Shades of Gray
on 21st Century Television* (McFarland, 2010)

EDITED BY LYNNETTE PORTER

*Sherlock Holmes for the 21st Century:
Essays on New Adaptations* (McFarland, 2012)

The *Doctor Who* Franchise
American Influence, Fan Culture and the Spinoffs

LYNNETTE PORTER

McFarland & Company, Inc., Publishers
Jefferson, North Carolina, and London

LIBRARY OF CONGRESS CATALOGUING-IN-PUBLICATION DATA

Porter, Lynnette, 1957–
    The Doctor Who franchise : American influence, fan culture and the spinoffs / Lynnette Porter.
        p.   cm.
    Includes bibliographical references and index.

    ISBN 978-0-7864-6556-9
    softcover : acid free paper ∞

    1. Doctor Who (Television program : 1963–1989)   2. Doctor Who (Television program : 2005–)   3. Torchwood (Television program)   4. Sarah Jane Adventures (Television program)   5. Television programs—Great Britain.   6. Great Britain—Civilization—American influences.   I. Title.
PN1992.77.D6275P67   2012
791.4575—dc23   2012035864

BRITISH LIBRARY CATALOGUING DATA ARE AVAILABLE

© 2012 Lynnette Porter. All rights reserved

No part of this book may be reproduced or transmitted in any form or by any means, electronic or mechanical, including photocopying or recording, or by any information storage and retrieval system, without permission in writing from the publisher.

On the cover: Promotional artwork for the sixth series of *Doctor Who*, 2010–2011. From left: Karen Gillan, Matt Smith and Arthur Darvill (BBC/Photofest).

Manufactured in the United States of America

McFarland & Company, Inc., Publishers
  Box 611, Jefferson, North Carolina 28640
    www.mcfarlandpub.com

Table of Contents

Acknowledgments vi
Introduction 1

1. The Culture of *Doctor Who* 9
2. Doing Business with the U.S. 37
3. The "Americanization" of British Television 59
4. Intertextuality and the Doctor 78
5. Intertextuality, Captain Jack, and the Future of *Torchwood* 89
6. "You Don't Kill Sarah Jane!" 119
7. Tweet Success: Social Media and Television Marketing 132
8. Friday Is Fez Day: The Popularity of Conventions 148
9. The Cosmos Is Their Oyster 164

Bibliography 179
Index 189

Acknowledgments

I thank the many people who talked with me about *Doctor Who, Torchwood,* and *The Sarah Jane Adventures* as I researched and wrote this book. Special thanks to *Torchwood* actor Kai Owen; Gillian Hanhart, Westminster Reference Library, London; Lewis Swan and Helen Thomas, Brit Movie Tours; Jarrod Cooper, Hurricane Who; and Jennifer Adams Kelly, Chicago TARDIS, for lengthy interviews. I appreciate your time and enthusiasm. Thanks, too, to the kind and generous volunteers, staff, and fans at Gallifrey One, San Diego Comic-Con, Wizard World, Chicago TARDIS, and Hurricane Who, who made my fan experience most memorable.

I must recognize and thank yet again my research assistant, Kirsten Peterson, who helped me keep tabs on media reports about the *Doctor Who* franchise and read many drafts of these chapters. Thank you, Kirsten, for all your help.

A Doctor's adventures through time and space would not be worthwhile without companions, and I am blessed with the best: Bart, Nancy, Heather, and Elvis. As always, I dedicate this book to you.

Introduction

During my sabbatical in Christchurch, New Zealand, in early 2007, I presented a seminar about "apocalyptic television" and series currently in vogue in the U.S. One series in which the protagonist was dealing with the aftermath of a genocidal war was the newly re-launched *Doctor Who* featuring the Ninth Doctor (Christopher Eccleston). At that time he was introduced as the lone Time Lord surviving a war-to-end-all-wars with the Daleks, and I commented on U.S. fans' preoccupation with homeland security in the aftermath of the World Trade Center attacks in 2001. (I also discussed other then-popular series such as *24* and *Jericho,* which were perceived as "purely American" series.)

During the Q&A session following my presentation, an indignant student questioned my use of *Doctor Who* in a discussion of science fiction (SF) series popular in the U.S. "How can you co-opt *Doctor Who*?" he asked. "That's a British series, and Americans just don't get it." Several students agreed and, indeed, seemed discontented with an American interpretation of the venerable SF series. Commonwealth countries, including New Zealand, apparently can rightly lay claim to the Doctor, but, according to these fans, he will always be a visitor in the U.S., not part of mainstream culture. Fundamental cultural differences, not only regarding the Doctor but the perceived "national personality," differentiate Americans and Brits.

In light of the introduction of "American" Captain Jack Harkness in the 2005 episodes "The Empty Child" and "The Doctor Dances," perhaps these students have a valid point. Although the former Time Agent/present con man currently going by the name of an American officer really is not from the U.S., the "American" personality traits given in these episodes to Captain Jack provide a clear contrast between him and the Doctor. Jack is brash, loud, swaggering, and supremely confident — at least until the Doctor points out the lack of humanity in his self-interest. (Jack's con inadvertently releases a type of plague on humanity, beginning with an innocent boy in wartime

London.) The Doctor's pro-Britain speeches exalting the resilience and dedication of ordinary British citizens during World War II also separates him from Jack, who seems to have little understanding of the world in which he lives beyond its immediate impact on himself. To confuse matters further, both the Doctor and Jack are competing for Rose Tyler's attention, although the Doctor correctly surmises that Jack is also interested in the him. In these and other ways, Jack's personality and his lacking sense of history make him seem different from Rose and the Doctor.

Even years later (in TV time), when Jack becomes the leader of Torchwood (and lead in *Torchwood*), the Cardiff-based series illustrates Jack's differences from the rest of the local population. His outfit is vintage middle America with remnants of his service in World War II. His generalized American accent also marks him as "other." Despite Jack's living in the U.K. for hundreds of years, he still looks, sounds, and acts "American."

Jack will always be an outsider, despite his long friendship with the Doctor and his association with Torchwood. His experience, framed in this description, is similar to the way U.S. fans are perceived by many Commonwealth fans and critics. *Doctor Who* is very much a part of British, not American, television history and, more recently, mainstream popular culture. Welsh *Torchwood* asserts that it is not English, but neither is it American. The *Doctor Who* franchise's roots are firmly planted in the U.K. But what does that mean to American fans?

In this book I apply an "American" concept of the franchise when I refer to the post–2005 *Doctor Who* and its most recent spinoffs, *Torchwood* and *The Sarah Jane Adventures*. The BBC's marketing strategy increasingly includes the U.S. through BBC Worldwide production (e.g., *Dancing with the Stars, So You Think You Can Dance, X Factor*) and BBC America's programming (e.g., SF series including *Doctor Who, Torchwood, Being Human, Bedlam,* and *The Fades,* as well as non-SF series like *Top Gear*). In the past few years, the *Who* franchise has begun a concerted effort to attract greater attention in America. As the U.S. market for *Doctor Who* grows and becomes more vocal, additional programming and special events will take place in the U.S., just as they have during a pivotal time in *Who* history.

Coming to America

Much of *Torchwood*'s development of the 2011 fourth season, *Miracle Day,* and the future direction of *Doctor Who* changed when showrunner Russell T Davies decided to live in the U.S. In 2009 the duo behind the re-imagined *Doctor Who,* Davies and Julie Gardner, relocated to Los Angeles. The balance of power for the BBC's most lucrative franchise shifted from Davies to *Doctor Who*'s next showrunner, Steven Moffat. As Moffat steered *Doctor Who* into innovative if controversial SF territory in the U.K., the Doctor developed a greater presence in the U.S., in part because of BBC Worldwide's and BBC America's marketing strategies.

At a gathering of *Who* fans in Orlando, Florida, in early December 2010, BBC Worldwide's Andrew Beach, the man responsible for gathering and identifying artifacts for the about-to-be-launched Doctor Who Experience, noted that the BBC long has wanted a U.S.-based drama, and *Torchwood* seemed poised to make that dream come true (Porter, "Doctor Who"). More recently, the BBC has collaborated with other U.S. cable networks (e.g., in 2011-12, with HBO, as well as Flemish VRT, to produce *Parade's End*, a product practically guaranteeing that the star of the BBC's *Sherlock*, Benedict Cumberbatch, would become more widely known in the U.S.). Nevertheless, the BBC-Starz arrangement to develop *Torchwood* as a jointly produced, jointly re-launched television series was a groundbreaking collaboration that blended U.S. cable television sensibilities and money with the BBC's characters and built-in audience.

From LA, Davies and Gardner began pitching ideas for TV dramas to U.S. networks. With the surprising success of *Torchwood: Children of Earth* in July 2009, Davies' focus turned to a fourth season of the newly acclaimed show that was generating a lot of new fans' and TV critics' attention internationally. When Fox rejected a *Torchwood* TV pilot story in 2010, the series began looking for another backer — amid fan consternation at the direction the series might take if it became a U.S. instead of U.K. production. Eventually the BBC partnered with U.S. cable network Starz to produce *Torchwood: The New World*. By January 2011 it had been renamed *Miracle Day*, an international production that nonetheless seemed heavily influenced by American tastes and production methods.

Throughout late 2010 and into early January 2011 shooting, *Torchwood* casting news and interviews from returning stars John Barrowman (Captain Jack Harkness) and Eve Myles (Gwen Cooper) kept online entertainment and SF sites busy, and Barrowman's comment that another seven years of *Torchwood* were being planned got a lot of attention from fans eager to see more (Bendoris). As filming began in Los Angeles but quickly returned to South Wales, fans on both sides of the Atlantic gleefully posted online their candid photos and star sightings.

Davies told the press that he was proud to show off the Gower coast to a new global audience ("New Torchwood Series"), but he also noted that about ninety percent of *Miracle Day*'s filming locations were in the U.S. When Davies glibly commented that he might leave the series because he is growing tired of SF ("Torchwood Writer"; Berriman), news outlets quickly spread this interesting tidbit, and fans questioned whether Davies was afraid the *Torchwood* venture would not succeed or if he had now established himself in the U.S. and wanted to create new projects only in Hollywood. (Davies began developing a new Showtime series, *Cucumber,* in 2011 [Kasperowicz]. Any plans to work with Starz on another season of *Torchwood* became dependent on his availability away from the new series, which, ironically, was announced two days before *Miracle Day*'s U.S. premiere. When Davies returned to the U.K. in 2011, however, because of personal matters, apparently plans for U.S. series were scrapped, at least for the time being, and in 2012 Davies and Phil Ford developed a U.K. children's series.)

The BBC-Starz joint venture came under close scrutiny as *Torchwood* took on new shooting locations, cast members, and type of story *and* as the U.K. network and U.S. cable channel pioneered a new model for television production. *Torchwood*'s degree of success also underscores cultural differences between the U.K. and U.S. and the geographic, cultural, and expectational "boundaries" *Torchwood* tries to span. Post-*Miracle Day,* both Starz and the BBC, as well as critics and fans, began to re-evaluate *Torchwood,* a process that further delineated what was perceived as right or wrong, American or British, about the co-production. By late 2011, with no word forthcoming from Starz or the BBC about further episodes, fans — and even series' star John Barrowman — declared *Torchwood* "in limbo," while Gardner claimed "only time will tell" what will happen to the show (Roco). Without the strong backing of Starz — and its financing — *Torchwood* seemed less likely to happen. I analyze aspects of *Torchwood*'s new hybrid nature — and fan response to it — in several chapters.

Torchwood was not the only BBC production to begin its new season on American soil. The year 2010 also saw the Eleventh Doctor (Matt Smith) film the sixth season premiere, "The Impossible Astronaut," in the U.S. The Doctor's visit to Utah became especially notable because of Smith's visit to late night talk show host Craig Ferguson's program on November 17. This was Smith's first time on a Los Angeles-based talk show, although the actor previously had promoted *Doctor Who* in New York and Hollywood during a mini-tour of the country. Following Smith's appearance on Ferguson's talk show, in 2011 *Who* actors Karen Gillan (Amy Pond) and Alex Kingston (River Song) also chatted with the host to help promote the series.

Smith's *The Late Late Show* visit became controversial because last-minute licensing issues precluded the broadcast of a special opening number, in which Ferguson and a dancing troupe of guest aliens boogie to the *Doctor Who* theme while a hand puppet explains the series' premise. Smith even pops in for a brief cameo. Although this opener could not be shown during the interview's initial broadcast because the BBC had not approved it ahead of time, the musical number made its way to YouTube, where, by early January 2011, it had received nearly 417,000 hits; by May 2012, despite the video also being uploaded to many other sites, the original YouTube video site had recorded more than 851,300 views ("Craig Ferguson — The Lost 'Dr. Who' Cold Open").

The American promotion of *Doctor Who* and *Torchwood* goes far beyond filming locations or periodic visits to U.S. talk shows. Personal visits from the Doctor, Amy Pond, and Captain Jack Harkness, for example, make entertainment news headlines around the globe when the actors and their fans meet face to face in the U.S. San Diego Comic-Con is one of the best places to market upcoming SF shows to the masses, especially given Comic-Con's overwhelming number of attendees, amount of media coverage, and growing reputation as *the* place to unveil the Next Big Thing.

In 2009, *Who*'s Davies and Tenth Doctor David Tennant, flanked by *Torchwood*'s Barrowman, chatted to the press and fans at Comic-Con, and Davies strongly hinted that *Torchwood: The New World* might be a panel for Comic-Con 2011. Indeed it was, with fans standing in line for hours in order to enter the huge convention hall. Although the seating capacity was in the thousands, hundreds of unhappy fans were left standing in the California sunshine — *Torchwood* attracted a huge audience and entertained them during the hour-long session. The 2011 panel, led by an exuberant Barrowman, introduced the new *Torchwood* team — Mekhi Phifer (Rex Matheson) and Alexa Havins (Esther Drummond) — plus returning cast member Eve Myles and guest star Bill Pullman (Oswald Danes). Scriptwriter Jane Espenson, whose tweets endeared her to *Torchwood* fans throughout *Miracle Day*'s run, answered questions during the upbeat Q&A session. Barrowman also participated in a *TV Guide* "superheroes" session, and the cast signed autographs for fans lucky enough to win a lottery set up to ensure that everyone in the autograph line would actually be able to meet the actors.

The 2011 *Doctor Who* panel was even more highly prized, and the largest room at the convention center, Hall H, was filled to capacity long before the waiting crowd of Whovians could find a seat. Smith and Gillan pleased the crowd during the Q&A session, but they, as well as Barrowman, gave media interviews throughout the convention that further spread the word about upcoming episodes. That the Comic-Con response to *Torchwood* and *Doctor Who* was overwhelmingly positive and enthusiastic was obvious to convention attendees, press, and the networks sponsoring the programs. These personal appearances are only part of increased marketing in the U.S. Billboards, trailers shown in cinemas, and print advertisements further reminded U.S. audiences that the Doctor is in — and far cooler than his bow tie, fez, or Stetson.

The Franchise's Uncertain Future

For all the positive promotion of both *Torchwood* and *Doctor Who* between 2010 and 2011, the franchise has suffered setbacks. With the loss of Elisabeth Sladen (Sarah Jane Smith) in April 2011, *The Sarah Jane Adventures* came to a close. Episodes filmed in late 2010 finally were broadcast in the U.K. in late 2011. Although *Doctor Who* fans also mourned the loss of Nicholas Courtney (the Brigadier) in 2011 — and the last episode of the sixth season includes a poignant scene in which the Doctor learns of his old friend's death — Courtney's death did not have as significant an effect on the future of the franchise. With no desire by producers or the network to replace Sladen in the role she had played off and on for more than four decades, added to the fact that the "children" in this series had reached university age and were thus leaving the nest, the *Doctor Who* franchise lost *The Sarah Jane Adventures*.

With *Torchwood*'s post–*Miracle Day* return seeming less likely, or at least seriously delayed, the loss of Sladen and her series, and the BBC's economic woes that seemed destined to limit the Doctor's appearances to a handful of episodes during 2012 and a Christmas episode, the *Doctor Who* franchise had gone from a record high of international attention and products specifically marketed to adults (*Torchwood*) or young children (*The Sarah Jane Adventures*) to a still highly visible profile but less certain future by 2012. Of course, the Doctor has survived setbacks and hiatuses before — and earlier spinoffs, such as *K9 and Company*, were disappointing and very short lived. However, with the 50th anniversary in sight, *Doctor Who*'s future seems less certain than it had been even a year or two earlier.

With the upcoming 50th anniversary of *Doctor Who*, now the longest running SF television series, the BBC seems eager to promote the Doctor and spread the *Who* franchise as far as possible, especially into the U.S. However, as BBC Worldwide finds other products that are more popular in the mainstream American market (e.g., *X Factor, Dancing with the Stars*), the need for the Doctor to determine his future — as a more mainstream international SF series or a British cult series — is becoming more critical. The 50th anniversary should be a time of celebration and unity among fans worldwide, and the BBC should be celebrating its venerable series while looking to the future. Certainly, whatever may happen after the anniversary, the period from 2009 to 2012 is a critical one in the history of the *Doctor Who* franchise, and the Doctor's variable fortunes are becoming increasingly tied to the fans, marketing strategies, and global appeal of this long-running SF series and its numerous product lines and television spinoffs.

What makes the *Doctor Who* franchise such a success story, and can it continue its winning ways at home and abroad? The following chapters illustrate some reasons behind *Doctor Who*'s longevity — its intertextuality (and that of its spinoff, *Torchwood*), the Doctor's and Captain Jack's many "regenerations" and shifts in character development, a broadened international marketing strategy, and the power of *Doctor Who* fandom. The fans, writers, and actors behind the series' popularity all share a voice in explaining how and why the Doctor is an important icon in popular culture, both in the U.K. and, increasingly, in the U.S.

Chapter 1

The Culture of *Doctor Who*

In February 2012, during a Gallifrey One convention session in February 2012 affectionately dubbed "*Doctor Who* for Newbies," American and British panelists suggested ways that long-time fans could best introduce their loved ones to the joys of *Doctor Who* fandom. Each guest selected episodes from the "classic" series that might correlate to episodes shown since 2005, when many U.S. fans began watching "New *Who*." Writer and dedicated *Who* fan Simon Guerrier noted that today's fans have it much easier than those who wanted to know the Doctor's backstory in previous decades and had to hunt for friends' videotaped copies of episodes. With the high number of episodes available on DVD and other platforms today, catching up with the Doctor is much easier. As well, the multiplicity of platforms on which his story is available, including new BBC-sanctioned audio stories from Big Finish, fill in gaps between episodes. Big Finish, for example, created a series for the Eighth Doctor, who had previously starred in only one television movie.

However, what is most interesting is the idea that at least one fan convention session was held about ways to introduce new American audiences to the long and varied history of *Doctor Who* and, in large part, to "erase" the perceived gap between the "classic" series (1963-1989, 1996) and "new *Who*" (since 2005). That Americans are far less likely, culturally, to know about the Doctor is evident in such sessions. Although the panel and its audience, and by extension a large part of the Doctor's continuing fandom, consider all episodes since the series' beginning in 1963 to be the "real" *Doctor Who*—with no distinction between "classic" or "new" needed or, indeed, appropriate, BBC America and other television programs frequently offer additional information to bring U.S. audiences, especially new or young fans who were not around in the Doctor's PBS (or even Sci-Fi/Syfy) days, to a greater rudimentary understanding of just who the Doctor is.

Being part of *Doctor Who* fandom is a culture unto itself, as academics like Matt Hills have illustrated in his book, *Triumph of a Time Lord:*

> *Doctor Who* has its own residual/emergent cult audience equivalent to the *Lord of the Rings* films (2001-3), but rather than Tolkien cultists transferring their attentions to film adaptations, here "old school" fandom of the classic TV series acts as a residual cult, with fan affect being carried over to the reimagined television series. And what I have termed emergent cult (-like) status belongs to "new fandom," where audiences become fans of BBC Wales' *Doctor Who* wholly without back-reference to the classic show (like fans of the *LOTR* films who have never read Tolkien) [218].

Certainly the residual cult of *Doctor Who* is familiar with pre- as well as post–2005 episodes, plus many other stories available on other platforms. New *Who* fans (or fans only of "new *Who*) have much more available to them, and selecting appropriate entry points was the focus of the Gallifrey One convention panel. Awareness of the "emergent cult" is a given among the "residual cultists" in the session's audience. Helping bridge the two seems to be an important activity for Americans in particular, if this session's attendees represent the larger fandom.

For fans like Guerrier, having so many episodes available is an opportunity that all fans should take advantage of; he mentioned that he cannot imagine *Doctor Who* fans, who have a wealth of history available to them (owing to the Doctor's intertextuality enhanced by current accessibility to so many episodes and other "texts"), not wanting to see the "classic" episodes as well as the new. A television series nearly a half-century old is worth celebrating in its entirety, not piecemeal by broadcast or copyright date.

Nevertheless, and perhaps particularly true in the U.S., where Hills' description of "cult" fandom is particularly apt, viewers who only recently "discovered" the Doctor seem to prefer the newest and shiniest information instead of gaining a deeper understanding of the show's mythology and history. Thus, the information provided specifically to U.S. audiences, or deemed unnecessary for them, takes on greater significance. A session like "*Doctor Who* for Newbies," in which longer-term fans discuss the best ways to introduce the program or character of the Doctor to their family and friends, is far more likely in the U.S. than U.K., and even the concern that a special approach may be necessary — or one method more successful than another — indicates that American audiences have far less mainstream cultural appreciation for *Doctor Who* but also that hardcore American fans find so much value in the series that they want to share their knowledge and fandom with others. They even seek advice on the best way to do so. In the U.K., just as the Doctor wearing a fez is cool, so is being a Whovian. It has not always been so, but now the Doctor is a well-known, mainstream popular culture reference in the U.K., where *Doctor Who*'s recent blockbuster popularity has enhanced the series' status and ensured its rightful place in television history.

Doctor Who Insider

As one way for North American fans (mostly in Canada and the U.S.) to catch up with the latest information about the series and to gain a deeper appreciation of the Doctor's long backstory, a new official magazine, *Doctor Who Insider,* debuted in 2011. BBC America's online shop encouraged presumably new viewers to "Satisfy your thirst for fascinating facts and behind-the-scenes stories about the phenomenally popular British SF series, from First Doctor William Hartnell in 1963, through Eleventh Doctor Matt Smith and beyond! In each issue: star interviews, character and monster guides, news, photographs, in-depth looks at the latest *Doctor Who* episodes, fold-out poster and more!" (BBC America Shop). A few interesting points can be derived from the creation of this special publication geared toward American readers: BBC America and BBC Worldwide determined the need for new viewers to gain important "catch up" or background information in order to get up to speed with the long-running series and its equally long-running fandom; producer Panini Magazines thought there would be a lucrative enough U.S. market in which to launch the publication; and BBC America, BBC Worldwide, and others invested in marketing *Doctor Who* to North America may have wanted this potentially huge market to feel special with a *Who* magazine geared toward this geographically specific audience. Although the magazine could be purchased outside the U.S. (and regular *Doctor Who* magazine purchased online as well as in some U.S. or Canadian bookstores and SF specialty or comic book shops), the audience for *Doctor Who Insider* was perceived as different enough to warrant a niche publication designed to complement, not compete with, well-established *Doctor Who Magazine*.

The first issue, launched in May 2011, welcomed readers with the opening question "What could be more British than *Doctor Who*?" Editor John Ainsworth assured them that the magazine was "British made but published in North America. This is surely a testament to the far reaching appeal of this unique TV drama that has enthralled and inspired viewers for nearly fifty years.... *Doctor Who* is no newcomer to America. However, since its debut on BBC America (and Space in Canada) it is now being watched by more people than ever before with new viewers discovering the series all the time" (Ainsworth). Even though the editor specifically wrote that the magazine was directed to all *Who* fans and would provide a mix of articles about the latest episodes as well as the series' history, the magazine quickly became perceived as an introduction primarily for new fans, because long-time fans already knew much of the historic information. If they wanted new information, they likely would turn instead to the "regular" magazine for fans, *Doctor Who Magazine*.

The title of the North American publication cleverly used the word *Insider* to make new fans feel included in what has been a cult fandom (pre–2005 in the U.K. and always in the U.S.) and now part of a burgeoning SF phenomenon. In addition, in his welcome message, editor Ainsworth signed off as "John," using a fan-friendly first-name approach to ensure readers know they are colleagues in fandom. In this new publication, readers presumably would be privileged with interviews and behind-the-scenes photographs to which they otherwise would not have access. That tone is used throughout articles to emphasize the "insider" aspect of this publication, sometimes to the point that it would be grating to adult or long-time fans reading the entire magazine. A first-issue article, "Mad Man with a Box," underscores not only the Britishness of the Doctor but the insider view being afforded North American readers. The first-person pronouns and present tense verbs, as well as first-name familiarity with the actor, also foster a "you are there" atmosphere through prose such as the following:

> I am indeed inside the most famous time machine in television history with the good Doctor himself—the very British Matt Smith. Being a fully-fledged *Doctor Who* insider, I've been behind the scenes and chatted to Matt on numerous occasions.... And what's more exciting than being in the TARDIS, with Matt Smith dressed as the Doctor? Why, getting the insider scoop on his second year in the iconic role of course [D. Scott 7].

Despite the inclusive language and immediacy of the style, the magazine, both in its Welcome message and its first feature article, also reminds readers that *Doctor Who* and the actor who play him are very British. This reminder sends a mixed message to American fans — welcome to our inclusive fandom *and* this television series is part of British culture, which is inherently different from Canadian or U.S. culture.

However, the reality of Internet fandom is that, especially through Twitter and Tumblr, but also on *Doctor Who* forums and fan sites, anyone who cares to look for the latest rumors or leaked photographs can easily find them online. Being an "insider" has more to do with a fan's interest level and Internet search skills rather than gaining access to official information through a BBC America-publicized and BBC Worldwide-sanctioned print magazine, even if it did live up to its guarantee to offer 100 percent original content in each issue ("Doctor Who Insider"). The tone and content, although well intentioned to reach new, probably young fans and bring them into the *Doctor Who* fold, put off other readers who could find less enthusiastic (noted by the number of exclamation points) prose elsewhere in official or unofficial publications.

Issue 9, published in December 2011, was the magazine's last. The Doctor Who News website cited Panini Magazines' email customer services specialist in relaying news of the *Insider*'s demise: "I am sorry to advise you that *Doctor*

Who Insider has ceased publication effective from Issue 9. Please be assured letters are on the way to our subscribers explaining this matter and offering either a refund or transfer to *Doctor Who* magazine. Once again I apologize for any inconvenience and disappointment caused in this matter" (Foster, "Doctor Who Insider"). The dissolution of the magazine in less than a year is less an indictment of North American (or the combined international) fandom than a misjudgment of the magazine's readership, an especially crucial error during a time of continued economic recession.

Some readers, upset upon hearing of the publication's end, commended it for being "more appealing to younger readers than *DWM* [*Doctor Who Magazine*]; my little cousin rather enjoyed it. Looked great, was a great read" (McGann Is the Doctor). Similarly, "Fish Fingers and Custard"—a fan whose name perhaps indicates a recent entry into *Who* fandom — praised *Doctor Who Insider* as "a nice balance of old and new *Who*. I sometimes find *DWM* a bit too in depth and this was a nice light read." In response to one fan's question about the reason behind the cancellation, an Australian fan speculated that "the problem with this mag was that it was too similar to *DWM* (with exception of a few region-specific articles/advertisements, etc.) and had the same target audience–and most people who had access to *DWI* were already buying *DWM*. Also, for comparison, *DWM* is about $17 in Australia, and *DWI* was about $11 ... so if you're on a budget, you're probably going to buy *DWM* as it has far more content for the price" (Mels). (The U.S. and Canadian retail prices for the first issue were $6.99, a few dollars less than the price of imported *Doctor Who Magazine,* which can run between $8.95 to around $11.95 per issue, depending upon vendor and shipping cost.) Yet other fans blamed the loss of *Doctor Who Insider* on the show's inability to financially support another official magazine.

As noted in the limited sampling of fan comments, several readers enjoyed the magazine and found it more accessible than *Doctor Who Magazine.* The problem became not that there are not enough fans in North America, or internationally, to warrant their own magazine, but that *Who* fans are not so easily regionalized (or separated by age) as BBC Worldwide may have thought. Even hardcore fans who tend to buy a wide range of products in their zeal for the series, it turned out, would not pay for a paper publication whose information they could just as easily buy elsewhere or access online.

Craig Ferguson's Doctor Who 101

Matt Smith's first appearance on *The Late Late Show,* on November 17, 2010, caused even more of a stir than anticipated among fans, including super–*Who* fan *Late Late Show* host Craig Ferguson. His plans to open the show with an introduction to *Doctor Who* and a surprise pre-interview cameo by Smith backfired when the show could not get BBC approval to use the *Doctor Who* theme. Despite grousing about the snafu, Ferguson amiably chatted with Smith and gave the actor his first U.S. guest appearance on a national talk show. Since 2010, Smith has returned to the series several times, apparently almost every time he is in LA.

In late July 2011, a week after San Diego Comic-Con, Ferguson showed episode clips, talked with Smith about the program, and exclaimed (more than once) that *Doctor Who* is his favorite television show. Smith admittedly enjoyed the American welcome, at Comic-Con and in the studio that evening, adding that the show "is really gathering a pace" in America. Similar to Smith's first appearance, when Ferguson had planned the show's opening segment to introduce unaware Americans to the Doctor (one unable to be shown until weeks later and now glorified on YouTube with more than 850,000 views to date), the host asked Smith to explain the series to an American who had never seen it. "It's about a man who time travels through the universe, saving different races that live on ... different planets, and sort of sweeps up companions and takes them on the way," Smith explained before turning the question back on the host. Ferguson obligingly rapped an homage to the Doctor while Smith beat-boxed ("Craig Ferguson"). During a subsequent appearance on October 18, 2011, Smith exultantly discussed winning Spike TV's Scream Award for Best Science Fiction Actor ("Doctor Who's Day Roundup"). Every time Smith is a guest on the show, it turns into a *Who* love fest. Not surprisingly, when BBC America began broadcasting *The Nerdist* on Saturday nights following episodes of *Doctor Who,* both Smith and Ferguson joined host Chris Hardwicke on the show (Schwarze).

In all these appearances, Ferguson works hard to make his fans aware of *Doctor Who* and provide a tongue-in-cheek Doctor Who 101. Of course, he has an eager audience of *Who* fans, as well as his own following, to clamor for more. When Smith was first announced as an upcoming guest, fans trekked to LA from across the country to be in the studio audience. Since then, *Who* fans look forward to Ferguson's *Who*-themed shows and take great pains to be in the audience when a member of the *Who* cast is a guest. Since Smith's first appearance in 2010, Karen Gillan (Amy Pond) and Alex Kingston (River Song) have also been guests.

Ferguson's method of introducing the Doctor to his studio and television audience is directed toward two groups: those in the know, who will laugh because they understand the information and put it into a broader context, and those who like Ferguson but have not watched *Doctor Who* and may become fans if they are intrigued by the information he presents. The overview

Ferguson gives to viewers is surprisingly similar to that provided by Amy Pond's narration at the beginning of *Doctor Who* episodes broadcast outside the U.K.— except Amy's narration is treated very seriously. Ferguson naturally takes a humorous approach. What do Americans need to know about *Doctor Who*? According to Ferguson, these are the pertinent facts. The host first announces that the evening's show will be different because it is "about a man who's not really a man. The Doctor, but he's not really a doctor. Like Doctor Phil, but awesome," he adds, providing a humorous reference to Dr. Phil McGraw and his talk show, *Dr. Phil*, that Americans are likely to understand. Ferguson next admits that "Most people in the United States of America have not heard of him," before adding the joke: "He's just like me in that regard." Although Ferguson, too, is a cult fave, his appropriately named *Late Late Show* is shown in the early hours of the morning, well past primetime. The core content follows this attention-getting rhetoric, played up by Ferguson's exaggerated, conspiratorial facial expressions and tone. The host finally provides key background about the Doctor: "In 1963 the BBC premiered a show about an alien who traveled through space and time, who tried to ward off evil.... The show has been popular in Britain almost fifty years with many different actors in the role of the Doctor." At this point, an alligator puppet pops in front of the camera with an additional comment: "Doctor doesn't die, just regenerates." Ferguson's lines provide a succinct description of the Doctor's popularity and the reasons for it: "One thing that's consistent, though, is why the show is so beloved by geeks and nerds. It's all about the triumph of intellect and romance over brute force and cynicism. And if there is any hope for any of us ... then certainly this is it, right, Doctor?" Guest Matt Smith then rushes in to deliver the final line, "Absolutely, Craig" ("Craig Ferguson — The Lost 'Doctor Who' Cold Open"). Although the audience knew that Smith would be a guest on the program, the studio group of fans was surprised to see "the Doctor" rush onto the stage to participate in the special opening segment. Because he addresses the host by his first name while in character, the humorous implication is that the Doctor and Craig Ferguson are on a first-name basis, as if both are characters on television. Although the opening is clever and visually appealing (hence all those YouTube views), it also smartly provides kernels of important information and presents Ferguson's talk show as the Doctor's special home on American television, one to which he or his companions would return in the following months.

Smith's and Ferguson's answers to the question posed to each — Who is the Doctor?— provide an interesting insight into their perceptions of who the character is meant to be. Whereas Smith summarizes the Doctor as one who saves people (and aliens) on distant worlds and travels with companions through time and space, Ferguson concludes his introduction with information about the series' theme: The Doctor uses reason far more often than weapons or violence; hope is a key element of the stories; and, especially in the recent past, romance has become much more prominent. Ferguson's final lyric about the Doctor's purpose was later incorporated into BBC America's official website description of the series, along with a note that it comes from this dedicated Whovian. Individually or collectively, done in jest or seriously, these are the elements deemed most important in order to attract new American viewers to *Doctor Who* and to provide them enough background to watch new episodes.

Amy Pond's "Meet the Doctor" Introduction

Given showrunner Steven Moffat's comment in April 2012 that *Doctor Who* is always the story of the companion during her or his time with the Doctor (Jones), Amy Pond's narration seems appropriate. She explains how she met the Doctor and why she travels with him. However, this addition has become a point of contention among non-U.K. *Who* viewers, because the introductory narrative, another version of Doctor Who 101, has been added only to the beginning of episodes broadcast outside the U.K. The BBC America version of *Doctor Who* begins each season six episode with the following voiceover: "When I was a little girl, I had an imaginary friend. And when I grew up, he came back. He's called the Doctor. He comes from somewhere else. He's got a box called the TARDIS that's bigger on the inside and can travel anywhere in time and space. I ran away with him, and we've been running ever since."

Viewers long familiar with the series found it annoying to have to hear such a preface to their favorite show, and even newer fans questioned the narrative because it makes *Doctor Who* seem to be all about Amy instead of the title character. Although Moffat may feel this way, not all fans believe that the companion should be the focal point of the story. Their complaints were addressed by an episode reviewer:

> Amy Pond's narration ... gives us the rundown of everything we need to know about *Doctor Who*. And it's come to my attention that some people don't like this. Some people: you are wrong. This season of *Who*, in particular, is not new viewer friendly, something that the past forty years have strived for. So any olive branch to a new viewer is important [Zalben].

What is more pertinent to American audiences is the information being presented. In the context of Amy's story, told over several seasons, this narrative is logical. She first meets the Doctor when she is a young girl; he returns when she is a young woman. During the interim, she believed in her "raggedy Doctor" and made up stories about him. Amy involves her childhood friend, Rory Williams, in this "make believe," just as she will someday include him in her real travels with the Doctor. Only to outsiders, who do not know that the Doctor is real, is the character about whom Amy dreams "imaginary."

The narrative, however, suggests that the Doctor is not "real" but merely a figment of a child's imagination come to life rather magically. The language in the narrative also is rather childlike: The Doctor comes from "someplace else" and travels in a "box" that is bigger on the inside (a running joke in the series). The most important details are that he travels through time and space — and he runs a lot. Without the context of episodes, "running" is extremely ambiguous — running from something? running toward something? The childlike storytelling cleverly plays on words — Amy runs away and keeps running with her formerly imaginary friend — but it presents a rather strange portrait of the Doctor.

Interestingly enough, of the impromptu description provided by Matt Smith on *The Late Late Show,* Craig Ferguson's lyrical introduction to *Doctor Who,* and an official version narrated by Karen Gillan as Amy Pond, only Ferguson indicates that the Doctor is not human (i.e., a man who is not really a man, a Doctor who is really not a doctor, an alien). Perhaps the implication that he can travel anywhere in space or time and comes from "someplace else" indicates he differs from Amy or the audience, but the only items, according to the show's international narrative introduction, that are most important are that she meets the Doctor twice and, upon the second meeting, she runs off with him to travel in the TARDIS. The key players are named: Doctor, TARDIS. However, Amy, the protagonist in this narrative, is not named. Of course, clips from previous episodes visually support the narrative and give more clues to the nature of the Doctor and the TARDIS, as well as young and adult Amy. By omitting her name, the narrative invites viewers to put themselves vicariously in Amy's place.

For a narrative that generated so much fan discussion online — often protesting the intrusion of a narrative and becoming irritated that the majority of viewers need such an introduction — it provides surprisingly little backstory about the Doctor or the purpose of his travels. Unlike Smith's definition that the Doctor saves others, the official narrative provides no context for the Doctor's need or desire to travel other than he is constantly running. Such a narrative provides a strange introduction for American or other international viewers and belies the rich history of the character and series. It does provide a quick entry into the episode for novice *Who* watchers, but the need for such an introduction also seems based on the assumption that some type of explanation is necessary for new audiences to understand what is going on. Amy's narrative could have been more helpful in that regard.

The BBC America's official *Doctor Who* page merely refers to the Doctor as a "mysterious time traveler" whose companions are human; together, armed only with a sonic screwdriver, they face "evil foes" (BBC America, "About the Show"). Even the character description page does little more to explain the Doctor, identifying him as an adventurer who often gets into trouble. Although viewers do not need to know about the Doctor's (or series') long past, the BBC America website and additional introduction to episodes provide so few descriptors of the Doctor that viewers may need to watch several episodes to grasp the complexity of the character. If they want additional backstory information, they need to go to other websites (especially fan sites) to find more specific character descriptors. BBC America may provide an easy entry into the series, but it conversely provides so little information about the Doctor that fans who want to learn more have to turn to other sources.

Talk Show and Media Interviews in the U.S.

Karen Gillan and Arthur Darvill (Rory Williams) attended a New York City screening of the first two episodes of season six ("The Impossible Astronaut" and "Day of the Moon"), which had been primarily filmed on location in the U.S. A few days before the sixth season's premiere on BBC America in April 2011, U.S. entertainment magazine *Entertainment Weekly* interviewed both actors.

Gillan described the sweeping shots of the Utah desert and the enhanced budget that allowed location filming outside the U.K. "It looked just like a film. I couldn't believe it was British television when I saw it," she told the reporter. She did not elaborate on that comment, but presumably she meant that the Utah landscape looks very different from any place in Britain.

Gillan also commented on the difference between her and the show's popularity in the U.K. and U.S. "There's quite a lot of hype around *Doctor Who* in the U.K. You get recognized a lot more as you're walking down the street." Darvill, however, recalled American fans tracking down cast and crew as they filmed in the desert, a surprise because they "really didn't expect to see anyone in America. I mean, the crews we were working with, most of them didn't really know what the show was." On the cast's first day, several fans arrived; they "had driven for hundreds of miles to sit by the side of a road and watch us walk between our trailers and the set and were perfectly happy to do so. I think there's something quite wonderful about *Doctor Who* fans. They'll always go the extra mile. Or the extra thousand miles" (Collis, "Doctor Who Cast Members"). Although the fans who seek location filming in Wales when the cast leaves the BBC Wales studios in Cardiff frequently track down the production during filming, the actors were surprised that American fans would take such initiative in staking out a location shoot, especially one taking place miles from the nearest town. The rarity of *Doctor Who* being filmed in the U.S. brought out the most dedicated fans (or the ones most motivated to find the film crew).

When the series again filmed an episode, this time for season seven, in New York City, fans flocked to Central Park, and photographs and videos of Smith, Gillan, and Darvill populated YouTube and *Doctor Who* fan sites. At a PBS advance screening of *Sherlock* on May 2, 2012, a few weeks after the *Doctor Who* location shoot, Moffat joked about the popularity of Smith and Gillan. He told a story about fans surrounding the van with Gillan, Smith, and Moffat. "'Karen, will you marry me? Matt, I love you,'" he said fans called as they frantically tried to take pictures through the vehicle's windows. "'Moffat, can you lower your head?'" the showrunner joked. The experience may have set up Moffat with a good joke, but the fact that fans surrounded the actors on location and paparazzi followed the cast during a shopping trip must have made them feel at home in NYC. Of course, British newspapers and tabloids also ran photographs and articles about the production's every move, even if an ocean separated the cast from reporters.

During special events, such as fan autograph events or screenings, American *Doctor Who* fans (and international fans traveling to the U.S.) are just as enthusiastic as their British counterparts. When Smith and Gillan appeared at Comic-Con in July 2012, the queue outside the largest hall in the convention center began hours earlier, and hundreds of Whovians had to be turned away. Fan behavior at such events may not be markedly different in the U.S. or U.K., but the fact that *Doctor Who* has begun generating U.S. press outside of fan-run sites does indicate the series' entry into American mainstream popular culture, if to a much lesser degree than in the U.K. The actors may be surprised that their American fan base is so attentive outside of conventions or special events, but the dedication of hardcore U.S. fans is equal to that of die-hard *Who* fans anywhere.

Nevertheless, when actors, such as Smith, Gillan, or Darvill, are interviewed on U.S. talk shows or in the entertainment press, they still must be introduced by name, character, and series. Unlike in the U.K., where so much media attention is focused on the series, the American public is not on a first-name basis with the cast. Even Steven Moffat, who has gained a higher profile in the U.S. through roles in running as well as writing episodes of both *Doctor Who* and *Sherlock,* is not a name or face readily recognized by mainstream television audiences. Moffat's appearance at the 2011 Emmy Awards, where *Sherlock* was nominated for a best writing award, went unheralded in the U.S. media, and his blink-and-you-miss-it moment on screen as the nominations were read would not be remembered by anyone who was not already a fan. *Doctor Who* may be gaining a wider audience and slowly entering mainstream popular culture, but it and its cast members or showrunners are not yet a fixture in American culture, a fact made obvious by the experience of highly popular (to *Who* fans in general and British television, film, and theater fans in particular) former Doctor David Tennant.

Cultural Resonance with Actor as Well as Role

Although *Doctor Who* fans in the U.S. recognize David Tennant and immediately connect him with the role of the Doctor, he is not a household name in America. In addition to Tennant's many stage roles in award-nominated productions, such as *Hamlet* (2008) or a modernized *Much Ado About Nothing* (2011), post–*Who* he has voiced characters in BBC radio dramas, audiobooks, and films (e.g., *How to Train Your Dragon*) and played a very un-Doctor-like role in *Fright Night*. Although he acted in other productions, these are the ones most casual *Who* viewers or film or theater buffs in the U.S. are likely to remember. Tennant analyzed the Doctor's appeal in a 2009 interview when *Doctor Who* moved to BBC America; his assessment of the U.S. audience could also be applied to their awareness of his role as the Doctor: "[*Doctor Who*] has never quite conquered America in the mainstream. Even now it's still not quite in everybody's consciousness, although the following it has is devoted. BBC America is keen to bridge that gap." The reason behind the Doctor's international popularity is his Britishness, which "may be part of its appeal overseas, in the same way of [Agatha Christie's] Miss Marple and other British brands. It's not sci-fi in the traditional American way; it's not jocks in space" (Collett-White). Tennant's talent as an actor is undisputed, but he fits no specific "American mold" for a television star, and in the U.S. his every move was not covered in the press and given national attention.

British actors, however, more frequently of late have gained roles in the U.S. that they would not have the opportunity to play at home, often to great success. Talking to the *Radio Times* shortly before his final episodes of *Doctor Who* were broadcast, Tennant noted that "British actors are more and more in vogue out there [in Hollywood]; look at Hugh Laurie [*House*]—he's just about as big a star as you get in the States and he's made it in a role he never would have been given here." Nevertheless, Tennant dismissed the idea that living in Hollywood is part of his greater career plan. "It's not a tactical move," although he mentioned the then-recent relocation of Julie Gardner and Russell T Davies to Los Angeles, "which I suppose makes it feel more possible" (Dickson 27).

Like many actors who leave home for a brief, but later sometimes extended foray into Hollywood after achieving success in the U.K., Tennant filmed a U.S. television pilot. During a December 2009 interview with the *Los Angeles Times*, Tennant enthusiastically described his leading role in *Rex is Not Your Lawyer* as "a great part. It's a very dramatic role, it's quite funny — you get to do a bit of everything, and that always appeals" (Lloyd). The series was less appealing to NBC executives, who turned down the pilot (with the reason rumored to be script problems), and Tennant soon returned to the U.K., where he played the lead of his next successful television series, *Single Father*.

The experience in the U.S., in hindsight, seems far different than what the actor anticipated. In an October 2010 *Radio Times* interview, Tennant mused about the nature of U.S. television and his inexperience with the system. "Los Angeles is an extraordinary place.... It's so full of opportunity that it does have that sort of wide-eyed American sensibility that anything is possible, twinned with this very harsh business sense where nothing is possible. It's a fascinating place and I found myself liking it more and more and loathing it more and more in equal measure." He found it difficult to interpret the political culture of network television, never knowing exactly who knew what, or what the information (or lack of) meant. "It's such a political minefield over here [in the U.S.]. You have to be careful about what you know, because everybody tells you things that they're not supposed to and you're not quite sure what's true and what isn't." After NBC declined the series, Tennant concluded that "America seems to be on hold for the time being" (Naughton 17).

Now that Tennant has established his family in London and has had even more success on radio, the stage, television, and film, another extended sojourn to Hollywood seems increasingly less likely. Although being recognized wherever he goes in the U.K. may be tiring, for the most part Tennant seems to bear up well as a role model for young fans and one of the most beloved Doctors, according to much of the series' fandom.

The British public's identification of Tennant as the Doctor, even years after he stopped playing the role, caused controversy in spring 2012, when Virgin Media introduced a television commercial that ran afoul of the BBC. As part of a multimillion-pound advertising campaign, the actor explains Virgin Media's TiVo video recorder and catch-up service. The controversy arose because, as an example of how to use the system, Tennant looks up *Doctor Who* episodes. In the background, Virgin Media's owner, Richard Branson, is shown using a time machine. The connection between Tennant and *Doctor Who* is instantaneous for British audiences — not just *Doctor Who* fans — even without the time machine reference to enhance the association. The BBC opposed the commercial because it seemed that the BBC (owner of *Doctor Who* and former employer of Tennant in the series) was endorsing or promoting Virgin Media's product. In response, Virgin Media pulled this specific advertisement but continued using Tennant in its campaign (Sweeney).

Despite increased popularity of *Doctor Who* in the U.S., it is highly doubtful that American television audiences would so readily identify Tennant with the series or understand why Branson uses a time machine in the commercial, but then, even if Virgin Media were advertising its product in the U.S., it likely would take a very different approach to selling the product. Neither Tennant nor the series resonates quite so much in America, and the instant identification of an actor with the role of the Doctor is not as likely outside the U.K. Achieving that type of instant identification in the U.S. would require a different cultural icon.

Twitter and Premiere Discussion: Differences in Time and Space

One place where U.S. and U.K. fans are getting together more often and sharing cultural references and comments is social media, which also help the Doctor to reach an ever greater international, and presumably younger, audience. Twitter, in particular, provides immediacy for fans wanting to share comments about what they are watching on television while they are watching it. River Song is not the only person to warn "Spoilers!" when fans watching *Doctor Who* as it is broadcast in the U.K. tweet to each other their immediate reactions. American fans who will be able to see new episodes a few hours later—or international fans who might not be able to (legally) see them until days or weeks later—either embrace the spoiler nature of Twitter talk or avoid social media until they can see the episodes for themselves.

Although several U.S. *Who* fans, and even high-profile British fans like BBC writer James Moran, pleaded with U.K. viewers not to spoil the show with specific tweets on the general feed (e.g., using general hash tags like #DoctorWho, #BBC), enough details leaked out during the sixth season premiere that astute fans worldwide had a good idea of what was happening minute by minute throughout the initial broadcast. As a likely result, the U.S. tweets a few hours later had fewer exclamations of surprise or confusion than British tweets, although certain high points of the episode (i.e., the Doctor's regeneration and death, the younger Doctor's presence in the story, the "Legs, Nose, and Mrs. Robinson" categorization of Amy, Rory, and River Song, the introduction of new monster the Silence, Amy's pregnancy) generated numerous tweets on both continents. When fans wrote about the key plot points, the content of comments was remarkably similar.

What differed were fans' reactions to variations in the way the premiere episode was broadcast. In the U.K., the first tribute to Elisabeth Sladen (Sarah Jane Smith) was shown before the episode began and an even longer tribute was broadcast immediately afterward on CBBC, the children's network that was home to *The Sarah Jane Adventures*. Such a tribute was missing from BBC America's broadcast, although a short memorial (i.e., Sladen's name, birth and death dates) ended the episode. Long-time *Who* fans complained about the lack of respect shown to Sladen and Sarah Jane, although BBC America programmers may have shortened the tribute because they believed fewer U.S. fans would remember Sladen, and a new audience — brought in by the increased publicity in the months leading to the April *Doctor Who* premiere — would not know the actor or character.

Similarly, another complaint arising on Twitter during the U.S. broadcast involved the voiceover narration by Gillan (Amy Pond), which was first introduced with the U.S. premiere of season six. Long-time *Who* fans complained about the (for them) unnecessary information that detracted from the scenes being shown. As one fan tweeted, "I hope that doesn't happen every episode."

Perhaps the biggest complaint on Twitter was the number of commercials inserted into the U.S. broadcast. Fans tweeted that commercials broke up the story every few minutes (e.g., 5, 6, and 8 minutes were specified in tweets). Not only did they dislike interruptions to an intense episode, one for which they had waited several months through plenty of media "teasing," but they became angry that BBC America misled them with promises of "limited commercial interruptions." Several fans tweeted their own definitions of that term during the apparently interminable commercial breaks; others simply typed profanities during yet another interruption. One U.K. fan "smirked" online that at least in the U.K. fans could watch the episode in one 45-minute block; only Americans had to deal with commercials.

Such a difference in approach to televising the episode underscores some basic differences between BBC One and BBC America and between U.K. and U.S. broadcast practices. In the U.K., citizens pay a license fee that permits them to watch national programming via BBC's many television or radio channels. BBC channels do not interrupt programming with paid commercial messages; *Doctor Who* fans benefit from watching a story in its entirety so that the tension can build and the suspense/terror rise until the episode's end. In the U.S., even cable networks frequently interrupt programs with paid commercials. Even though U.S. citizens generally pay for cable or satellite service, they have the option of whether to buy programming, such as cable packages that offer BBC America; "public broadcasting" (i.e., PBS) may be free to audiences, but it is diminishing in frequency across the U.S. because of equally diminishing government and public monetary support. All other channels support their programming with advertisements. The result is a fragmented viewing of *Doctor Who* (or any other series' episodes). Every few minutes the story is interrupted for several more minutes of commercial messages; the story lacks a continuous flow and may even be further disrupted by poor editing. One fan bitterly complained on Twitter that BBC America inserted a commercial into the middle of a character's sentence. Such interruptions make it more difficult to follow the story or to feel dramatic tension within the episode's plot arc. Instead of being a 45-minute story, the U.S. version follows the common practice of being a one-hour program with commercial breaks.

The differences in programming reflect more cultural issues, as did some tweets. BBC America's assumptions about the U.S. *Doctor Who* audience indicate that it is newer and not as culturally invested in the "classic" series or even the Davies' era of storytelling. They change the story — what is added, what is deleted — for the widest common denominator, not the long-time *Who* fan. Although they make it easier for more people to enter the story during the current season's episodes, they also frustrate fans who already know background information or, for example, look forward to what they know has already been broadcast in the U.K., such as the Sladen tribute. (Of course, within a few hours, the missing-from-the-U.S.-broadcast tribute appeared on several fan sites and YouTube, so Americans could find another way to see it. If the BBC hoped to avoid downloads or file-sharing among fans, the omission on BBC America actually encouraged fans to go online to get the missing content.)

As well, some U.S. fans wanted to see the episode a second time to make sure they completely understood it or could "decode" all the clues about time lines, a key element of Moffat-scripted stories. During a first viewing, fans often are caught up in the emotional content — in this case, the Doctor's death, the horror of a new monster — and find the "timey wimey" aspects of the story more difficult to grasp. Multiple viewings help ensure that fans understand all the nuances of the episode and intellectually as well as emotionally interact with it. U.S. fans who tweeted at the episode's conclusion, more than their U.K. counterparts, indicated they needed to see the episode again — perhaps also a commentary about the way the episode was interrupted by commercials that tended to distract the audience from the plot by breaking their concentration.

There also were cultural differences in the details fans noticed, as reflected in their tweets during the respective broadcasts. British viewers commented on the American accents and laughed at the fact that the aliens were portrayed as Americans. A few derogatory comments mentioned that Americans are patronizing, which made the aliens all that much more realistic. In the U.S., tweets often commented on the program's choice of locations. One fan wrote that everything in the U.S. is reduced to the West coast or New York, although the Doctor was shown in Utah's Monument Valley, Cocoa Beach, Florida's space center, and the president's Oval Office in Washington, DC. Other fans wondered about street names and whether they were real places in Florida; another commented that there are no tunnels possible in Florida "to go down," as the Doctor indicated, because the state is at or just above sea level.

More than geography concerned fans tweeting from either side of the Atlantic. One U.K. fan commented that, of course, Americans would have guns; the comment refers to laws in the U.S. (but not U.K.) permitting citizens to own or carry firearms. (Two British *Doctor Who* fans I met in London in 2011 pointedly asked me if I felt safe living in the U.S. because of the presence of so many guns and the level of gun violence. They questioned whether they would travel to the U.S. because of the prevalence of gun-related incidents reported in the news.) In response to the tweets about guns, a U.S. fan suggested that the BBC realize that the sound effect present when a gun moved is unnecessary: "If a moving gun makes a noise, you're dead."

Some fans liked specific U.S. references to *Star Trek*, Stetsons, convertibles, and Richard Nixon, although fans everywhere thought the actor playing Nixon looked nothing like the president. The "Mrs. Robinson" comment, appropriate to a story set in 1969, when *The Graduate* was a recently (1967) popular movie, garnered a lot of LOL comments, but the Doctor's question about who was president in 1969 gained more questionable comments from U.S. fans. "I know who the Queen was in 1969," wrote one. "Why wouldn't the Doctor know who was president then?" Of course, whether that fan also knew the identity of the Prime Minister in 1969 was not mentioned.

For many fans, no matter where they live, the U.S. references were comfortable, as were the American accents. Iconic images like Stetsons (i.e., cowboy hats) and red convertibles fill the episode. It is interesting how the U.S. is summarized by three key locations in this episode: the vast open spaces of the American West, historically a great determiner of U.S. character; the Oval Office in Washington, DC, a place of political policy making as well as political intrigue; and the space program, both a reminder of American technological ingenuity and a required location given the story significance of a moon landing and an astronaut. Ironically, the masked astronaut who kills the Doctor prompted some viewers to ask (before the astronaut's identity was revealed in a later episode) if America is ultimately responsible for killing the Doctor.

However, iconic U.S. locations were not the sole topic of tweets. U.K. and U.S. fans alike cheered the Doctor's mention of Jammie Dodgers, a famous U.K. cookie (i.e., biscuit) with which Anglophiles in the U.S. would be familiar. Twitter helped fans everywhere "bond" on this important premiere date, but the types of comments indicate some cultural differences depending on where and when the audience was watching the episode.

What Is the Secret Behind the Doctor's Popularity?

Fandom incorporates hobbies and businesses as fans find ways to share their experiences and make meaning of them, individually and collectively. During 2010-2012, I attended several conventions where I talked with *Doctor Who* and *Torchwood* fans; I also took *Doctor Who* tours in London and Cardiff. In this section, U.S. and U.K. fans who have been immersed in *Doctor Who* culture for many years offer insights into why the *Doctor Who* franchise is unique and meaningful to so many.

One increasingly popular fan activity is cinematic tourism, and London-based Brit Movie Tours operates both a half-day *Doctor Who*-themed tour and a full-day tour to Cardiff, with *Who*-related stops (e.g., Amy's village or Farrington farm locations) along the way. Helen Thomas, my guide on a private tour in May 2011, is a *Doctor Who* fan/scholar who can happily and unerringly discuss episodes or characters; she closely follows the series but also attends fan meetings in London and keeps up with the latest news. She explains the tours' are popular because "people get to see behind the scenes of their favorite show. They can see how a regular street in Cardiff or London is turned into an alien world or another country, or how it's made to look how it was hundreds of years ago. *Doctor Who* fans get together at conventions all the time to discuss the show and share their love of it.... Going on a tour of locations is a great way of seeing places with other fans and is kind of a *Doctor Who* convention on the go."

Brit Movie Tours' founder, Lewis Swan, estimates that 600 fans, some who dress up as their favorite character, took a tour in the company's first fifteen months of operation. Because "overseas *Doctor Who* fans form the core of our *Doctor Who* tour business," April through October, when most international visitors take their vacations, are the most popular months for these specific tours. Swan realizes that fans sometimes want to "escape" into the world of a television series that offers them not only fantastic stories but a different way of looking at the world. By visiting location sites, or possibly re-enacting scenes filmed there, cinematic tourists develop a personal connection not only to the series but to real-world locations.

Like the fans she has guided to former filming locations, Thomas knows exactly why she continues to follow the Doctor and why the series has been successful for so long. In addition to the Doctor's ability to travel in both time and space, which opens up story possibilities, and his and the show's ability to regenerate into something different, Thomas praises the "richness to the story of The Doctor; there is so much history to the show and the character whilst there still is a mystery around who he is. I can't think of another TV show where you don't even know the main character's name! After nearly fifty years, it's still a question: Doctor Who? I like the mystery of this, and each thing we find out about The Doctor is really exciting."

Thomas also enjoys the show because of its "Britishness," and although she follows and enjoys several American television series, *Doctor Who* "feels different from American shows. The Doctor himself has that quirky, British eccentricity, and [the series] has a different type of humor. I mean, in what other show would you see the world saved by a cup of Jackie Tyler's tea?!"

In a PopMatters interview in early 2011, writer and perennial *Doctor Who* fan Simon Guerrier explained that, in addition to the Doctor's ability to travel anywhere and anywhen, the program's premise is "such a brilliant idea. You take this box, and wherever the box lands, you're in the story. The Doctor always arrives just as the story is beginning. Steven Moffat refers to people like the Doctor (and Sherlock Holmes and James Bond) as people to whom adventures just happen anyway, so you're always off running" (Porter, "Yet Another British Invasion"). The nature of the Doctor's character opens up the story's possibilities.

Chicago TARDIS convention programming director Jennifer Adams Kelley has been involved in *Doctor Who* fandom for much of her life and interacts with actors, writers, and directors who have worked on *Doctor Who, The Sarah Jane Adventures,* and *Torchwood*. Kelley believes that the series' theme is integral to the show's longevity and cultivation of fandom. The important point is "that one person can make a difference. You don't have to be part of a military operation (or even a quasi-one) to affect real change in the world. It's a person-driven story more than a military-driven one. (I mean, I love *Star Trek* to pieces — it was my fist SF fandom — but it all comes down to the might and power of Starfleet.) It's not this one guy going around putting right what once went wrong (to borrow from *Quantum Leap*)."

Although the Doctor sometimes travels alone in time, like *Quantum Leap*'s Sam Beckett, his story is not bound by a single lifetime (e.g., Sam's) or by location. The Doctor makes a difference, but his actions often are not perfect — he cannot solve all of humanity's (or any species') problems. Whereas *Quantum Leap* ended each episode that at least one person's life had been changed for the better and offered a "happy ending," *Doctor Who* does not always provide such closure, and disputes between species or people tend to crop up in later episodes. Yet, as Kelley astutely points out, the Doctor does make a difference, which, strange as it may seem, given the plethora of monsters and sometimes quirky scenarios in which the Doctor finds himself, allows *Doctor Who* to be more realistic — not all problems can be solved once and for all, but a single person can make a difference.

Before a *Doctor Who* session at a 2011 Wizard World convention in Chicago, Jim Droese discussed his return to the fandom and the reason why he thinks the series is so popular in the U.S. Although a fan during the Tom Baker years on PBS, Droese's interest had waned until 2007, when he was reintroduced to the newly reimagined program and became a self-described "rabid" fan during David Tennant's time as the Doctor. Droese attributes the series' ability to hook American fans, who, he notes, are not culturally brought up with the series as many fans are in Britain, on a simple fact: the show reaches out to more than one demographic. "America doesn't usually have shows that do that anymore. It used to be TV was open to everyone. Now *Mad Men* is aimed at a certain demographic. *Desperate Housewives* is aimed at a different demographic. So, to America, *Doctor Who* is different, because it's a show you can watch with your children and feel completely comfortable. ... Because the writing is superior, they can create different levels [of meaning in] stories." Science fiction stories can analyze social situations in a way that can "go under the radar for the average public" (or perhaps children), but fans interested in the analogy between the Doctor's world and their own can find deeper meaning to the stories.

Doctor Who has been able to develop a fan culture that, although incorporated differently into popular culture by region (e.g., once cult but currently more mainstream in the U.K., gaining in popularity but still cult-like in the U.S.), attracts fans internationally because of the range of possible stories and the ability to "regenerate" as necessary. Thematically, the series shows how an individual can make a difference and can do so without violence or military intervention, relying instead on intellect as well as bonds of friendship and love. Fans may have different ways of expressing their appreciation for the series, but their continuing involvement with the Doctor at different points in or throughout their lives illustrates their devotion. Such a strong, continuing fan base is yet another reason why *Doctor Who* continues to thrive.

Two Surveys: Academic Fan/Scholars and Social Media Fandom

In 2010 and 2011 I developed a series of short surveys for specific, sometimes quite small, target groups or about specific television series, in order to get a broader perspective of fans' interpretation of the popularity of *Doctor Who, The Sarah Jane Adventures,* or *Torchwood*. Responses also indicated whether fans think a series is becoming "Americanized" and how "Americanization" might be defined. Behaviors, such as frequency of viewing a series or participation in fandom-based activities, formed the basis of other questions. Because the response rates were low for some surveys, the results cannot be generalized to the entire fandom. Nevertheless, they provide some interesting insights into fan opinions and behavior.

The first survey was emailed to nine academics (i.e., teachers, researchers) scheduled to present papers in the *Doctor Who* or *Torchwood* sessions of the Popular Culture Association's April 2011 conference. The second survey was made available online and advertised on fan websites, as well as through Twitter and Facebook; almost 600 fans responded to this survey and represented a much more diverse group.

A Survey of Popular Culture Association Participants

The Popular Culture Association invites collaboration among teachers, students, and researchers who analyze popular culture and study it as a discipline. During the April 2011 conference held in San Antonio, Texas, sixteen academics presented papers in a specifically themed *Doctor Who/Torchwood* subsection of the Science Fiction genre celebrated each year. These presenters were invited to take a brief survey about their use of *Doctor Who* or *Torchwood* as a text within their courses and, because they work with students in the U.S., Canada, or U.K., also to comment upon any differences they have observed between fandom in North America and Europe. Of the sixteen invited, nine agreed to participate in the survey, which certainly makes it far less than scientifically valid but does provide some insights into the ways that *Doctor Who* and *Torchwood* are considered worthy of study in popular culture and these professional pop culture analysts' perceptions of the series' fandom. Because the number of respondents is so low, both the number of people and the percentage of respondents providing each response are listed, because the percentage alone would seem highly misleading.

Seven (77.8 percent) respondents teach in the U.S., with one (11.1 percent) teaching in Canada and one in the U.K. Eight (88.9 percent) are employed by universities, and 1 (11.1 percent) by a community college. These faculty teach a variety of courses within their institution, and each institution labels its popular culture courses differently. According to these respondents, they teach or have taught the following courses within the past six years: humanities (4; 44.4 percent); communication (3; 33.3 percent); English, film studies, literature, or popular culture (2; 22.2 percent); and media studies or cultural studies (1; 11.1 percent). These faculty seem well educated in a variety of disciplines that would be able to include a study of television series as part of students' analysis of a variety of "texts."

Two faculty members replied to a question about series' texts (e.g., television episodes, television specials, novels, non-fiction critical evaluations of a series) that they did not use any of the listed *Doctor Who* texts in their courses, likely because they don't "teach" *Doctor Who* specifically, although their PCA presentation indicates the series interests them as a subject of research. However, seven (77.8 percent) reported that they show and/or discuss episodes in class. Other *Doctor Who* texts were used appreciably less often: non-fiction books in which *Doctor Who* is discussed (3; 33.3 percent), Christmas specials (2; 22.2 percent); online interviews with cast, crew, or creators (2; 22.2 percent); and novels, comic books, *Doctor Who* magazine, or radio plays (1; 11.1 percent for each).

Torchwood has been used less often, but, to be fair, it is a younger series and has more of a niche audience; five respondents (55.5 percent) do not use or have not used any *Torchwood* texts their courses. Nevertheless, four academics reported using *Torchwood* texts: episodes (4; 44.4 percent); non-fiction books in which *Torchwood* is discussed (3; 33.3 percent); comic books or *Torchwood* magazine (2; 22.2 percent each); and novels, journal articles in which *Torchwood* is discussed, and radio plays (1; 11.1 percent each). If *Torchwood* is used appreciably less by faculty who teach popular culture-related courses and participate in a specific *Doctor Who/Torchwood* conference section, it may be safe to draw a conclusion that they perceive the series as less popular or less significant to analyze.

Academics enjoy analyzing fan culture, and these respondents' comments about *Doctor Who* and *Torchwood* fandom are more intriguing than their use of the series as objects of study. In response to the question Do you think there are differences between being a *Doctor Who* or *Torchwood* fan in the U.S. and being a *Doctor Who* or *Torchwood* fan in the U.K.? seven (77.8 percent) said Yes, one (11.1 percent) said No, and one (11.1 percent) was unsure. The follow-up question asking for an explanation of a Yes answer resulted in these comments, which I have grouped by reason for a difference in fan behavior by geographic region.

Responses that indicate a difference in fan behavior because there is a barrier to understanding or appreciating the series (i.e., inability to understand the language/dialect/vocabulary, inability to gain access to the series):

"One thing that has surprised me is how much even quite dedicated US fans miss because of comprehension barriers in culture, dialect and accent. I think this is true to some extent of Canada, too."

"Cultural references; it took me a whole season to realize 'chips' were French fries."

"U.K. fans have more texts available to them, have more *Doctor Who* or *Torchwood* news, and can see the actors in other roles far more easily than fans can in the U.S."

"UK fans have years more in-depth exposure to the show."

"In the U.K., *Doctor Who* is commonly accepted. In the U.S. it's still a novelty." (perceived as an "access" problem, although it could also be understood as a difference between mainstream and cult popularity and added to the following section)

Responses that indicate Doctor Who as embedded within the culture and being a mainstream cultural influence (i.e., a different way of thinking about the series):

"The major difference is that as an American television writer who teaches television writing, I fell for the show because of its writing and that is what I stress in my teaching. I use 'School Reunion' for theme and 'Blink' for thinking outside the box of the structure or format of a show. I think, from those I've met in Cardiff, London and Bath, that U.K. fans look to the show with a sense of national pride, almost the way Americans loved the early years of *The West Wing*."

"*Doctor Who* is part of British culture, whereas in America, it's a television show, like any other."

"US fandom seems less nostalgic, less completist and (dare I say it) less sexist. UK fandom is very tied up with people's childhood and family viewing experiences, and is not considered to be particularly niche. The 'my doctor' concept seems to be a much more dominant feature in UK fandom.... I have noticed that Anglo-American debate around *Doctor Who* tends to focus on whether the programme could/should/shouldn't be made more American, whereas Canadian and Australian fandom is more focused on what elements of the existing programme already resonate with their respective cultures."

This latter comment is similar to my fan experiences and discussions outside academia. Elements of the "American personality" perceived by fans outside the U.S. are straightforwardness (also referred to as bluntness), eagerness to share opinions, and interest in "bigger and better," the latest technology, and status from wealth or celebrity. Quotations from fans, actors, and writers throughout this book support these notions of an American national character or an American influence on television.

The last two survey questions asked these academics to consider whether the nature of fandom differs between continents: In general, do you think there are differences in television fandom between fans in the U.S. and U.K.? More than half (5; 55.6 percent) were unsure; three (33.3 percent) said Yes; and one (11.1 percent) said No. Perhaps these SF television scholars are much more invested in and aware of *Doctor Who* than other series but have not studied or participated in the series' fandom enough to feel comfortable making a determination. The three respondents who perceive a difference between U.S. and U.K. fans in general wrote these follow-up comments:

"U.S. fan conventions may have more panels with actors and more discussion of television series. U.K. events seem to be more signing events or fan-run activities. Also, I think U.S. fans tend to be more excitable and passionate about their TV series."

"American fans are more vocal, but with the widespread use of social media across countries nowadays, the differences aren't as great as they once were."

"Americans tend to sexualize the series, whereas in Britain is viewed as family friendly." [Indeed, as examples in later chapters illustrate, "family viewing" is a key component of *Doctor Who*'s appeal in the U.K., and deviations from it — e.g., "sexy Amy," Captain Jack's explicit sex scenes in *Torchwood*— often result in complaints to the BBC.]

These responses point to a perception of *Doctor Who* as a family-friendly, easily accessible, commonly viewed series in the U.K.— part of the national popular culture — whereas U.S. fans often respond to the series as something new or different (even though the series was available on PBS for decades, and many long-time fans trace their entry into *Who* fandom to the 1970s or earlier). Perhaps the series' reboot, as broadcast on Sci-Fi/Syfy or BBC America, has become the version with which U.S. fans are most familiar or that which provided their entry into the series. U.S. fans may be looking for ways to "Americanize" the series or make it relevant to their different cultural experiences. Fans in Commonwealth countries (e.g., Australia, Canada) as well as in the U.K. may share cultural elements that U.S. audiences do not and thus may be able to emphasize the cultural similarities across national borders. Cultural differences (e.g., chips or fries, region-specific accents or dialects) may create a barrier for some U.S. fans, but others may find these differences less of a barrier and more of a selling point, simply because they are outside the viewer's everyday experience.

The Doctor Who/Sarah Jane Adventures/Torchwood *Survey*

To attract a larger, more general group of respondents, I made available online a 10-question general survey of fans of the *Doctor Who* franchise, including *The Sarah Jane Adventures* and *Torchwood*. In addition to asking about length of tenure as a fan, the survey inquired about fan activities and opinions whether *Doctor Who* has become "less British" and whether *Torchwood* has become "Americanized," terms used in several online articles published since 2010. Although these descriptors are indeed vague, as fans posting on the Gallifrey Base forum noted, the terms used by online media in discussing *Doctor Who* and *Torchwood* should make the concepts understandable to fans who have been reading critics' articles about both series. The survey took place in late June and early July 2011, around the time *Torchwood: Miracle Day* premiered and when it was frequently discussed in entertainment news.

As well, *Doctor Who* had recently broadcast the first half of season six episodes, and Matt Smith's and Karen Gillan's upcoming San Diego Comic-Con session was receiving a great deal of publicity. Thus, fans who keep up with *Doctor Who* in the news, and who are probably more likely to want to take a survey about the franchise, may have stronger opinions about the episodes being reviewed or previewed in the news during or close to the time of the survey.

To gain a bigger response and possibly a wider *Doctor Who* fan audience, I posted the survey link on my Facebook page and via Twitter and encouraged people to share the link (as several fans reported on Facebook and via tweets that they had done). I also posted the link on *Torchwood* and *Doctor Who* fan pages on Facebook and on the Gallifrey Base fan forum. The results of 592 surveys are included by question.

1. *Where do you live (i.e., country of residence)?*
    55 percent (324) United States, United States of America, USA, US of A, US, or America
    40.5 percent (240) United Kingdom, Britain, England, Scotland, Wales, or UK
    2.7 percent (16)) Australia
    1.3 percent (8) France, Germany, or New Zealand
    Less than 1 percent (4) Canada, Croatia, Ecuador, Finland, Italy, or Northern Ireland

2. *What is your age?*
    34.5 percent (204) 40-49
    24.3 percent (144) 30-39
    18.9 percent (112) 20-29
    10.8 percent (64) Under 20
    8.8 percent (52) 50-59
    2.7 percent (16) Over 60

3. *When did you become a* Doctor Who *fan?*
    60.1 percent (356) Before 2005
    31.8 percent (188) 2005-2010
    8.1 percent (48) Since 2010
    0 percent (0) Not a Fan

4. *Are you a fan of* The Sarah Jane Adventures?
    35.8 percent (212) Consider myself a fan, but I haven't seen all episodes
    28.4 percent (168) Watch all episodes and am a fan
    21.6 percent (128) Seen it, but I'm not a fan
    14.2 percent (84) Never seen it

5. *Are you a fan of* Torchwood?
   65.5 percent (388) Watch all episodes and am a fan
   16.2 percent (96) Seen it, but I'm not a fan
   14.9 percent (88) Consider myself a fan, but I haven't seen all episodes
   3.4 percent   (20) Never seen it

6. *In what type of* Doctor Who *fan activities have you participated at least once?*
   83.4 percent (494) Purchase series-related merchandise (e.g., magazines, DVDs, audiobooks, comics, action figures, t-shirts)
   70.0 percent (414) Post a message in an online fan forum
   50.7 percent (300) Read or write fan fiction
   44.4 percent (263) Attend a fan convention
   37.2 percent (220) Meet or have a photo taken with a series actor
   36.8 percent (218) Attend a fan meeting (not a convention)
   20.6 percent (122) Create a costume
   12.1 percent (72) Help organize a fan meeting
   11.2 percent (66) Create or distribute a fan video
   10.3 percent (61) Participate in cosplay
   9.4 percent   (56) Help organize a fan convention
   8.1 percent   (48) Create a fan website

7. *Do you think that* Doctor Who *is becoming less British?*
   70.9 percent (420) No
   12.8 percent (76) Unsure
   9.5 percent   (56) Yes
   6.8 percent   (40) No opinion

8. *Do you think that* Torchwood *has become Americanized?*
   29.1 percent (172) No
   28.4 percent (168) Unsure
   25.7 percent (152) Yes
   16.9 percent (100) No opinion

9. *If, as expected, the series continues, do you think you will watch* Doctor Who *in the next two years?*
   89.2 percent (528) Yes
   4.7 percent   (28) Not sure
   4.1 percent   (24) Not if new episodes are similar to those in the most recent series/season
   2.0 percent   (12) Only if new episodes are similar to those in the most recent series/season
   0 percent   (0)   No

10. *If, as expected, the series continues, do you think you will watch* Torchwood *in the next two years?*

    66.9 percent   (396)   Yes
    15.5 percent   (92)   Not sure
    6.8 percent   (40)   Not if new episodes are similar to those in the most recent series/season
    6.8 percent   (40)   No
    4.1 percent   (24)   Only if new episodes are similar to those in the most recent series/season

From the demographic information provided, this group of respondents is older and has been involved in *Doctor Who* fandom for many years. The minority of respondents are younger or new fans (since 2005, the year of the Doctor's return, or 2010, the year of the shift to the Eleventh Doctor and showrunner Steven Moffat). Fans who have been watching the series for several years (and are an older audience) are more likely to be aware of many shifts in the franchise, not only the coming or going of spinoffs but also changes as a result of network or budget, actors portraying the Doctor, characterizations of the Doctor, or preferences of showrunners. Perhaps this audience has more firmly ingrained perceptions of what makes *Doctor Who* or *Torchwood* "British."

To compare more closely fans' perception of Questions 7 and 8 about different perceptions of whether *Doctor Who* is still as British as it ever was or whether *Torchwood: Miracle Day*'s mostly U.S. production signaled the Americanization of the series, I matched responses to these questions with country of residence. (There were no other significant correlations between age or country of residence and response to other questions.)

Of the 240 U.K. respondents, 168 (70 percent) responded No to Question 7; they do not think that *Doctor Who* has become less British. Thirty-four (14.1 percent) responded Yes, 19 (7.9 percent) Unsure, and 19 (7.9 percent) No opinion.

Of the 324 U.S. respondents, 240 (74 percent) responded No to Question 7. Forty-two (13 percent) were Unsure, 23 (7 percent) responded No opinion, and 19 (6 percent) answered Yes.

In this survey, the vast majority of U.S. and U.K. respondents have a similar response: to them, *Doctor Who* is not becoming less British.

Torchwood, however, invites a difference of opinion between U.K. and U.S. fans. Of the 240 U.K. respondents, 84 (35 percent) responded Yes to Question 8 Do you think that *Torchwood* has become Americanized? Sixty-seven (28 percent) were Unsure; 58 (24 percent) said No; 41 (13 percent) had No opinion. Granted, that is not a high percentage, and many respondents had no clear-cut opinion. Of the 324 U.S. respondents, 108 (33 percent) responded No, 92 (28 percent) replied Unsure, 64 (20 percent) replied No opinion, and 60 (18.5 percent) responded Yes. Roughly a third of U.K. fans responded that *Torchwood* is becoming more Americanized, whereas third of U.S. fans think that is not occurring. The results indicate a lot more uncertainty within the response group about *Torchwood*'s Americanization, but, according to these respondents, more British fans than American fans are likely to think that the series has made this cultural shift.

In their enthusiasm for the series and the types of fan activities in which they participate, American and British fans are remarkably similar in their appreciation of *Doctor Who*. How others — notably the BBC, BBC Worldwide, and BBC America — perceive fans by geographic area does differ, especially in the amount and type of information provided about the Doctor and the series or franchise in general. The fans themselves are the best indicator of cultural differences, whether through surveys or social media, including Twitter. Fans' immediate responses to news or episodes are one of the best ways to interpret cultural differences and the ways that fans in other nations perceive each other.

Chapter 2

Doing Business with the U.S.

When BBC Worldwide produced its annual revenue report in July 2011, the news was good: profits were up. Chief Executive of BBC Worldwide, John Smith, announced that 2010–11 "was BBC Worldwide's most successful year ever in championing great U.K. content around the globe. By offering world-class British programming and brands that resonate with global audiences, we were able to lift revenues beyond a billion pounds for a third year in succession and also deliver impressive results" (BBC Worldwide Press Release). Noting BBC Worldwide's marketing emphasis on English-speaking countries, primarily the U.S. and Australia, Smith further noted a 37 percent increase in the number of primetime U.S. viewers ages 25 to 54.

Whereas the U.S. *Doctor Who* audience increased in April 2011, the number of U.K. viewers seemed to decrease appreciably. BBC America reported that the sixth season opener, "The Impossible Astronaut," received the network's highest ratings ever: 1.3 million viewers watching live or on DVR the same day. Certainly the immediacy of the broadcast encouraged more Americans to watch the episode as soon as possible, which was still something of a novelty to U.S. fans long accustomed to waiting for new episodes. "The Impossible Astronaut," like the previous year's Christmas episode and the remaining season six episodes, were shown in the U.S. within hours of their BBC broadcast.

Although ratings numbers were later adjusted in the U.K. to reflect more viewers watching *Doctor Who*'s series six premiere on DVR and iPlayer in the days following its initial broadcast, ratings for "The Impossible Astronaut" fell short of expectations. An unusually warm holiday weekend and an early Saturday evening broadcast time (as well as thunderstorms causing power outages at that time in some areas of the country) were possible reasons given for the lower-than-expected overnight ratings in the U.K., which indicated 6.5 million watching the episode live or soon after on iPlayer (Westbrook). The size of the audience was still admirable for U.K. television, but far fewer people watched the first episode of series six than series five, which introduced Matt Smith as the Doctor and Karen Gillan as companion Amy Pond (Cable).

The U.S. ratings are especially impressive because they further indicated an increase of more than 71,000 viewers from BBC America's previous high-ratings setter—*Doctor Who*'s fifth season premiere. The series' U.S. audience was growing, even though the Doctor was relegated to cable network BBC America, which has fewer potential total numbers than a national broadcast channel like ABC, CBS, or NBC, for example. Nevertheless, BBC Worldwide's marketing department clearly is doing something right.

Coming to BBC America: Broadening British-oriented Fandom

As its name explains, BBC Worldwide markets BBC programs internationally, and the programming is not limited to SF. Reality series such as *Dancing with the Stars* bear the BBC Worldwide distribution logo, but the BBC also has been looking for ways to produce and market dramas in the U.S. BBC America is a logical place for BBC programming to find a home, but it is far from the only place that mainstream U.S. audiences can see the BBC logo.

The programming of BBC America naturally reflects favorites from the U.K. that were originally broadcast on the BBC. *Torchwood* reruns and first-run episodes of *Being Human* and *Primeval*, for example, were transplanted to BBC America. *Doctor Who* logically became the lynchpin of the network's "Supernatural Saturday" lineup, which, in 2011, included not only the Doctor but scary sci-fi series like *Bedlam* and *The Fades*. However, other British imports, such as *Top Gear*, also gained a good share of BBC America's audience throughout the weekly schedule. According to a report from BBC Worldwide, in 2010–11, the three most popular British television exports were *Doctor Who*, *Sherlock*, and *Top Gear* (BBC Worldwide Press Release). Two of the three are helmed by Steven Moffat, whose latest iterations of iconic characters the Doctor and Sherlock Holmes have become more internationally popular than ever. Although BBC America presents *Doctor Who* and *Top Gear*, *Sherlock* instead was bought by public broadcaster PBS. Despite their lack of mainstream network presence, all three series have gained dedicated followings and consistently earn high ratings for their respective networks.

The Internet obviously boosts the popularity of British series shown in the U.S., whether on BBC America, PBS, or Sci-Fi/Syfy (which once broadcast the latest *Doctor Who* episodes and still shows previous seasons' stories; it also briefly introduced audiences to *The Sarah Jane Adventures*). Forums and fan sites, as well as the BBC's official program sites, make more people aware of these television series and help to cultivate fandom and create an immediate demand for programming. According to BBC Worldwide, "the *Top Gear* and *Doctor Who* pages on Facebook have over 11.8 million fans, and an average 68 million visitors per month visit its websites" (BBC Worldwide Press Release). These numbers reflect only the number of visitors to official BBC program sites, not the numerous fan forums, fan-run television or actor websites, and fan-shared news and fanfiction sites populating YouTube, Tumblr, Dreamwidth, or Live Journal, for example. As more viewers become involved with fandom, they want more programming — new episodes available for consumption at a faster rate. Part of fans' frustration with all BBC programming is its availability, a problem discussed in a later section in this chapter.

In addition to social media and the Internet helping fans new or old share information about the Doctor, as well as help BBC and BBC Worldwide cultivate a dedicated fan base, BBC Worldwide's marketing strategy includes more traditional advertisements in public places to make people aware both of *Doctor Who* and BBC America. Before the season six premiere, billboards in major cities across the U.S. showed Matt Smith as the Doctor and prominently displayed the BBC America logo. Spring 2011 screenings of British actor Simon Pegg's comedy, *Paul*, were treated to a *Doctor Who* trailer. Targeting *Paul* audiences was a shrewd move. Not only would Pegg's fans (who probably include a high percentage of Anglophiles) be reminded of another British actor and series, but *Paul* is the story of two friends who visit San Diego's Comic-Con and, during a subsequent drive across the U.S., encounter and begin traveling with an alien. Science fiction or cult-media fans attracted to *Paul*'s premise also would likely be intrigued by *Doctor Who*. Such advertisements are part of a typical marketing strategy, but they indicate BBC Worldwide's interest in gaining the venerable television series a much larger U.S. audience.

In early May 2011, NBC's *Today* anchor Meredith Vieira showed a video of her visit to the *Doctor Who* set in Cardiff. The segment was part of an Anchors Abroad series in which *Today* hosts visited several countries and sometimes performed strange activities. Vieira played a brief role as an on-air reporter for an upcoming *Doctor Who* episode, and although she teasingly tried out different British accents, she was encouraged to stick with her standard American broadcast voice. During the visit, dubbed Who 101, Vieira learned about the Doctor, the TARDIS, and River Song (Alex Kingston), with whom she compared designer shoes (Vieira).

Back in the studio after the segment had been broadcast, Vieira admitted she had never heard of *Doctor Who* before the visit. (Colleague Al Roker had.) Vieira seemed amazed at the way the series was filmed inside Cardiff's BBC

Wales studios. She noted that the BBC set was much smaller and less complicated than she was used to. Not only this comment about bigger and more expensive productions (echoed when *Torchwood* began filming in the U.S.), but the lack of general knowledge about *Doctor Who* seemed to be typical comments from mainstream American entertainment news.

In fact, the Who 101 fluff piece, while fun to watch, illustrates how little the majority of *Today* viewers were likely to know about the long-lived television series. Via Vieira's questions as a reporter trying to learn more about the Doctor, she helped the U.S. *Today* audience understand that he travels in time and space, the blue-box TARDIS is his time machine, and River Song is a time-traveling companion. A BBC America blogger picked up on the tone of the "interview" by reiterating the discussion about shoes: "Meredith asked Alex Kingston what it takes to be a really good time traveler. Alex's response? 'You have to have a pair of Louboutin shoes.' Awesome" (Wicks).

Certainly the piece was fun to watch, and it underscores the increased publicity of *Doctor Who* through mainstream media, like *Today*, which reached 5.7 million viewers each day during the week of the *Who* segment (Ariens). Nevertheless, this segment also illustrates just how far outside mainstream media *Doctor Who* remains in the U.S., despite its increased popularity and high ratings on BBC America. The *Today* segment was part of a media effort to "educate" Americans about the series and get them more interested in it. The short Anchors Abroad piece explained the basic premise of the series, acknowledged its long history, and visually introduced to audiences Matt Smith and Alex Kingston and their characters. Perhaps that brief overview enticed some viewers to watch the series on BBC America or DVD. It certainly made the U.S. *Doctor Who* news, as fans who missed the broadcast watched it online.

Marketing the Doctor in 2011 is very different from the PBS days, which relied on viewer support and fans' positive word-of-mouth campaigns to get new(er) episodes broadcast in the U.S. Today's mass-marketing campaigns must cover multiple platforms: print advertisements in television and entertainment magazines, such as *Entertainment Weekly* and *TV Guide;* trade publication advertisements and news articles; billboards; promotional television spots on BBC America; movie trailers; actors' guest appearances on British-friendly television shows like *The Late Late Show with Craig Ferguson;* and panels at widely publicized and media-covered conventions like San Diego Comic-Con. Such a marketing plan is designed to generate more interest among casual viewers, television critics, and media outlets that report TV trends. *Doctor Who* fans do not need to be convinced that the program is worth watching. BBC America and BBC Worldwide have to gain the attention of the unconverted masses.

Offsetting Marketing: Continuing Problems in Supply and Demand

Popular BBC programs often have supply-and-demand problems that affect international sales. The BBC's annual Showcase event, where BBC Worldwide shows off new and continuing series and sells them to international markets, takes place each spring. The event not only promotes BBC programming and touts Worldwide's sales and international marketing strategy, but it alerts viewers about new series or episodes headed their way. The problem for the BBC has been providing enough high-quality programming, especially of returning series, to meet demand not only in the U.K. but overseas, an increasingly difficult situation because of cutbacks to the BBC's budget offset by an increasing need to show a greater profit from its programs.

If television series are not readily available to audiences who want to watch them — no matter where they are in the world — then viewers have two choices: find something else to watch (at least until more episodes of their favorite programs become available) or find alternate ways of viewing programs the BBC is not yet making available to them. Increasingly, tech-savvy fans find ways to circumvent the BBC's online restrictions for downloading episodes from their iPlayer. A global pay-as-you-go download system has been promised but not yet delivered, and not all fans wait to order DVDs from the U.K., even if they have region-free players on which to watch them.

To help avert the problem of illegal downloads and file sharing of BBC programs soon after they are broadcast in the U.K., the BBC began offering more programs sooner to BBC America. As previously mentioned, the much-anticipated 2010 *Doctor Who* Christmas special was broadcast at its traditional Christmas night time slot in the U.K., but only a few hours later was broadcast in the U.S. on BBC America — a channel that previously had to wait a week or more for a new *Who* episode after its British premiere. Add to that the BBC's announced intention to allow U.S. citizens the opportunity to download programs for a fee, initially theorized to begin in 2011 with the return of *Torchwood* (it didn't), which was suggested to help alleviate the time lag between the continents' programming. American fans of *Sherlock*, for example, found themselves waiting several months after the second season episodes were broadcast in the U.K or, indeed, much of the rest of the world. Although casual viewers likely waited from January to May 2012 to watch *Sherlock* on PBS, hardcore U.S. fans found other ways of seeing the episodes, whether through illegal downloads, software that circumvented the IP-country problem of logging onto BBC's iPlayer, or the purchase of Region 2 DVDs that could be played on region-free DVD players or laptops. Although *Doctor Who* notably benefits from less broadcasting lag, it still is a BBC America program, which means that audiences who do not subscribe to a service provider offering this channel still have to wait for DVDs or use other means to watch new episodes.

Torchwood: Miracle Day faced a different problem — U.S. fans who subscribed to Starz could see the episodes almost a week before they were broadcast by the BBC in the U.K., a time lag that angered British fans and encouraged *Torchwood* showrunners to interact with U.K. viewers more often and in different ways in order to ameliorate the discontent.

Despite the logistical problems and business models that determine how, when, and where a British television series will arrive in the U.S., British imports are currently in vogue, not only among ex-pats or PBS lovers but among more formerly "cult" TV watchers who love good SF or fantasy. All in all, it is a good time to be a British import, especially one associated with the *Who* franchise. BBC watchers only hope that the broadcaster can continue to afford to produce such highly promoted and globally watched programs as *Doctor Who*.

A February 2011 article in *The Guardian* notes a pressing problem for British original programming: economic downturns and resulting cutbacks. The article explains that the "great worry is that the BBC is now embarking on years of cutbacks and retrenchments as the cost of out-of-London transfers mounts and the reality of the new license fee settlement kicks in. [The BBC relies on license fees paid by British audiences. The most recent agreement prohibits any increases in the fee until 2016–17.] ... [W]e are in danger of being short-changed, by a BBC already having problems giving us what we want — quality in more quantity" (M. Brown).

Some showrunners are often stretched beyond the bounds of time, energy, and funds to run the type of high-quality programming BBC fans want. *Sherlock* "had audiences begging for more, and co-production funds pouring in; but Steven Moffat, its co-creator, is apparently too stretched making the next series of *Doctor Who*" (M. Brown). Co-production funds seem to be a key ingredient in the commissioning of popular series, as *Torchwood* creator Russell T Davies found out. Although global demand in light of *Children of Earth*'s increased ratings and critical acclaim seemed to make a fourth season of *Torchwood* highly likely, it took more than two years and consideration by more than one possible co-production partner (e.g., Fox and Starz as the two publicized contenders) before the series went into production in January 2011 after the joint Starz-BBC production was announced in June 2010. When the series failed to live up to either partner's ratings expectations (and with Davies' changing priorities in light of personal issues and other television series), by late 2012 *Torchwood* was once again in limbo.

Programming considerations in the U.K. are now affecting product placement in the U.S. more than ever before. Whereas some BBC Worldwide productions, such as U.S. series *American Idol, Dancing with the Stars,* and *X Factor,* are late arrivals after success in the U.K. (where they were known as *British Idol, Strictly Come Dancing,* and *X Factor*), the delay seems more acceptable because an American version follows the British version. It takes time to revamp a series for American production. As well, shows like *Dancing with the Stars* or *X Factor* are reality programs that typically require less budget and production time and are thus more likely to be exported.

BBC dramas require a bigger budget. After *Doctor Who* splurged on a road trip to the U.S. to make "The Impossible Astronaut," for example, later episodes like "The Girl Who Waited"—filmed on sets with little dressing—illustrated a greatly reduced budget. Nevertheless, early seventh season episodes were filmed in Almeria, Spain, once the filming location of classic Westerns *The Magnificent Seven* and *A Fistful of Dollars,* as well as in New York City. Set photos from Spain showed the Doctor riding a horse, and the script from Toby Whithouse was described as having a "Wild West theme." Even when foreign travel was not specifically to the U.S., some fans felt that "Americanization" was inherent in the Wild West motif (Conor) and a reason behind foreign travel, something that Moffat has repeatedly denied.

Dramas also require more production time, which affects broadcast schedules as well as budget. Although the international demand is high for high-quality British drama, and usually only the best shows (e.g., *Doctor Who, Sherlock, Downton Abbey*) are bought as imports, these series are far less likely to be quickly produced, especially in the current economic climate. A lag of a year or more is not uncommon, as *Torchwood* fans have learned. The gap between season two and *Children of Earth* was over a year; the air date for "Exit Wounds," the second season finale, was April 4, 2008, and "Day One" of the following miniseries first was broadcast in the U.K. on July 6, 2009. In the hiatus between the end of *Children of Earth* and the premiere of *Miracle Day,* the BBC formed a production partnership with Starz; the viewing gap for U.K. viewers (and a similar time period for U.S. audiences) was two years (July 10, 2009 to July 8, 2011).

The Christmas specials help dispel *Doctor Who* fans' frustration with a long hiatus between episodes grouped into two distinct seasons broadcast during the same year. Season six, for example, provided a block of seven episodes between April 23 and June 4, 2011, with the remaining six episodes broadcast between August 27 and October 1, followed by another hiatus until the Christmas special. Season seven began filming in February 2012 with a projected broadcast schedule beginning in autumn 2012 and concluding in 2013. Although dedicated fans are willing to wait for high-quality new episodes, casual fans, especially those in countries where entertainment news is less likely to cover the Doctor or Matt Smith throughout the year, may be less likely to retain their enthusiasm for a program or even to return once new episodes are ready for broadcast.

Even with the promise of high-quality episodes at a later date, the threat of budget cuts seems to be a sword hanging over many British imports. *Doctor Who Confidential* was one casualty of the BBC's budget cuts. The cancellation drew fan ire, although the BBC justified the cut because behind-the-scenes information provided since 2005 through *Confidential* now is being provided online, not only by the BBC but by fans. However, British fans viewed the loss of *Confidential* (which was never shown in the U.S. but became available as DVD extras) as the first step in cuts to *Doctor Who* in general (McCabe).

Questions about *Doctor Who*'s recent U.K. ratings also generated what some critics called faux anxiety about the series' future. With a reduction in the number of episodes announced for 2012, fans wondered whether the BBC was beginning to cool once more on the idea of continuing *Doctor Who* past its upcoming 50th anniversary in 2013. With so many austerity cuts looming, could a television series, even one so much a part of U.K. popular culture as *Doctor Who*, survive indefinitely? Offsetting questions about U.K. ratings and a limited number of episodes leading into the anniversary year was the success of the Doctor Who Experience, which did well in London in 2010–11 and then moved to Cardiff, near the new BBC Wales studios. Such a move, fans reasoned, indicated that the Doctor was going to stick around Cardiff for at least a few more years. The 50th anniversary and the anticipated special programming to commemorate it will surely be a cash cow for the BBC, who could milk it for at least a year or two, even if they only produce a series of specials or limited number of new episodes. The new BBC Wales studios near Cardiff Bay indicate that series made in Wales — including *Doctor Who* — will continue, as long as their cost can be justified with enough critical awards and global markets clamoring to pay for more episodes.

Nevertheless, *Doctor Who*'s U.K. ratings for seasons five and six seemed troubling enough in the media that science fiction stalwart, British *SFX* magazine, devoted an article to the concern about ratings. The report begins with the *Daily Mail*'s headline reflecting a further ratings slide from the sixth season's first episode to its second, "Day of the Moon." *SFX* provides an opposite point of view and assures readers that it is not using the fallback "you can prove anything with statistics" argument. The magazine concludes that, despite some vocal fans venting their confusion about or dislike of the current season, the majority are "calmly and sensibly" using facts to discuss the ratings issue. *SFX* explains that the consolidated ratings figures including in the total those people who recorded and later watched "The Impossible Astronaut" had increased the original tally "from an overnight of 6.5 million to a final figure of 8.86 million," which, the author reminds readers, is "pretty much in line with the final consolidated viewing figures for every series opener bar the phenomenon that was 'Rose,'" the first episode of the rebooted series (Golder, "Why Doctor Who's Falling Ratings").

SFX makes some important points. If media choose to quote only the most vocal fans or those upset immediately after an episode is broadcast, then the audience will seem to be leaving a show. If not all audience members are counted because the measuring system is outdated, then a series will seem to be less popular than it actually is. Both have been problems with *Doctor Who*.

Science fiction audiences may be expected to be early adopters of technology. Even those U.K. viewers who wait a year or more for the latest gadget probably have DVRs, download episodes (preferably legally) to a computer or portable device, or otherwise find ways to watch a new episode within a week of its BBC broadcast. Overnight ratings do not take these audiences into consideration. The more the public chooses when and how to view their favorite programs, the farther behind traditional ratings measures, especially those conducted overnight, will lag in accurately reflecting the total numbers.

When a series such as *Doctor Who* or *Torchwood* is sold globally and, in fact, is prized because it has a worldwide audience, traditional ratings measures in one country cannot provide a full picture of who is watching the *Who* franchise. Nevertheless, if U.K.-only ratings are equaled to revenue, fans may be rightly concerned that the BBC might withdraw its support for a series and leave it in the hands of a partner or cancel it altogether.

The *SFX* article also brings up a final point well worth broadcasters' consideration. Is a program only worthwhile to be made if it is written to gain the widest possible audience? If the objective is only to gain viewers (ratings), then a lowest-common-denominator approach to television production is highly desirable. (The trend toward reality programming in the early 2000s attests to this fact, as does the recent trend that the majority of British series exported to mainstream U.S. networks — such as Fox and ABC — are reality music or dance programs.) However, SF stories often are meant to be dark, frightening, prophetic, and enlightening — all at the same time. More than any other genre, SF can safely provide audiences with multiple "alien" or "future" perspectives and ideas that challenge the current status quo. When *Doctor Who* provides a darker story line or asks questions that are difficult to consider, much less answer, perhaps that does not mean that the series is faltering or becoming less family friendly. Perhaps it is doing exactly what good SF should do — challenge the audience to think, not only to follow plot developments but to consider the ideas embedded within the action. That "mission" may be questioned, however, when BBC Worldwide is challenged to sell more products internationally. The U.S. is, after all, a very large market.

Torchwood: The Great Experiment of a U.K.–U.S. Joint Production

Doctor Who spinoff *Torchwood* moved even farther afield of its parent with *Children of Earth* and *Miracle Day,* but it still is considered part of the "family" and technically remains part of the franchise, even in its latest version. Perhaps because *Torchwood* has become more of its own SF series, instead of paralleling *Doctor Who*'s story lines or having crossover episodes in which Captain Jack briefly travels with the Doctor or assists him during a two-part story, the latest episodes include only brief reminders that *Torchwood* is indeed a spinoff series. Its greater physical distance from Cardiff and the studios it once shared with *Doctor Who* reflects the narrative distance between the two shows, which makes *Torchwood* far more likely to be adapted as a joint U.K.–U.S. production than is *Doctor Who*. Although Captain Jack or *Torchwood* does not share the "culture icon" status of the Doctor or *Doctor Who,* they still faced a great deal of culture conflict when they moved—at least temporarily—to the U.S. for *Miracle Day.*

After the acclaim of *Children of Earth,* an abortive attempt to relaunch *Torchwood* on Fox, and the BBC's decision to find a U.S. production partner, *Torchwood* finally was announced as a joint production of U.S. cable network Starz and the BBC. Almost immediately, the press and fans began to question, sometimes rather loudly, whether the partnership indicated that *Torchwood* would become either a completely American remake or an "Americanized" continuation of the original series. Many fans feared that *Torchwood* would be altered so much that it would not bear any resemblance to its Welsh-based first two seasons in particular or even the more globalized but still Cardiff- and London-set *Children of Earth.* Almost from the get-go, *Torchwood* seemed ensnared in a tug of war between cultures and countries. Whether the BBC's great experiment in co-producing a television series with Starz would lead to similar future partnerships on other series (it did), or whether *Torchwood* would be a casualty of culture clash (it was), haunted reports of filming and fan commentary, beginning with *Miracle Day*'s first days of filming in January 2011 through the cast's 2012 comments about *Torchwood*'s future and even its place within the *Who* franchise.

In early January 2011, the fourth season of *Torchwood* filmed its first scene in Los Angeles. During the next few weeks, the production returned to its original home, Cardiff's Bay area, where once again Captain Jack Harkness, Gwen Cooper, Rhys Williams, and Andy Davidson filmed scenes on their old stomping grounds. With locations in and around Cardiff and the Gower coast, *Torchwood* paid tribute to its Welsh roots, but by then, the divide between fans for or against the production was as wide as the Atlantic.

During *Torchwood*'s more than two-year hiatus from television, and the production's much longer absence from Cardiff (where filming of *Children of Earth* concluded in October 2008), fans had plenty of time to vent their anger at the loss of Gareth David-Lloyd's Ianto Jones, build a shrine in the character's memory, and share their frustration in fan forums, on BBC web sites, and in the press. *Children of Earth,* however, also gained *Torchwood* a much larger global audience and much-needed critical acclaim.

Although Russell T Davies' efforts to shop around for a new home for his series turned out to be more difficult than he or the BBC likely anticipated, with the Starz-BBC alliance in place by summer 2010, *Torchwood*'s publicity machine began rolling out new hyperbole about every step of production. Casting notices especially gained notoriety in entertainment news, such as when a big name like Bill Pullman joined the cast. In early 2011, actors tweeted about the first days of filming, the BBC issued updates online about the new series, and fans shared candid photos and stories of their encounters with John Barrowman (Captain Jack) or Eve Myles (Gwen Cooper) on set — whether that set was along a rocky Welsh coastline, back on Cardiff Bay's Roald Dahl Plass, or outside Los Angeles' City Hall. As one blogger commented, fans more often could stand around and watch filming in Wales than in the U.S., even when scenes were shot in public locations, and far more *Torchwood* sightings were posted online whenever filming took place in the U.K. The mood surrounding the cast and crew seemed markedly different in the two countries, with the "home team" in Wales getting the most fan kudos for allowing onlookers to watch the filming, as the Doctor Who News emphasizes in its weekly summary: "Unlike in the U.S., production in the U.K. has not been shrouded in heavy security, and with a (mostly) U.K. production team in attendance, the traditional approach to filming that fans here are used to [has] continued." The *traditional* approach is the U.K. method of allowing quiet, respectful onlookers to watch what is happening in a public filming location; the American production "shrouded in heavy security" is unfavorably described as an atypical and far less friendly way of dealing with fans. The U.K. way "has, of course, meant that the public have been able to witness more of the proceedings than in the previous fortnight, so this week's [news] roundup includes many of their observations as well as the cast and crew's usual tweets!" (Foster, "Torchwood"). The ability for fans to be treated nicely and allowed to watch filming taking place outside of a studio is cause for celebration (indicated by the exclamation mark) at the "business as usual" approach to dealing with fans.

Calling Gwen Cooper and Captain Jack Harkness "modern legends," Russell T Davies glibly discussed *Torchwood*'s fourth season when he was back in Wales during the series' early weeks of filming. *Torchwood* was "home" for two weeks, during which time Kai Owen (Rhys Williams) ended his current stint in the story, tweeting fans about his schedule and recent developments on set. Original cast members Tom Price (Andy Davidson), Owen, Myles, and Barrowman, filmed scenes in and around Cardiff. Once again, the Cardiff waterfront became the setting for new episodes, as did the nearby Coal Exchange — previous filming locations well known to *Torchwood* fans but used sparingly in *Miracle Day*. Perhaps the most prominently photographed shooting location was Rhossili Bay, on South Wales' Gower coast, where fans and the media took photos of huge explosions, as well as helicopters flying above *Torchwood*'s famous black SUV rocketing along the beach ("Torchwood: Week Three Filming").

Despite the number of Welsh settings captured on camera in January 2011, as the following hook into a Welsh news article about *Torchwood*'s local filming indicates, the series is now considered much more American: "Makers of the new series of *Torchwood* seem to be getting the most from their American-sized budget." The article closes with a comment that Wales only received two weeks' filming, whereas the majority of the series was shot in the U.S. (Turner, "Dramatic Torchwood").

In Wales, *Torchwood* is more than just exciting — it is a community event. Although the local press grumbled about American money and filming locations, it also documented the appearance of numerous fans who stood near a former butcher shop along Frogmore Road in Swansea's Sketty district, which had been turned into the set of a pharmacy, one quickly damaged during a high-speed collision. The shot took almost a day to set up, but fans and neighborhood onlookers watched while the scene was set and filmed. *Wales Online* noted that Davies grew up nearby, and Myles also is from Swansea (Turner, "Dramatic Torchwood").

Davies proudly boasted that he likes to show Wales to the rest of the world, and tourist-friendly locations like Rhossili Bay and Cardiff tend to attract fans who like what they see on screen. The Welsh coast also provides a startling contrast to Los Angeles-based scenes, which, during early weeks of filming, seemed to take place in and around public buildings downtown. The culture clash also made its way into the scripts; Davies could not resist telling the local media covering the Rhossili shoot that he "quite enjoyed the little jokes in the show about Brits feeling lost in America and Americans not knowing where Wales is" (Turner, "Torchwood Touches Down").

Interesting for a showrunner who seemed eager to bring *Torchwood* back — and into American living rooms, Davies announced only a few weeks into filming that he might leave the series, even if it were successful in its fourth season and received orders for further episodes. "Personally I think I'm coming to the end of it now and I've saved the world and blown up the world too many times, and I hope I leave *Torchwood* in rude health, and then I'll probably move onto something else then" (Brew). Comments like these worried the series' fans, who tried to read between the lines to see if Davies believed *Torchwood* was already in trouble, if he simply wanted out of this series in order to more firmly establish himself on other series in the U.S., or if *Torchwood* was being handed over to American showrunners.

Starz and the BBC showed only confidence in *Torchwood* and vigorously promoted it long before the first episode was broadcast. Beginning in late 2010, when casting announcements began appearing in the media, through the U.S. and U.K. premieres in summer 2011, seldom a day went by when *Torchwood* was not in entertainment news headlines.

Marketing *Miracle Day*

Similar to the marketing plan for *Doctor Who*, *Torchwood*'s publicity was a combined effort. Starz, BBC Worldwide, and the BBC got out the word that new *Torchwood* episodes would arrive in July 2011. Splashy articles in (U.K. and U.S.) national newspapers like *The Guardian*, *Wall Street Journal*, and *USA Today*, among hundreds of (often rehashed) interviews with the series' creators and cast, encouraged potential audiences to watch *Torchwood: Miracle Day*. Set visits, online and television trailers, billboard advertisements, and magazine advertisements (including, in the U.S., those in *Entertainment Weekly* and *TV Guide*) helped alert audiences to *Torchwood*'s return. Far more than most BBC programs or Starz original series, *Torchwood: Miracle Day* became the focus of an international marketing campaign, including advertisements and publicity, that would take its cast to big events like the MIPTV promotional event in Cannes, France, during spring 2011; special screenings of the first episode at London's British Film Institute and in Swansea, Wales, in late June; and San Diego Comic-Con in late July.

Starz and the BBC each had its own promotions to introduce the series to new audiences. For Starz, that included a behind-the-scenes video introducing the characters. For the BBC, clips from upcoming episodes were included in a summer trailer of BBC programs, concluding with a shot of Gwen Cooper (Eve Myles).

The majority of interviews and promotional events emphasized the returned series' "bigger and better" production values owing to a larger budget and the international scope of the story. In light of *Children of Earth*, a polarizing story in *Torchwood* fandom, such a marketing campaign may have seem warranted to get long-time fans back on board after basically wiping out many series' characters, as well as the setting and scenario that originally attracted them to the show. The 2009 miniseries' greater production values, a tighter five-episode story arc, and a setting change from Cardiff to London, with an international plot, won new audiences as well as critical acclaim and television nominations or awards. Seeking to capitalize on the gains made by *Children of Earth* in ratings and audience share, *Torchwood: Miracle Day* needed to bridge a two-year gap since the last time audiences had watched new episodes and try to regain the momentum lost during such a long hiatus. The resulting publicity for the new series took a multilayered approach to 1) reassure fans who did not care for the miniseries, 2) assure fans of the miniseries that *Torchwood* would be even better next time, and 3) entice new international audiences to begin watching. The publicity surrounding *Torchwood*'s return and *Miracle Day*'s filming determinedly kept the series in the public eye in the months leading to its television debut in July 2011.

According to fans and critics who blogged or posted on forums their qualms about *Miracle Day* long before it made its way onto television screens, the tone of press conferences suggested a pervasive American influence on new episodes. Even the way the series was presented to the public during a Television Critics Association tour in early January 2011 seemed more American in the amount of information revealed and the press tour presentation. One blogger complains that "at first I was a bit annoyed that [Davies] revealed so much, considering how relatively little we knew before *CoE* about what would happen. I hate to quote *Doctor Who*, Moffat Edition here, but 'Spoilers!'" During Davies' interview, a major plot point — that no one on Earth can die as a result of the "miracle" — was revealed. Even if that point would quickly be revealed in the first episode, some fans who wanted to be surprised were blindsided by the unexpected revelation before the first episode was broadcast. The blogger then turns his attention to a perceived cultural difference: "*But there was no way that they could sell this revamp, at least in America, without revealing something juicy* (emphasis added). And there's a lot that those of us who are *Torchwood* fans can chew over in the next few months, like how the man who can't die and just watched two of the people he'd loved most in his hundreds of years of life die will deal with an immortal world" (Franks). Once again, fan attention is on Captain Jack and the way his post–*Children of Earth* grief (and future character development) would be handled in *Miracle Day*.

This fan also encouraged other *Torchwood* fans to watch the new episodes. While acknowledging the many changes the series has undergone, he provides some "encouragement" that might not seem all that positive an inducement for all *Torchwood* fans to watch the new series: "Don't you want to see Jack flirting with every living creature on multiple continents? And don't you want to at least see if this new cast can keep up with him and Gwen and their two loyal compatriots? For me, the answer is yes. I hope you come along for the ride" (Franks).

In response, thirty-three comments were posted to the article, and forty Facebook fans Liked it. The first comment establishes the tone of much of the rebuttal to Franks' plea. Tesa posted that "Torchwood was Cardiff and the Hub and all that went with it. I am not so shallow that I want to see Jack naked and shagging his way across the U.S." Pinkpolyanthus concurred: "the old TW will not exist–this is the all new U.S. version with a tad of Wales thrown in to keep the Anglophiles happy! Of course it is total BS–it now has a worldwide storyline–a bit of which is set in Cardiff/Wales–but it is most American ... and that means Americanised ... and we have all seen what they do to Brit programmes."

Lawsontl perhaps best expresses the argument that, for many fans, *Torchwood* is Wales, although several points of contention exist between fans of the first two seasons and the series' creators. This multi-pronged argument, as the writer emphasizes, has been made "over and over" and is the sticking point for many onetime fans who look askance at the direction the series took with *Children of Earth:* "within the space of five episodes we lost ⅗ of the primary cast, the Hub, Cardiff, the SUV, the quirks like a pet pterodactyl and freaky house aliens, and even the rift in time and space that justified TW Cardiff's entire existence. The only things that remain of the show most of us fell for are Gwen, Jack, and giant plot problems." What most television critics and fans new to the show think of as improvements to the television series are the very reasons why fans "fell" for the series. The first two seasons' episodes may be unevenly written and include elements that require a great deal of suspension of disbelief, but they gave the series its quirky charm and "guilty viewing pleasure" appeal, often because the audience liked the characters and their relationships and were willing to overlook plot problems. Lawsontl elaborates on another reason why some viewers take issue with more recent *Torchwood* miniseries — the number of characters who are killed off by the story's final scene. The writer expects to see "two secondary characters we can pretty much ensure are going to die, if not this season, then the next. With these stats [regarding the deaths of major and minor characters], why invest in the new cast of red shirts?" (a *Star Trek* reference to the original television series in which "disposable" characters wearing red uniform shirts usually die on missions). The final problem involves the expected "Americanization" of *Torchwood* because of its many *Miracle Day* filming locations and story lines set in the U.S. Lawsontl concludes that U.K. fans may not care for new American characters because they "are going to be on such familiar turf for American fans. Many of us gravitated to TW specifically because it was NOT set in America. Hell, Cardiff was downright exotic compared to the usual DC/NY/LA triumvirate."

Although fans who from as far away from the U.K. as New Zealand added comments to express their desire to see Jack again, about half of those who posted were negative about the just-announced plot and concerned that anything Welsh from the original series had been lost in translation to an American audience. Of course, the arguments against watching involved other reasons, too, ranging from the death of Ianto Jones in *Children of Earth*, to the multiple deaths in recent episodes, to loss of the original series' quirks that made *Torchwood* unique, to Davies' and even Barrowman's published responses to fans mourning Ianto. What is surprising is that, more than a year after *Children of Earth*, fans — new or long-time, pro- or anti–Ianto, pro- or anti–Davies — took the time to compose long, often well-written statements about their feelings toward *Torchwood*'s past and future seasons and their reasons for watching or not watching *Miracle Day*. Whatever else *Torchwood* may be, it is a barometer of fan culture, the passion with which fans react (either appropriately or inappropriately), and the multiple rhetorics it inspires. Not surprisingly, the move from Cardiff to LA is more than a geographic shift to these fans, some who specifically lament the loss of a program that seemed to be uniquely Welsh and fear that their former favorite show will become something typically American. All of the hype surrounding *Miracle Day* could not overcome many vocal fans' concerns about the new episodes.

The Problems with Partnerships

The Starz-BBC partnership seemed destined to generate as many questions as it solved problems. What would happen, *Torchwood* showrunner Russell T Davies wondered in the press, if *Torchwood* became a hit in the U.S. but not in the U.K., which was scheduled to receive episodes days later than they were shown in the U.S.? Conversely, what if the ratings outside the U.S. were good, but Starz failed to get the numbers justifying its investment? These types of questions highlight the flip side of international production partnerships that join networks with very different thresholds for determining success. Davies looks forward to new BBC Worldwide-style offerings filmed in the U.S. but questions what might happen if the BBC cannot or does not want to continue to fund series that are not hits at home. He introduces several interesting questions about *Torchwood* after *Miracle Day*: "[W]hat if it does well on Starz but doesn't do well on BBC1? Or if the BBC1 money is tight and they have to take money away — does it become entirely a Starz production, which means they have to own the rights? Would the BBC ... actually give away rights to an existing property?" (Frost).

Jane Tranter, head of Los Angeles-based BBC Worldwide, encourages such partnerships and seeks new ways for the BBC to collaborate with cable networks. Davies is on board with this trend, telling *The Guardian* in July 2011 that both the BBC and premium cable channels (i.e., those subscribers pay for separately, such as HBO, Starz, or Showtime) have similar objectives; they want "dramas that aren't just doctors and nurses and lots of happy endings" (Frost), certainly a plan that Davies followed in both *Children of Earth* and *Miracle Day*. This future model for U.K. television may rely heavily on U.S. partners, and *Torchwood*'s inaugural collaboration may yet determine how new arrangements are brokered or what types of partnerships need to be avoided.

Although *Torchwood* has become estranged from *Doctor Who* since 2010 (some would argue 2009, with *Children of Earth*), it still is a *Doctor Who* spinoff. Even *Miracle Day* alludes to the TARDIS and the Doctor, although no one unfamiliar with *Doctor Who* would realize there is a connection between these series' latest iterations. If the BBC would give up rights to *Torchwood*, the implication is that the broadcaster might also be willing to give up rights to other failing or flailing series as a way to make some profit from what had become a loss at home. It is highly doubtful that the BBC would ever give up rights to *Doctor Who*, whose fortunes have risen and fallen several times in the past half century but who keeps coming back to generate more income for the BBC. *Torchwood*, or any other series that budget cuts cannot promote adequately or produce at a quality high enough for audiences to watch, would be far easier to sell off or cancel if it failed to meet expectations at home or abroad.

U.S. ratings for *Miracle Day*'s first episode, "The New World," which premiered on July 8, 2011, were deemed "a decent start" (Ausiello, "Ratings"). During its first screening from 10 to 11 P.M. on Starz, not even a million people watched, but the combined numbers from that hour and a repeat of the first episode immediately following, from 11 P.M. to midnight, earned *Miracle Day* 1.5 million in total U.S. viewership. Industry newspaper *Variety* termed these numbers "modest" and broke down viewership to specific numbers: 819,000 for the first hour, 687,000 for the repeat (Levine).

Considering that subscribers pay for the premium cable channel and that Starz has fewer subscribers than HBO, for example, this total seems adequate but not exemplary. Among Starz' original series (which included new-to-them *Torchwood*), *Miracle Day* fell short of *Spartacus*' record 1.1 million for a first viewing (with total viewership increased to a total 1.9 million with figures added from the immediately repeated episode). *Torchwood* equaled *Camelot*'s premiere from earlier in the year (Ausiello, "Ratings"). The bad news for *Torchwood* was that *Camelot* had just been canceled when *Miracle Day* debuted.

The problem with almost-instant ratings published for the public was that viewers in other Northern Hemisphere countries where *Miracle Day* had not been shown may decide to stay away (i.e., not waste their time, especially in summer, on a series apparently destined to fail). Even more than reviews, which were mixed in U.S. online and print periodicals, ratings indicate what people actually watched. Potential audiences may not agree with reviewers or may wonder if critics might not have their own agenda in choosing which programs to promote or demolish. Ratings, on the other hand, seem far more objective.

Granted, not every viewer considering whether to watch *Miracle Day* checked the ratings first. With so much media publicity leading up to *Miracle Day*, its name was frequently mentioned in entertainment news, and thus headlines announcing it as an immediate hit or as a possible failure also became newsworthy. Anyone following *Miracle Day*'s press promotion would probably notice at least the headlines of articles touting ratings.

Whereas the audience response seemed less than overwhelming in the U.S., Space, Canada's channel for science fiction/horror programming, declared *Miracle Day* "a death-defying debut." Channel Canada's headline announced the "Premiere of *Torchwood: Miracle Day* Smashes Series Record on Space and Space HD." Certainly the tone of Canadian ratings announcements differed greatly from that in the U.S. Channel Canada wrote that the episode put "a death grip" on audiences (a phrase ironically indicating something good — that audiences could not turn away from watching the episode) and further describes the drama as "gripping" ("Premiere of *Torchwood: Miracle Day*"). The emphasis on mesmerized audiences and high numbers led into a dramatic preview of the next episode.

Canadian audiences received *Miracle Day* before viewers in the U.K., and Space broadcast the first episode only one day behind the U.S. Its ratings for "The New World" were the highest ever for the specialty channel: on average, program viewership is 432,000, but 929,000 watched at least part of "The New World." The audience for *Miracle Day*'s premiere also was 55 percent greater than that for *Children of Earth* ("The New World: Canadian Ratings"). A specialized channel does not draw nearly as many viewers as stalwart Canadian networks CBC or CTV, and Canadian audiences are smaller than U.S. audiences for any program. Nevertheless, by Space standards, *Miracle Day* was a hit, whereas it was only a moderate success on Starz.

In the days following their respective first screenings, Starz and Space provided audiences further opportunities to see the initial episode. Starz broadcast it on a rotating schedule for several days, whereas Space ran the episode on the Tuesday following the Saturday debut and made it available on their Spacecast.com online network. These screenings preceded the BBC's Thursday night premiere (July 14).

To help generate excitement for *Miracle Day,* a few days before the new television episodes were shown in the U.K., BBC Radio 4 broadcast three new *Torchwood* plays, recorded during the last days of *Miracle Day* filming in Los Angeles. *Torchwood: The Lost Files* presents two stories set before *Children of Earth. The Devil and Miss Carew* is a pleasant little story recalling the series' first two seasons of alien hunting in Cardiff. It drew special attention because of the return of Gareth David-Lloyd as Ianto Jones, a character killed off during *Children of Earth.* Ianto fans flocked to listen online or on radio. Although the first story is an interesting enough adventure, the next two offerings, *Submission* and, in particular, *The House of the Dead,* drew larger audiences because they expanded canon regarding the relationship between Jack Harkness and Ianto Jones.

Fans around the world who planned to avoid a Ianto-less *Miracle Day* made a special effort to listen to the radio plays, likely the last canon stories to feature Ianto or the Cardiff-based, alien-fighting *Torchwood* team. Unlike BBC television programs, which require access to the BBC's iPlayer in order to view them online, anyone who can figure out the time zone difference can listen to BBC 4 radio through their website. Perhaps boosted because of the number of international listeners, as well as hardcore Ianto fans, the ratings for these dramas surpassed those of previous years' *Torchwood* radio dramas.

Americans are not in the habit of listening to radio dramas, and usually have fewer options for listening to original programs presented daily by a national broadcaster (such as NPR). BBC radio plays broadcast in 2011, featuring such popular television stars as John Barrowman (*Torchwood, Tonight's the Night*) in the *Torchwood* series of plays and Benedict Cumberbatch (*Sherlock*) in the latest season of *Cabin Pressure,* attract a faithful international following among an actor's fans as well as fans of a television or radio series. The programs could be played for a week after their initial broadcast, which further increased the number of people who listen to these stories and thus improve the overall ratings. The audience share for a radio play broadcast on a weekday afternoon — or early in the morning in the U.S.— is always smaller than that for a television series. Nonetheless, the fan fervor for *Torchwood*'s radio plays in 2011 indicates a different audience, one primarily in the U.K., although dedicated fans living outside the U.K. made a point to hear the stories.

A Den of Geek reviewer wrote what many *Torchwood* fans feared most about the upcoming "American" edition, *Miracle Day:* "So there we have *The Lost Files.* A mixed bag for sure, but never less than entertaining, and concluding with an absolute classic. If you are curious about how the Torchwood team operated before its American influence, you could do a lot worse than check out these stories" (Coupe). Fans worried about undue American influence on what had been perceived as primarily Welsh and secondarily

British *Torchwood* listened to "their" version of the series one more time before the television series was irrevocably changed.

After all the concern about how U.S., Canadian, or Australian viewing numbers might affect the U.K. audience, *Miracle Day*'s overnight ratings from the July 14 premiere were very good. U.S. television series typically are expected to have a larger audience than that for a U.K. series, simply because of the greater number of potential viewers in the U.S. However, the reverse is true of the potential audience for *Torchwood: Miracle Day*; the potential BBC audience is far larger than the number of Starz subscribers. "The New World" received 21 percent of U.K. viewers, meaning that 4.8 million people watched the first episode. The numbers were lower than for *Children of Earth*, which had 5.9 million viewers for its first episode. However, *Children of Earth* was seen first in the U.K. ("Torchwood: Miracle Day Opener Ratings"). It would be difficult to measure how many U.K. fans, disgruntled by the BBC's days-later broadcast of *Miracle Day*, already had seen the episode before it was shown at home. Davies' concern about *Torchwood* becoming a hit in the U.S. but not in the U.K. seemed unfounded, but it brought up future questions to be addressed by *Torchwood*'s partners.

As well, *Miracle Day*'s numbers indicate a global audience wanting more *Torchwood*. Because of the networks on which it is broadcast — such as niche-oriented Starz or Space — the series may never gain a huge following of something like a *LOST*, which garnered huge U.S. numbers even before it was shown in other markets. Nothing in the *Who* franchise can achieve those ratings. However, *Torchwood* can succeed, especially in the U.S., as a "cult" favorite with a much bigger audience base than it enjoyed as a "cult British" favorite. The fans of cult series are truthfully cultivated to buy additional products beyond DVDs of episodes. They will purchase other merchandise related to their series and create or attend conventions featuring its actors. *Torchwood* has not yet tapped into a specifically North American consumer market, although its intertextuality is well established in the U.K., where novels and audiobooks, as well as action figures, have been popular for years. Starz and Space viewers, for example, may be tempted to purchase *Torchwood*-related merchandise and attend within-country conventions, rather than ordering products online or traveling overseas to meet the actors of their favorite series.

Torchwood also has moved away from its original premise by becoming what Barrowman calls "psychological" science fiction. The stories of *Children of Earth* and *Miracle Day* are indeed dark and frightening. With *Torchwood*, however, the question was not whether the series should become more serious, but if it would lose all sense of fun — and destroy the elements of setting and character that gave fans their primary reason to watch episodes. Most critics have considered the majority of *Doctor Who* scripts since 2005 as better written than those for *Torchwood*, although Davies has been praised for the themes interwoven in *Children of Earth* and *Miracle Day*.

Doctor Who's greater claim to British popular culture and its history of disappearing for a while only to return to a waiting audience makes it more likely that, should its budget be cut and number of episodes reduced (or if it is canceled after the anniversary), it will return in some form in the future. Its intertextuality and marketability make it much more viable to survive ratings fluctuations than could *Torchwood*.

Results of the Great Experiment: Implications for Starz, the BBC, and *Torchwood*

By mid–2012, a year after *Miracle Day*'s debut, *Torchwood*'s fate was still undecided but open to interpretation. Barrowman and Myles expressed their hope that *Torchwood* would continue in some form, perhaps as a film. Adding that nothing could happen before 2013, Myles told *Cult Box* that in "every series we've changed our format. We've always had a gap in between, so fingers crossed, because we've got such an outstanding loyal fan base. They deserve *Torchwood* to go ahead with something else to draw a line under it, for the fans to have a bit of closure" (Martin).

Whereas some fans applauded the series' return to an overly dramatic finale in which Captain Jack once again offers to sacrifice himself for humanity and manages to save the day (and the planet), others detested the possibility of an American spinoff, as indicated by the newly granted immortality to American CIA agent Rex Matheson. The first post–*Miracle Day* audio drama on CD, *Army of One*, released on March 8, 2012, features Gwen Cooper and Rhys Williams in Washington, DC, and further cements the idea that *Torchwood* may indeed be international in scope, but at least some future stories will be set in the U.S. The cover of a second CD drama, *Fallout*, pictures previously Cardiff-based Andy Davidson, as well as Gwen Cooper, standing before a London backdrop — bringing *Torchwood* back to the U.K. Although novels published in 2011 include some stories based in Wales, most notably *Long Time Dead*, involving Suzie Costello, a first-season character killed off twice during *Torchwood*'s early episodes, one novel (*The Men Who Sold the World*) revolves around Matheson and the other (*First Born*) around Gwen and Rhys. The apparent shift from Captain Jack to Rex or Gwen as the impetus behind future *Torchwood* stories made long-time fans fully aware that the series was never likely to return to Cardiff on a permanent basis.

Even if Davies and *Torchwood* ultimately fail to benefit from the BBC-

Starz collaboration, the production partners found the collaboration worthwhile. *Deadline Hollywood* reported that Starz Entertainment and BBC Worldwide Productions signed a multiple-year agreement to co-develop and also co-finance several television series. This agreement could produce more than 100 hours of television dramas. The distribution rights were divided as follows: "Starz gets distribution rights for the U.S. and English-speaking Canada, while BBC Worldwide will distribute the series internationally. The deal essentially gives Starz a (non-exclusive) production arm without the large cost associated with overhead as Starz is looking to compete against its more established pay-cable competitors on a far smaller production budget" (Andreeva). The BBC needs an influx of cash to continue to produce more hours of high-quality programming, and Starz needs a partner in order to be a competitor of bigger networks and to see its business grow. Although the arrangement may not have worked particularly well for *Torchwood,* television critics pointed the finger of blame at an inconsistently developed plot and at least one lead character to whom audiences never warmed. The business side of production seemed more likely to achieve greater success as the number of partnered projects increases.

Without Davies' commitment to more *Torchwood* episodes, at least for the foreseeable future, because of, first, his desire to return to the U.K. while his partner received medical treatment, and later, his involvement with a new children's television series, *Torchwood*'s future remains uncertain. Davies more than hinted that *Torchwood* is no longer his priority, either in the U.S. or the U.K. *Torchwood* no longer seems a likely project for Davies to gain a firm foothold in Hollywood.

However, he may feel confident leaving any future seasons in the hands of capable (perhaps American) writers such as Jane Espenson, who effusively praised the series and her collaboration with Davies when she was interviewed throughout production and before *Miracle Day*'s premiere in July 2011. Nevertheless, *Torchwood*'s place in the *Doctor Who* franchise seemed to be changing dramatically by late 2009, and by 2012 its future, in or outside the franchise, was highly questionable and apparently subject to the whims of creator Russell T Davies as much as the BBC or Starz.

Chapter 3

The "Americanization" of British Television

The differences between the perceived quality of American and British television is often debated and stereotypes about what constitutes a "typical" British or American show often the source of humor. British television is praised for being intellectual or daring in ways that U.S. television is not, but British budgets are often the butt of jokes. In contrast, American television is frequently deemed flashy and superficial, with a big budget but no substance. In his speech to introduce the winner of the 2012 South Bank Sky Award for TV Drama, Steven Moffat's other series, *Sherlock*, actor Jason Isaacs (Lucius Malfoy in the *Harry Potter* franchise) humorously described his life in Hollywood, "that great mecca of culture and intellectual pursuit." At awards events he attends in California, he explained, the audience has a distinctly "American" look; "their hair is thicker and the teeth are whiter and the cleavage is a lot deeper." The California crowd seems interested in displays of conspicuous consumption, one exaggerated example being "a car with a jacuzzi in it."

The cultural differences go beyond superficial images, however. Isaacs suggests a deeper difference in cultural mindset, what he termed a "difference in ambition." He next addressed those who make excellent British television programs being recognized with an award: "I look around me at these extraordinary individuals..., and I know that you want to be part of the national conversation that forms the fabric of our daily life, ... to help us connect with what is most human in ourselves and each other.... And that [difference] is no better well represented than in the extraordinary television that we make." After this praise to his immediate audience at the awards presentation, the actor added one final comment about cultural differences before actually presenting an award: "I sit in my house in America, flicking through 100,000 channels of mind-numbing pap, and I think things still look very, very shiny over here" ("Sherlock Wins").

Isaacs' comments drew polite laughter, and he also poked fun at the British tabloid *Sun* in comparison with the *Times,* but his U.S.–U.K. television comparison draws upon accepted perceptions of both industries. The image of Americans, as represented by the Hollywood elite, emphasizes beauty (even if it is enhanced instead of natural) and wealth, as well as the best technological toys that underscore an individual's status — in a word, flash. In contrast, the television programs, and the people who make them, being applauded at the South Bank Sky Awards are more favorably summarized as being purveyors of high quality and substance. The programs they create can make a difference and further the human connection. The British ambition indicated in this speech — which seemed sincere, despite the jokes — is turned toward depth of content, not superficiality, and seems far loftier than Americans' perceived ambition to achieve beauty, wealth, and fame for oneself. British ambition is implied to be more outwardly directed and to have an impact on the "national conversation."

Although *Doctor Who* may not be accorded the same level of intellectual or critical acclaim as *Sherlock*, the SF show is perceived by American fans as equally British and representative of a different expected style and quality. *Doctor Who* may be thought of as entertainment incorporating monsters to tell scary tales, but it also emphasizes the Doctor's ingenuity in finding alternative solutions to problems and illustrates loyalty and friendship. At times it tackles more topical issues, such as depression (as shown in "Vincent and the Doctor"). Of course, *Doctor Who* is family entertainment, but it also embeds some core human values and represents that need "to connect with what is most human." When audiences in the U.S. or U.K. consider the "Americanization" of anything, it often is not a compliment, and because *Doctor Who* is such a cultural touchstone in the U.K., the thought of "Americanizing" the parent or its offspring seems particularly abhorrent.

"Americanization" of a British television series can take many forms, and, if *Doctor Who* and *Torchwood* fans are reliable indicators of fears of television's cultural contamination or globalization resulting in a lack of distinctive cultural markers, both British series face the danger of losing at least part of what makes them identifiably British, for better or worse. Because *Doctor Who* is one of BBC Worldwide's top-selling exports, the fears of "Americanization" are these: The possibility is greater that episodes will be edited to make them more understandable to American audiences or to fit commercial-laden time slots; the content of stories or the direction of future story arcs will be changed to make them more palatable for international audiences. The use of U.S. filming locations and the greater visibility of British actors in the U.S. media or during promotional tours might introduce greater American influence on a series' production. Even worse, the lure of Hollywood might tempt showrunners and actors to move to California.

Questions about the meaning and consequences of "Americanization" compete with those about British ethnocentrism in casting and the quality versus quantity of television programming. *Doctor Who* and *Torchwood* have become part of an ongoing international discussion about differences between the U.K. and U.S. casting, production methods and values, episode content, and even the elements that make up a culture. Fans, cast, crew, and critics all contribute their opinions about what makes *Doctor Who* inherently British, *Torchwood* culturally Welsh, and American television "bigger and better" but not as culturally specific — all emotionally-charged assumptions and expectations that can affect the *Who* franchise.

What Characterizes an "American" Show?

In the months prior to the premiere of *Torchwood: Miracle Day*, critics often questioned whether new episodes would be a reboot of the series, last seen in first-run episodes in summer 2009. The next obvious question, at least to television critics and reporters, was whether *Torchwood* would be "Americanized" because of the Starz connection. With two returning cast members, John Barrowman (Captain Jack) and Eve Myles (Gwen Cooper), having prominent roles in the new episodes, the series might be considered a reboot (i.e., a return of a former series with a continuation of its mythology, including the main character) but clearly was not a remake (i.e., a new version of the series, with completely new cast and location). However, *Torchwood: Miracle Day* was something different.

It was not a reboot, as Davies had done with *Doctor Who* after the series had been off television for a decade. *Miracle Day* is listed as *Torchwood*'s fourth season, which means it is not a reboot, like *Doctor Who,* which began renumbering its seasons with 2005 as the first (after a long hiatus).

It also was not a remake in the sense of the BBC's *Being Human* or *Law & Order U.K.* When *Being Human*, for example, became a U.S. series, it truly was "Americanized." The setting switched from the original Bristol, England, location to Boston. Although the three roommates involved in the story — vampire, werewolf, ghost — were only slightly modified as far as backstory, their names were changed. The plot of many of Syfy's *Being Human* episodes closely followed the first season plot lines of the BBC's *Being Human.* Syfy's characters were American and reflected American culture, language, and history, just as their British television ancestors lived and worked within British culture.

Law & Order: UK took a series in the other direction, from the U.S. to the U.K. The long-running *Law & Order* franchise in the U.S. had a well-established roster of characters and told stories about crimes taking place in New York. Episodes showed the interplay of police investigators with prosecutors who later tried the case based on evidence provided by the police. *Law & Order: UK* copied this concept with episodes similarly structured. A story begins with a crime being investigated by the police; the latter part of an episode involves the trial. Even the familiar "dum-dum" sound effect as an aural transition between scenes and the block titles alerting viewers to a change in time and setting for the next scene made the transfer from U.S. to U.K. *Law & Order: UK*, however, became a "British" series with an entirely new cast, new characters, and London setting. Not only language and culture, but legal procedures, had to be changed to create a plausible reality for the British version.

Torchwood: Miracle Day is unlike either of these series. It is a hybrid: with both Welsh and American filming locations, both U.K. and U.S. actors in the cast, and a plot that spans Torchwood's historic past, much of it involving Captain Jack Harkness, the series' recent past, and the present plot. Russell T Davies continued as showrunner, and, as in previous seasons, he wrote some but not all episodes.

Nevertheless, Davies and U.K. cast members went out of their way to assure BBC audiences and the original U.K. fan base that they are still highly prized and the series had not sold out to American money. Trying to interest new audiences globally and placate somewhat sensitive U.S. or U.K. fans of previous seasons' episodes became an interesting exercise in diplomacy. Articles in specifically U.S. publications, such as *USA Today*, *TV Guide*, or the *Wall Street Journal*, catered to "newbies" unfamiliar with *Torchwood*, whereas BBC-related publications, such as the *Radio Times*, emphasized the continuing British content of the series.

Some U.S. reviewers felt that the series definitely had an American vibe. A Philadelphia *Inquirer* review suggested that "nothing says 'made in America' quite like putting the fighter pilot president from *Independence Day* and one of the stars of *ER* in your cast" (Gray). Based on comments like these in the press, an "American" show may be defined as having these characteristics that distinguish it from a same-genre "British" show:

- Bigger budget
- More and better special effects (e.g., explosions)
- Young, physically perfect actors
- Emphasis on gay characters (a recent shift in U.S. programming that reflects story arcs rather than merely the number of LGBTQ characters in a series)
- More explicit sex scenes (another recent shift in U.S. programming—and then only on cable series)

- Unique language or culture
- Commercials on network television (a traditional aspect of an hour-long U.S. broadcast hour, but one not applicable to programs shown on cable platforms like Starz)

Not surprisingly, when Davies and the cast insisted during interviews that *Torchwood* is not becoming an American series, they touched on these points to show that what was once "Welsh *Torchwood*" is still part of *Miracle Day*. Nevertheless, the checklist of what might be termed a successful U.S. action-adventure series, in science fiction or another genre, seems to have been used as a blueprint for *Miracle Day*. Point by point, the following sections illustrate the cast's acknowledgment of what it would take for *Torchwood* to return to television after *Children of Earth*. Unfortunately, the BBC's economic climate in 2010–11 was not conducive to a more expensive *Torchwood*. As well, by the time *Children of Earth* received so much attention in the media, the series' creators no longer lived in the U.K. but had moved to the U.S. *Torchwood: Miracle Day* becoming a BBC production shared with Starz provided the budget permitting ten more episodes to be filmed. Therefore, the first consideration of whether *Torchwood* has been "Americanized" is budget.

Big-Budget Television

U.S. television series, such as one-time hit *LOST*, often are known for their big budgets, which allow numerous special effects or multiple (or exotic) locations. *LOST*'s two-hour pilot episode, made in 2004 at a cost estimated to be between $10 and $14 million, at that time was the most expensive pilot ever made for U.S. television (T. Ryan). More recently, Fox's television series *Terra Nova*, burdened by production problems and CGI-heavy scripts, led to a reported total cost of $70 million. Compared with figures like these, *Doctor Who*'s estimated budget of £13 million per season (about $20 million U.S. in 2012 dollars) seems modest; even reality show *X Factor* costs approximately £2 million per episode (Bettridge). The production values of some U.S. series come close to blockbuster movie quality, and the concept of "bigger and better" often is attributed to American entertainment.

The BBC's partnership with Starz afforded *Miracle Day* a much larger budget, even bigger than the one provided for *Children of Earth* to make the jump from BBC Two to primetime BBC One (and a huge leap in budget and prestige from its original home on BBC Three). In April 2011, publicity surrounding the cast's interviews at the MIPTV event in Cannes, France, revealed that *Miracle Day*'s budget had tripled; later reports in July suggested it had merely doubled. In either case, the production benefited from more money, presumably provided by Starz ("Torchwood Budget"; Bulkley).

The continued presence of U.S. money became evident even before *Miracle Day*'s premiere. In early June 2011, the California Film Commission announced twenty-seven recipients (down from thirty-two the previous year) of tax subsidies for the 2011 tax year. If *Torchwood* continued production in California for what was called its second season, the project would receive a share of the $100 million tax subsidy. Because the number of applicants for funding increased from 70 in 2010 to 176 in 2011, *Torchwood* was indeed fortunate to be one of the 27 winners (Block). If ratings or other factors precluded new episodes, then the funding would go to another project. Presumably, because *Torchwood* remained in limbo in 2012, this funding was indeed lost. However, the announcement about a month before *Miracle Day* premiered heavily suggested that further U.S.-based production was being planned at the time.

Another source of revenue for Starz is the fee paid by subscribers who want to see its programming. Although *Miracle Day* was part of BBC programming paid by citizens' license fees, American viewers also had to pay for the privilege of seeing the episodes. Although many viewers pay to get BBC America, *Torchwood: Children of Earth*'s broadcast home, as part of a cable subscription, Starz is a premium channel that requires an additional fee. Just prior to the U.S. premiere of *Miracle Day*, Barrowman told potential audiences that "[t]his is an amazing series you're about to see. So you will be happy spending the money ... to get Starz" (Jeffery, "John Barrowman").

More and Better Special Effects

Blowing up stuff costs a lot of money. So does production on two continents. For *Miracle Day* to have that "bigger and better than ever" quality the creators and cast touted in interviews, the production values needed to reflect the globalized story and higher expectations for the series' overall look. When insiders talked about what was new or improved in *Miracle Day*, they often mentioned special effects, including the use of helicopters, bazookas, and aerial footage of an action sequence filmed at Rhossili Bay, along the South Wales coast.

Other explosions and chase scenes were filmed in and around Los Angeles. Although filming in multiple locations had been hinted back in 2010, location filming took place in Wales mostly in January 2011, from Cardiff to Rhossili Bay, and then in Southern California, with the addition of other U.S. locations in specific scenes. Although Washington, DC, footage could be used to establish the setting, actual filming took place in LA, with Orlando standing in for DC during an airport sequence, for example, and Denver-area locations were used to film medical-conference scenes.

Young, Physically Perfect Actors

Barrowman and Myles (or Captain Jack and Gwen) are the cover faces on the *Radio Times* issue for the week of July 4, 2011. Getting the cover is serious business, as Myles mentions in a behind-the-scenes video of the photo shoot released that week. The video, linked to the BBC's website, emphasizes *Miracle Day*'s British connection and importance to the broadcaster. No U.S. actors (e.g., Mekhi Phifer, Bill Pullman) are shown, even in the background, of the issue, and the story clearly is focused on *Torchwood*'s original stars.

Definitions of beauty are, at best, subjective and, at worst, subject to criticism and worthy of analysis and sensitivity. It is probably a fair statement, however, that the way "beauty" is portrayed and promoted on U.S. television often has been criticized, especially when it suggests such high standards that young women in particular feel they cannot achieve without dire measures. Youth and physical attractiveness are often deemed a U.S. obsession.

When my students in humanities classes watched *Torchwood*'s early episodes (or *Doctor Who* episodes from 2005 to 2010) during the 2010–11 academic year, they often commented on the actors' appearance. Some students picked apart the looks of female actors in particular; Myles' gap between her teeth and the shape of her face received criticism, but Captain Jack's shirtless chest also was scrutinized. Weight, height, teeth/smile, and facial features often bear the brunt of students' criticism, and British actors sometimes are unfavorably compared with American actors in terms of beauty. One student suggested that, should *Torchwood* ever become an American series, a different cast would need to be hired if they were to pass inspection from hypercritical U.S. viewers.

The *Radio Times* article addressed this issue by focusing, not surprisingly, on female beauty: "there have been no demands from Starz executives that Myles lose weight or firm up to conform to the glam tyranny of U.S. TV" (McLean). Nonetheless, Barrowman lost weight before filming began, and his trademark coat also slimmed. Costume designer Shawna Trcpic revealed that she remade the coat in new material better suited for filming in Los Angeles and created a tailored silhouette while keeping the coat's cape-like qualities. "I brought in the waist 24 inches. He's [Barrowman] lost weight, but the other coat was quite billowy" (M. Ryan). Whereas Myles' and Barrowman's appearance is praised in the *Radio Times* article, the issue was at least important enough to bring up.

More Gay Characters

Years ago, back when Davies was best known as the creator of British series *Queer as Folk*, British television seemed far more likely than U.S. television to include LGBTQ characters. With the recent popularity of primetime American shows ranging from comedy *Modern Family* to musical dramedy *Glee*, or even to Neil Patrick Harris' rousing musical opening number at the 2011 Tonys, "It's Not Just For Gays Anymore," U.S. television at least superficially seems more welcoming to characters of any sexual orientation.

Davies attributes the shift in sensibility to the popularity of award-winning *Glee* and *Modern Family*. "The portrayal of gay, bisexual, and lesbian characters [in America] is currently way ahead of Britain.... The kids on *Glee*, the beauty and detail of that couple on *Modern Family*. We've got nothing like that" (Hibberd). Undoubtedly, Captain Jack also is a role model, something that entertainment website Squidoo noted in its description of this TV character: "The character itself has become a role model for young gay and bisexual people in the U.K., and I think for many in the U.S. as well" ("Captain Jack Harkness").

Torchwood's second season episode "Kiss Kiss, Bang Bang" includes a scene in which Captains Harkness and Hart (James Marsters) engage in rather enthusiastic kissing. "Kiss Kiss, Bang Bang" or even a kiss-and-grope scene in "Adrift" are far less graphically portrayed than the sex scene in *Miracle Day*'s episode "Dead of Night." A few episodes later, "Immortal Sins" again showed a sexually explicit scene of Captain Jack in bed with a male partner. The increasing level of sexual explicitness in scenes depicting Captain Jack's homosexual liaisons continues to push the boundaries of television, although Starz, home of the even more sexually explicit *Spartacus*, is far less likely than the BBC to censor Captain Jack.

Explicit Sex Scenes

When Fox was considering whether to greenlight *Torchwood*, Captain Jack fans feared that he would either "turn heterosexual" on the conservative network in a conservative U.S. viewing climate or only briefly visit a completely American cast before leaving for good. Either way, fans speculated that Captain Jack as shown in the BBC's *Torchwood* would cease to exist. The concerns prompted Barrowman to reiterate in several interviews, before and after Starz acquired *Torchwood*, that he would not want to play Captain Jack if the character's sexuality were changed. No one wants a neutered Captain Jack.

Starz' reputation for sexually explicit programs indicated that sex scenes would be de rigueur (and rigorous) in *Miracle Day*. Barrowman also publicized the scenes, noting his delight in going to work to have sex with a 24-year-old man. The scenes are filmed so that plenty of flesh is visible and specific sex acts can be easily identified, but even Starz avoided full frontal nudity.

Miracle Day emphasizes Jack's homosexuality (although his previous sexual relationships have included women and alien species, meaning he is omnisexual, despite the homosexual emphasis in the latest episodes). In addition to a one-night stand with Brad, references are made to past male sexual partners, including Ianto Jones. However, Jack also indicates his attraction to Gwen, who, despite her abiding fondness for Jack, is a married woman committed to her husband and child. The door is left open for Jack to entertain future sexual partners of either gender (or any species).

Starz permitted *Miracle Day*'s scriptwriters to more explicitly show Captain Jack's (as well as Rex Matheson's) sexual encounters. In the case of Captain Jack, however, audiences had often been told about but had seldom seen the good captain in action. *Miracle Day* allows Jack's sexual prowess to become real for viewers who could voyeuristically observe the character participate in a variety of sexual acts.

Starz' reputation also increased the likelihood that Barrowman would be asked about sex scenes and partners during *Miracle Day*'s publicity. Interviewers encouraged Barrowman to discuss Jack's sexual nature and, as a secondary topic, his experiences as a gay man living several months a year in the U.S. Such interviews are sure to titillate potential viewers and gain more publicity for the series.

The legality of same-sex marriage differs by nation, and although some states recognize legal unions between same-gender partners, the U.S. lacks the uniform legalization of civil unions found in the U.K. In a June 2011 interview, Barrowman commented on the legal differences between U.K. and U.S. as a result of a recent experience with U.S. Customs (and, arguably, customs). The actor and partner Scott Gill arrived in the U.S. so that Barrowman could film *Torchwood*. However, they could not go through Customs together because their civil union is not recognized in the U.S., which angered Barrowman and provoked him to challenge the authorities. Barrowman complained that "all of a sudden Scott comes over here and we don't have the same legal rights as we do in the U.K. And while I'm fortunate enough to have an American passport and my dual nationality, he's not recognized as my partner, and so he doesn't have the same benefits that I do over here, which I think is absolutely ridiculous" (Duralde). *Miracle Day*, in real life as well as on screen, challenged differences between U.S. and U.K. social norms and cultural expectations.

Unique Language or Culture

Another area of cultural difference is terminology, reflected in the different vocabularies of characters speaking British (Br) or American (Am)

English. During an awkward scene in an early episode, Gwen returns from a shopping trip with (Br) crisps (Am — chips), bought with cash from a (Br) cashpoint (Am — ATM). She also has to stop for (Br) petrol (Am — gas). American Esther Drummond translates for her. Gwen complains that her canned lemonade is not what she expected. Drummond explains, "It's fizzy in the U.K. and flat in the U.S." (Espenson and Davies). Such scenes tend to flatten the buoyant nature of *Torchwood* by pointing out rather clumsily the cultural differences in language and products.

Even local landmarks, in the U.S. or U.K., can provide symbolic or cultural references as well as serve as geographic identifiers. Just as Big Ben is a landmark and symbol of London, so does the Washington monument represent Washington, DC. Although on-screen text identifies the city for those unfamiliar with the landmark, the choice of the tower dominating Washington's landscape helps audiences recognize the change in setting from the U.K. to the U.S. One of the most popular Cardiff landmarks is the water tower on Roald Dahl Plass, which, until *Children of Earth*, was an entrance to Torchwood's Hub. Switching from one tower to another as a visual shift from Cardiff to Washington makes the monument an especially apt choice.

The Severn bridge is another symbolic landmark used both in *Children of Earth* and *Miracle Day* to illustrate differences between Wales and another country. When Gwen leaves Wales for a quick trip to England on "Day One" of *Children of Earth*, she laughingly tells husband Rhys "Goodbye forever!" as they end their (Br) mobile (Am — cell phone) conversation. He previously teased her about having the right currency as well as inoculations before she goes into England (Davies, "Day One"). Even viewers outside the U.K. could understand by context the cultural difference and national pride in making a distinction between what is Welsh and what is English. Similarly, during the BBC's 2011 promotion of *Miracle Day* in the U.K., a scene in which an American sneeringly calls Gwen "the best the U.K. has to offer," Gwen slugs her while replying, "I'm Welsh" (BBC).

In *Miracle Day*, American Rex Matheson drives from England across the Severn bridge into Wales. He makes disparaging comments about the bridge and then balks at having to pay a toll before he can enter Wales. Getting into Wales seems provincial (and expensive) to the American. It even serves as a final joke late in the episode when he lists his complaints about his life since the "miracle": not knowing if he is really dead or alive after being impaled, learning about Torchwood and not yet getting the answers he seeks from them, and paying the bridge toll (Davies, "The New World"). Not knowing that Wales is separate from England seems to be a comment about "typical Americans" ignorant of other nations' geography or history.

Conversely, when Gwen gets into a getaway car during an escape from a Washington, D.C., airport, she balks at the tiny car (Egan and Davies). Ironically, the large Torchwood SUV drove the team around South Wales for more than two seasons. Gwen's complaint flips common assumptions that Americans drive big, gas-guzzling vehicles, whereas compact, fuel-efficient cars are the norm for the U.K.

Comparing what is considered to be typically "American" with what is typically "Welsh" is often mined for humor, especially in *Miracle Day*. The series tends to get these comparisons out of the way early on, but viewers who want to see elements of Welsh (or British) culture or language may be disappointed at the way cultural differences are handled. Davies acknowledged the limited use of cultural differences: "I could bore you to tears with a million cultural differences between Britain and America but actually [Captain Jack and Gwen would] kinda look like [Br] arses [Am — asses] if they couldn't cope in America! There's a lot of bad dialogue I'm really glad we haven't chosen to do — there's some funny lines from Gwen about it in episode three, but not for long" (Berriman).

In addition to these obvious cultural comparisons, a few symbols more subtly make their way into *Miracle Day*. When Gwen chats with former police partner Andy Davidson in a hospital, a vase of bright yellow daffodils sits prominently on the desk. Americans likely will not realize that daffodils are the national flower of Wales. Adding this little detail to a Cardiff-filmed scene asserts the episode's Welshness in a way that U.K. audiences, particularly those living in Wales, could recognize.

When the cultural references are subtle, such as flower symbolism, they are usually left into an episode and are not a topic for humor. More obvious comparisons of language or lifestyle form the basis of humor, but the joke only works if everyone understands both cultural references. *Miracle Day* provides many types of cultural comparisons, but it still may not be as "British" as Anglophile American viewers would want.

Commercials and Advertising

Although U.S. network television is beset with nearly 20 minutes of advertisements per hour, BBC audiences watch an entire (usually) 45-minute drama without interruption. Cable-based Starz also shows an episode in its entirety, which leveled the viewing field for *Miracle Day* audiences.

Selling airtime is only one aspect of paying for a series or promoting a product. In *Torchwood*'s case, a more important consideration was the amount and type of advertising and promotion afforded *Miracle Day* as a result of the U.K.–U.S. collaboration. Both countries utilized billboard campaigns to make people aware of *Miracle Day*. Trailers abounded on the Internet, increasing in frequency and including episode footage in late spring 2011. As well, Starz and the BBC promoted the series, using different clips or images, to alert their viewers about new *Torchwood* episodes.

The U.S. benefited from additional screenings in major markets, such as Boston, New York, Chicago, Atlanta, and Los Angeles, on July 5 and 6 (Starz). Screeners (advance copies) with the first three episodes went out to television critics and other entertainment professionals who could promote the show with their reviews or online/in-media comments. Starz provided subscribers with an on-demand five-minute behind-the-scenes promotional video. On the U.S. premiere date, July 8, hundreds of newspapers carried articles and reviews promoting *Miracle Day*. Starz even provided an early viewing online at midnight on July 8.

In the U.K., special screenings took place at the British Film Institute in London, where the cast and series' creator answered questions after the first episode had been played. A few hours later, another screening in Swansea, Wales, followed by another Q&A, allowed the press and fans to interact with Barrowman, Myles, and Davies, in particular. The event seemed to be a "return of the conquering hero" whereby the cast could "bring home" their gift of new episodes to their home-country fan base. During the first week of July, Barrowman appeared on several U.K. talk shows, where he could promote his two BBC series premiering only a few days apart: *Torchwood* and the second season of *Tonight's the Night*.

Whether paid advertisements, promotion on their own networks, or related publicity and marketing promotions, both the BBC and Starz supported campaigns to make sure a global audience knew that new episodes were coming. The intermittent flurries of press releases and publicity in effect gave *Miracle Day* more than a year's build-up to the first episode's broadcast, a level of promotion *Torchwood* had never had.

This promotion began as soon as the Starz-BBC partnership was announced in June 2010 and continued with frequent updates about production news. Casting calls and announcements of new, frequently well-known actors hired for the new season began in autumn 2010 and continued through spring 2011, well into *Miracle Day*'s filming schedule. Mekhi Phifer (formerly of *ER*) received a great deal of interest when he was cast as Rex Matheson, *Torchwood*'s American lead. Announcements of the casting of former *Ghostbuster* Ernie Hudson and *Star Trek*'s Q, John de Lancie also earned a flurry of SF-related online articles. The biggest casting coup was film actor Bill Pullman, perhaps best known for *Independence Day*. *Torchwood*'s ability to attract many well-known actors boosted its credibility as "event" television, something for which Davies rapidly was developing a reputation in SF programming.

When filming began in January 2011, more articles and interviews appeared on the Internet. Teasers arrived online by April, when *Miracle Day*'s cast attended the MIPTV television-promotion event in Cannes, where entertainment reporters interviewed the stars and took advantage of numerous photo ops. True advertising, in the form of more specific trailers involving footage, new promotional photographs, and billboards, increased more than a month before the premiere, especially after the official U.S. (and world) premiere date was set for July 8.

The frequency of international advertising and publicity made U.K. fans eager to get the broadcast date from the BBC, which withheld the information until late in June. Building up interest in the returning (or new-to-many-viewers) series became a multi-year project, leading some critics to wonder if *Miracle Day* could live up to its hype or whether audience anticipation of new episodes would lead to viewers feeling somewhat letdown when seeing the complete product. The trailers featured rapid cuts among chases, explosions, and concerned faces. The promotional poster consisted of the world as a bomb with a lighted fuse. Starz' promotional character interviews, in which the main U.K. and U.S. characters talked into a camera about life after the miracle, were dramatic and suggested a horrific apocalyptic event. Such build-up, especially when online articles swarmed around newly released teasers or potential spoilers, kept *Miracle Day* in the public eye far longer than most new or returning television series. For some fans, the increased money spent on such promotion indicated a further shift toward "Americanism"—lots of money for publicity, a blockbuster event, and media saturation.

The resulting "checklist for Americanization" created from the BBC's, cast's, or crew's response to media questions about *Miracle Day* suggests that, despite what the original cast members proclaimed to the press, *Torchwood* had undergone a series of changes during the production of *Miracle Day*. Whether the resulting episodes were indeed "bigger and better," as the series' stars and creator had promised, was left up to television critics and international audiences to decide.

Is Captain Jack American?

Captain Jack seems a natural character to guide *Torchwood* to the U.S. because he sounds and acts like an American. Scriptwriter Jane Espenson even mentioned in one interview that Captain Jack Harkness *is* American. Fans familiar with *Doctor Who* and *Torchwood* canon immediately pounced on this comment, wondering if it signaled a change in what was to be considered canon or if it indicated a lack of understanding of Jack's backstory by one of *Miracle Day*'s scriptwriters and most vocal proponents.

Technically, in *Doctor Who* canon, the former rogue Time Agent poses as an American RAF volunteer during World War II and later mentions that at home, on the Boeshane Peninsula, he had once been the Time Agency's poster boy, nicknamed the "Face of Boe." *Torchwood* canon includes the information that Jack appropriated his current name from a real American volunteer, but the time traveler's true name is unknown. References to Jack's 51st century pheromones and physical differences to "ancient" humans on Earth in the 21st century further layer early *Torchwood* audiences' understanding that, although Jack sounds "American" and has developed a cover story consistent with this persona, he is, in fact, an "alien" from the future.

Miracle Day audiences may not know this backstory, although they are told in "The New World" that Jack was immortal but now is mortal — and furthermore, apparently the only mortal human after the miracle occurs. The Captain's immortality (or lack of) is one of the primary ways in which Jack stands out from the people living around him. He often seems "other" to natives where he lives (e.g., as an "American" living as a Welsh citizen but retaining his accent, as a man wearing an RAF coat [or suspenders/braces] in the 21st century).

In *Miracle Day* he is able to blend in linguistically better than Gwen, whose accent and vocabulary are obviously Welsh instead of "mainstream American." When Jack infiltrates a hospital to gather information about the miracle, he dons a shirt, tie, and overcoat appropriate for the role he plays as an FBI agent. When he dresses as himself, he reverts to the wardrobe most familiar to *Torchwood* fans: cape-like coat, blue work shirt with white t-shirt underneath, braces and belt, and dark trousers. Such attire causes sharp-dressing CIA operative Rex Matheson to nickname Jack "World War II."

Despite Jack's attempts to blend into either U.K. or U.S. culture at various points in the character's continuing story, an underlying theme of every episode is that the real Jack looks or acts different from the man others perceive him to be. The layers of Jack's backstory are gradually peeled back to continue to intrigue even long-time fans who know all details presented in previous episodes. For that reason, when Espenson or Davies refers to Jack as "an American," hardcore fans wonder if the canon is about to be conveniently changed to fit *Torchwood*'s shift to the U.S. Calling Jack "American" as a matter of convenience for new audiences who do not need to know the entire canon surrounding Jack is one thing, but changing "canon" to make a key character possibly more desirable to an American audience creates more of a problem for long-time fans.

However recent comments are construed, the fact remains that Captain Jack Harkness, especially in *Doctor Who*'s 2005 episodes and the first two seasons of *Torchwood*, illustrates many characteristics associated with "typical Americans." As one British *Doctor Who* fan explains, the cultural difference among citizens of the U.S. and U.K. or Commonwealth countries may be described as being "forward foot" or "back foot" (Hanhart). Americans often lean forward when they talk with others. They are less hesitant to provide an opinion or ask a question. They may be louder in conversation. They are forthright and more likely to jump into a discussion or volunteer an idea. In contrast, British citizens or those from Commonwealth countries often are more reticent or softer spoken. They "take a step back" and consider information and options; they listen and observe before offering commentary.

If viewed in this way, Jack Harkness seems very American. He often is loud and brash; he commands attention and seems larger than life. He seldom hesitates to express an opinion, volunteer to leap into action, or take charge of a situation. Perhaps that is another reason why Captain Jack and Rex Matheson have a tug-of-war over who is in charge. At first, CIA agent Matheson is in charge and forces Jack to travel to the U.S. Once there, though, Jack's experience with Torchwood shifts the balance of power, a fact that Jack likes to rub in. Both characters seem equally "American" in their desire to take charge. They do not like anyone to stand in their way, and they visually and verbally express their displeasure when their orders are not followed immediately.

In *Doctor Who* episodes like "The Empty Child," when the Doctor praises British ingenuity and determination to survive during the Blitz, the series seems more nationalist and patriotic. In this context, Captain Jack, con man and self-proclaimed American, stands out as outspoken, brash, and impetuous. He often acts before he thinks of all the ramifications. In such an episode, the cultural differences, politically and socially, between Yanks and Brits can be easily compared in a historic context.

Miracle Day emphasizes more superficial differences, such as terminology, but manages to compare Captain Jack with a real American, Rex Matheson. In such a comparison, Jack still seems "other," but for different reasons. He is able to seem American because of language, accent, and knowledge, but his experience, shift between immortal and mortal, and even wardrobe suggest that, even in the U.S., Jack will never completely fit in. In *Torchwood*, he will always be somewhat of an outsider, no matter how successfully he can display an American persona.

New viewers may assume that Jack is really American, although he lived in Wales and was a member of Torchwood for decades. Long-time fans who balk at Jack being seen as really American, as opposed to simply continuing to masquerade as one, may feel that Jack-as-true-American is moving the series itself toward Americanization.

Begging the Question: Has *Torchwood*'s Balance of Power Shifted Westward?

Do all these differences equate to an "Americanized" *Torchwood*? The subject comes up frequently enough during interviews that one Australian reporter mentioned Barrowman becoming "tetchy" about discussing it yet again. In that interview, Barrowman is quoted as saying, "We had to look elsewhere [because of budget, perhaps; definitely after *Children of Earth*] in order to keep the integrity of the show.... It seemed the correct progression to be a bit more epic" (P. Brown). Nevertheless, the actor insisted, all the elements that made *Torchwood* unique are still in place.

It is a sentiment that Myles echoes in an article targeted specifically for British fans unhappy with the U.K. lag in broadcasting the series. Myles emphasizes U.K. fans' importance not only to the series, but to her, Barrowman, and Davies. She told unhappy British fans that "[w]e never, ever, ever wanted to take this show away from the original fans." Instead, the cast and production team wanted to give fans "a gift every year, something wonderful .... We've made you the best, best series yet. And it works out that it will be a week after the U.S. showing. And obviously we have nothing to do with that — me nor John [Barrowman] or [showrunners Russell T Davies and Julie Gardner] ... We want [fans] to sit back and enjoy it, be proud of it like we are, and to stick with us" (A. Ferguson).

Not only did Barrowman and Myles attempt to reassure British fans (i.e., the "hometown" crowd) that they are important to the original stars but that the series would retain its Welshness, even in *Miracle Day*. The language in this message is especially interesting; Myles reminds fans that the showrunners and cast do not control the program's scheduling — the BBC does. As with the use of Twitter throughout *Miracle Day*, messages like this one help align the cast and showrunners with the fans. If fans feel there is an "us" and a "them," the series' creators and actors consistently indicate that they feel camaraderie with fans. These messages never say anything against the BBC, but they subtly side with fans on the issue of *Miracle Day*'s broadcast schedule.

Although Myles and others' messages may not have made fans feel better and certainly did not affect the series' scheduling, the actors continued to reach out to their fans. Even in 2012, when future *Torchwood* episodes seemed far away if they materialize at all, Myles commented in the press that the series' fans are loyal and that she and Barrowman would eagerly return to film another, likely final story.

Espenson also has continued to discuss *Miracle Day* with *Doctor Who* and *Torchwood* fans. Most notably, she tweeted during the episodes as they were broadcast in the U.K. and tried to offer additional content to British audiences. (See Chapter 7 "Tweet Success" for further discussion of Espenson's use of Twitter to attract more viewers to *Miracle Day*.) At the February 2012 Gallifrey One *Doctor Who* fan convention in Los Angeles, Espenson, as well as other *Miracle Day* scriptwriters and actors, talked with fans about the show and expressed their enthusiasm for the project. The cast's and crew's interaction with fans, through official media as well as Twitter, provided a personal touch that was far more effective than Starz' or the BBC's attempts to maintain the series' fan base.

Changing the Context: *Doctor Who* for Newbies

Torchwood may be far more likely classified as "Americanized" than *Doctor Who*, but the venerable parent program also has been modified for the U.S. market and, more important in the long run, has faced controversy over the disparity between U.K. and U.S. ratings. As well, with season six filming taking place in the U.S. and the American West subtly influencing the Doctor's style, plus Amy Pond's controversial voiceover narration to BBC America's episodes, even the very British series seems to be accommodating the American audience more than it has in the past.

Strangely enough, showrunner Steven Moffat's approach to storytelling in some of season five and the first part of season six often seems oppositional to BBC Worldwide's attempts to get new viewers to watch the show, because some plot threads tie together multiple episodes and require viewers to pay attention to more than one episode in order to understand the complete story. Not every episode in the fifth season is part of an ongoing story (e.g., "Vincent" is a good example of a standalone episode that pleased viewers new or old), but many episodes are part of a larger, overarching story arc. To understand the complete story requires audiences to see all the episodes pertaining to the continuing plot thread.

Season six begins a River Song-themed arc that concluded just before a summer hiatus with the announcement of River's true identity. Although the serial format was heavily used in "classic" episodes' story arcs prior to 2005, only shorter (usually two-part) story arcs had become the recent norm, but the majority of episodes could be viewed out of order within a season without audiences becoming confused. Moffat has not returned to a truly serialized format like the "classic" serials of several episodes clearly forming only one story. Instead, character relationships are developed over a series of episodes, with a revelation before a hiatus; clues introduced in a series of episodes eventually pay off with an "ah ha" realization; a continuing mystery leading to audience questions (e.g., Who is in the astronaut suit? Is the Doctor really at the end of his regenerations?) is at least partially solved or most questions answered by the end of the season.

While U.S. publicity strives to bring more viewers to the show, Moffat seemed equally determined to tell good stories without undue concern about writing for new viewers or designing only stand-alone episodes that would be easily understood by audiences wanting to sample only one or two episodes. During controversy over the press' alarm at *Doctor Who*'s ratings in spring 2011, Moffat seemed unconcerned about criticism. He writes scripts for an intelligent audience who should easily be able to follow what some critics and fans deem convoluted plots. When the *Radio Times* asked for whom he writes *Who* episodes, Moffat answered with a question: What makes a great story? "I write it to entertain me. You can't write to entertain anyone else, because then you are making assumptions about what other people would like" (Millard).

Telling a good story is paramount, and the *Who* franchise often excels at telling gripping stories that attract audiences worldwide. The way *Doctor Who* was established as a series back in the '60s makes it far more adaptable to the changing fortunes of the BBC or the whims of the public. Moffat and, before him, Davies have always seemed confident that a good story will find its audience.

Giving audiences a different perspective on the Doctor apparently is one of Moffat's objectives. Having the youngest actor in the role play the oldest Doctor creates some intriguing story possibilities, which Moffat seems determined to explore. Although long-time fans often compare Smith's Doctor with Doctors from the "classic" years, especially Second Doctor Patrick Troughton, new viewers are more likely to compare Smith with his immediate predecessor, David Tennant. That Moffat took *Doctor Who* in a different direction may actually help some new fans get involved with the series — they, like everyone else, are finding Moffat's vision for the Doctor to be different from the series' recent past, even if it also resonates with elements of classic *Who* storytelling and characterization.

Although Amy Pond has been a polarizing companion — fans either seem to love or hate her — American audiences (especially men) tune in to see "sexy Amy." The relationship between Amy and the Doctor often seems sexually suggestive, especially before her marriage to Rory Williams and the many trials and separations the couple endures during season five, but the Doctor never pursues her. Nevertheless, in the first two episodes of the Moffat era, the Doctor has disrobed in front of Amy and Rory (but only Amy grins and watches), and Amy has thrown herself at the Doctor, wildly kissing him. The Doctor always manages to disentangle himself from Amy and, before long, to include her long-time (and long-suffering) boyfriend-then-husband Rory in their travels. However, Amy's penchant for wearing short skirts coupled with her former job as a kiss-o-gram made some British parents question *Doctor Who*'s place in children's or family programming on national broadcast network BBC. In the U.S., the series' increased sexiness seemed to improve ratings. Adding Amy to the program made the Doctor seem more grown up and likely to appeal to a wider audience.

Of course, the "dark" stories, which Moffat also favors in seasons five and six, appeal to BBC America audiences who like the network's other SF series broadcast on Saturday nights, such as *Being Human, The Fades, Outcasts,* or *Bedlam.* Although U.S. and U.K. audiences both watch *Doctor Who* on Saturday nights, BBC America has cultivated an audience wanting supernatural series or scarier SF on that night (although adding Graham Norton's talk show to the programming mix in 2011–12 diminished the impact of SF-only programming previously established on "Supernatural Saturdays"). In the U.K., the early Saturday evening time slot turns *Doctor Who* into far more of a family-friendly program. BBC America viewers are more likely to think of *Doctor Who* as an adult SF series rather than family entertainment.

Because of the perhaps-contrived "sexy Amy" controversy of season five and the "too dark" story arc of season six, critics began to question in print just how these trends factored into ratings. Articles questioned whether British ratings actually were declining or only seemed that way because of some reporters' interpretation of the numbers. What the media and fans agreed upon was the fact that the Doctor, assisted by Amy Pond, was reaching more viewers than ever in the U.S., no matter what the ratings indicated in the U.K.

This dichotomy between the need to entice new, perhaps more international audiences to the *Who* franchise and keep true to a series' original premise and mythology became more evident not only in *Doctor Who* but with *Torchwood* in 2011. That year, more than any since 2005, became a watershed for the *Who* franchise. *Doctor Who* began a greater marketing presence in the U.S., plus filming of both *Doctor Who* and *Torchwood* took place on two continents, and both series' stars made appearances at fan events in the U.S. They also courted the media, whether through late-night talk show appearances or more standard newspaper or magazine interviews. Both series became global entertainment entities (and advertised more frequently in the U.S.) more than they had been in the past. To some fans, these trends equated to "Americanization," despite showrunners' comments to the contrary.

Chapter 4

Intertextuality and the Doctor

In his book *Triumph of a Time Lord: Regenerating* Doctor Who *in the Twenty-first Century,* fandom and popular culture scholar Matt Hills defines intertextuality as "the integrated transmedia development of the *Doctor Who* brand across mobile phones and websites." It presents long-time fans with a "consistent, multi-platformed hyperdiegesis, or narrative world" that appeals to newer, or "emergent cult-like fans, who could follow *Doctor Who* across platforms as a matter of interactive 'tele-particpation,' without necessarily even thinking of themselves as including traditional 'cultists'" (219). Building on this definition, I consider *intertextuality* to include multimedia formats, from print publications (e.g., novelizations, comic books, magazines, posters), to audiovisual platforms requiring a specific playing device that may not be mobile for all viewers (e.g., television episodes, webisodes, radio dramas, videogames, CDs, DVDs, Blu-ray discs), to tangible objects (e.g., action figures, t-shirts, collectible plates, coffee mugs, other fan-purchased official or BBC-sanctioned ephemera), as well as the transmedia Hills includes in his definition (e.g., smartphone-, iPad-, iPod-, etc.- downloadable or accessible media, websites).

Although many other television series have developed a web presence about a television series, in addition to a plethora of merchandise, *Doctor Who* is one of the best examples of intertextuality, using my expanded definition. Its long history provides a wealth of television and print texts in particular. Additionally, BBC can promote or create new *Doctor Who*-related texts through its multiple broadcast arms (BBC Three, Two, and One television, BBC Radio) and BBC-related publications, such as BBC Books.

Long before other television series offered a plethora of products, and in the days before the Internet made television series' websites a required fan resource, the Doctor's non-televised adventures abounded in other media, whether through novelizations, comic books, magazines, or yearbooks. One hundred fifty-six *Doctor Who* novelizations, published under the Target imprint, began with *The Abominable Snowman* in 1974 and ended with *The Paradise of Death* in 1994 (DrWhoGuide). Virgin's series of sixty-one *Doctor Who* adventures primarily center around the travels of the Seventh Doctor, with one story featuring the Eighth. These are only the beginning. Other book, CD and audiotape, and comic book stories help fill in gaps between canon stories or hiatuses in television broadcasts, and fan creations further add fanon to canon.

Since 2005, BBC Books has published hardback novels further exploring the travels and relationships of the Doctor and his companions. Instead of being novelizations, the novels tell new stories of the Ninth, Tenth, or Eleventh Doctor and his companions. Six novels feature the Ninth Doctor, with companion Rose Tyler for the first three and Rose and Captain Jack Harkness joining them in the final three stories. The Tenth Doctor stars in an impressive thirty novels, with Rose continuing as his companion in the first six. Martha Jones is the Doctor's companion in thirteen novels; Donna Noble travels with him in only three. The Doctor loses not only Rose but Martha (who decides to leave him) and Donna (whose sacrifice of her mind in order to save humanity means that she can never remember the Doctor). True to his self-imposed isolation in the television series, the Tenth Doctor travels alone during the final seven novels. By June 2012, the Eleventh Doctor already had shared adventures with Amy Pond as his sole companion in four novels and with "the Ponds" (Amy and boyfriend-then-husband Rory Williams) in ten more, with at least one more hardback arriving before year's end. Beyond the hardback novels, the Darksmith Legacy, also published by BBC Books, involves the Tenth Doctor in a ten-part series of young adult novels. The Eleventh Doctor and the Ponds tackle adventures more suitable for younger readers in a series of paperback novels. Other sanctioned ongoing print series return to earlier regenerations.

In describing "What Fandom Did for Doctor Who," Den of Geek's Andrew Blair describes the period between *Doctor Who*'s cancellation in 1989 and the series' return in 2005 as the era that "produced some of the greatest *Doctor Who* stories ever told, helping young writers go on to great things, from *The League of Gentlemen* to *Action Comics*. Fans have argued ... that without keeping *Doctor Who* alive in this way, the show would never have returned in 2005." The fans created the demand, which first Virgin books and, beginning in 1997, BBC Books supplied, as did *Doctor Who Magazine* and Big Finish.

The BBC logo-bearing books are only the beginning of the Doctor's long history of intertextuality. The lag time between a book's release in the U.K. and its availability in the U.S. has understandably shortened over the years, but books far more than other *Doctor Who*-related merchandise have been easier for American fans to find on their bookstore shelves, even before online ordering made downloadable books and audios or overnight shipping an even faster way to follow more of the Doctor's non-televised travels.

Over the years, reliance on only television or paper texts decreased as intertextuality branched out into different media through which the Doctor's adventures could be presented: CDs, radio plays, and in-person appearances (by the character, not the actor appearing as himself). Children in Need specials and proms provided additional ways for fans to see characters in real-life-related skits. Proms featured the Doctor's companions (e.g., Freema Agyeman as Martha Jones) as hosts to an intergalactic event involving monsters and mayhem integrated with music and special effects. More recently, interactive events revolve around high-tech depictions of the Doctor, such as the Doctor Who Experience that opened in London before relocating to Cardiff. U.K. fans more than U.S. fans benefit from in-person appearances or interactive events, but online interactive sites and games, as well as fan-instigated role playing and cosplay, add to the number of total texts and experiences, official or not.

As Mark Campbell noted in his episode guide to *Doctor Who*, fans "have never had it so good." Although some *Who*-related texts he mentioned in his 2007 book no longer exist (e.g., *Doctor Who Confidential*), and the magazine directed predominantly to American fans, *Doctor Who Insider*, stopped production in 2012 after only a year, the fact remains that, since 2005, "[a]fter decades of squandering marketing opportunities, the BBC have at last realized they can make a bob or two from the programme, and while *Doctor Who* and its assorted offshoots remain popular, this should continue indefinitely" (11). The variety of merchandise made available through the BBC or producers of sanctioned products does more than make money from *Doctor Who* and its spinoffs. It also makes more texts more available for fans, even those in the U.S., where for many years merchandise other than books (or, later, DVDs) has been difficult to find or purchase.

Buying DVDs, CDs, novelizations, collectibles, and so on directly from the U.K. through eBay and Amazon or online stores like Forbidden Planet is far easier now than ever before, although American fans buying *Doctor Who* or *Torchwood* merchandise from overseas pay a higher price than their British counterparts, owing to a weak U.S. dollar and shipping costs. Nevertheless, the web's interactivity and immediate access to fan-created (unofficial) and BBC (official) texts have given American fans nearly as much access to the complete range of *Doctor Who* texts as fans have in Britain. All they have to do is work a little harder to find what they want and to be patient while non-downloadable texts are sent to them.

Since 2005, the market for *Doctor Who* merchandise, which increases the number and variety of texts through which fans learn about the Doctor, has changed dramatically from the "old days." Simon Guerrier, a long-time *Who* fan, frequent convention guest, and writer of Big Finish dramas, among other *Doctor Who-* or BBC-related works, explains that "before the show came back, *Doctor Who* merchandise was a relatively small but lucrative area, mainly based round adult collectors. Now it's a huge and broad market" (Blair).

Unfortunately, the market seemed too "British" for American buyers around the time that *Doctor Who* returned to television. Mal Young, another long-time *Who* fan who became the BBC's Controller of Continuing Drama Series in 1997, recalled that "Julie Gardner and Russell [T Davies] headed off to LA to pitch [the series] as a potential co-production to hopefully make up the shortfall [in budget needed to produce the series to meet expectations] ... US Networks were looking to reinvent their own brands like *Battlestar Galactica*" and *Doctor Who* "was seen as too British." When *Doctor Who* became a hit, BBC Worldwide was "able to sell it all over — especially to the Americans" (Blair). To generate more interest in the returned series — that is, to remove the impression that the brand had been tarnished by a long hiatus or old preconceptions about production quality, as well as to interest new viewers — meant offering additional "texts" so that new viewers could enjoy (and buy) plenty of products and perhaps go back to see what they had missed in the "classic" series. Young noted that "the books and audio plays helped convince everyone there could still be an audience.... We knew we had to attract audiences outside of the core fan base" (Blair). The American audience, which also includes the core fan base, nevertheless became a largely untapped new market for additional products.

The Perils and Perks of Intertextuality in the *Doctor Who* Franchise

Not only does *Doctor Who*-related intertextuality promise a variety of age-appropriate or media-specific products or interactive experiences and events for all ages and levels of fan involvement, but it also allows fans to continue to bask in the presence of their favorite Doctor, even if he regenerated long ago. New adventures of former Doctors continue to be published or recorded (or released on disk) each year. BBC official or approved events and merchandise (those bearing the BBC logo) supplement *Doctor Who* episodes and enrich fans' understanding of individual "Doctors" as well as the composite character — after all, no matter that fans tend to number them (e.g., Eleventh Doctor, played by Matt Smith) or showrunners and actors differentiate their version of the Doctor from others who developed the role, the Doctor is only one character. Understanding how he has looked and what he has done in the past can help inform audiences about the current television iteration. Fan-generated "texts" (e.g., fiction, videos, role-playing games, cosplay) present yet another layer of intertextuality. In this chapter, however, the emphasis is on BBC official (i.e., radio plays, television episodes) and sanctioned (e.g., novels or comic books bearing the BBC logo) texts and the ways that intertextuality may affect audiences' interpretation of a character.

Character Development Across Texts

Ideally, character growth means that audiences/fans develop a more complex understanding of a character and a shared history that adds to their depth of understanding and greater personal meaning attributed to characters and television series. The more an audience knows about a character, the greater they may become invested in a television series and more likely to stick around to learn even more.

Just as continuity of monsters or nemeses, companions (i.e., Sarah Jane Smith), the TARDIS, and — most important — a regenerating Doctor have helped ensure *Doctor Who*'s television longevity, intertextuality has helped the franchise survive and thrive, even when the parent series' or spinoff's television episodes or seasons fail to live up to fan expectations. It is not a coincidence that the most recent spinoffs gained audiences in the U.K., or even made it to America, because their main characters have a rich intertextual background. Both Sarah Jane Smith and Captain Jack Harkness began as the Doctor's companions, but they also star in tie-in novels, magazine articles, recorded audio adventures, and live radio dramas. They developed and continued to build on their core characterizations introduced in *Doctor Who*, but they evolved into lead characters of their own series, becoming transformed as they took on new roles. Sarah Jane became a mother and mentor. Captain Jack became a citizen of Earth and an integral part of Torchwood. Just as their roles expanded, so too did their multimedia stories. Although intertextuality is key to the *Doctor Who* franchise's success, it is also one measure of a spinoff's success in the U.S.

Penguin turned to novelizations of episodes when it published paper or e-books about *The Sarah Jane Adventures*; eleven were produced between 2007 and 2010. Because the "New *Who*" books are novels, not novelizations, *The Sarah Jane Adventures* thus shares yet another link with its "classic" parent: Target also published novelizations of much earlier *Doctor Who* episodes. Even after the death of Elisabeth Sladen, two audio adventures completed the series of ten, including BBC radio dramas and stories developed only for the audio books. In 2012 the complete set of audio stories was made available on disk.

Online ordering sites like Amazon.com, for example, offer the novelizations and audio books, but they were never as readily available in stores. American fans of this series needed to be aware of these additional texts; casual *Doctor Who* fans in the U.S. were far less likely to run across them or know to look for them online.

Whereas *The Sarah Jane Adventures* did not become well established in the U.S., *Torchwood* was clearly developed as a joint British-American production with the U.S. audience in mind. Between July and October 2012, several web, radio, or print texts helped serve as a transition between the television episodes comprising *Children of Earth*, which began *Torchwood*'s transition to a global, rather than a purely British television series, and *Miracle Day*, the BBC-Starz co-production. These texts became even more important to the spinoff's success, but they also took *Torchwood* far away from its parent television series. New texts not only had to keep Captain Jack recognizable to long-time fans but also had to introduce him to and quickly establish his character for a new television audience. The problem with intertextuality may come when, because of so many available texts offering different perspectives or depictions of the same character, fans may become confused by competing or contradictory versions that cannot easily be explained away.

For example, if the Captain Jack of "The Doctor Dances" seems very different from the Captain Jack of *Miracle Day*, at least some changes can be attributed to the character's growth because of a wide variety of experiences and, in Jack's case, centuries of time between his initial meeting with the Doctor and Rose and his meeting with Rex Matheson. As well, Jack's role in each story is different. In *Doctor Who*, he is a supporting character; in *Torchwood*, he plays a much larger (usually leading) role. Although "The Doctor Dances" and the *Miracle Day* miniseries involve crises, they are of different types and have different potential consequences. Such differences in time frame and plot may reasonably explain character growth or even temporary "out of character" behavior. If, however, in *Torchwood* texts, Captain Jack strays too far from what is expected, given fans' knowledge of his long history and their own experience with multiple texts involving Jack, the dissonance may be too great, and fans (readers/viewers/listeners) may not accept that text or its depiction of the character.

In contrast, the Doctor can display a wider range of behaviors before viewers declare them too uncharacteristic to be believable. Intertextuality has helped keep the Doctor alive during television hiatuses and is one reason why *Doctor Who* is nearly a half-century old. Torchwood as an entity, just like the Doctor as a "composite" character, may continue indefinitely. Both might end for a while on television, only to be brought back later; they could "retire" from television but remain alive through BBC-sanctioned products, including new print and audio adventures. Granted, the Doctor is far more likely to return, in the U.K. or even U.S., than Torchwood, but both *Doctor Who* and *Torchwood* have proven to be malleable and attractive to different audiences at different times.

Whereas the Doctor's — or Torchwood's — intertextuality is theoretically unlimited, even internationally, that of Captain Jack may face limitations. The actor, for example, may decide to no longer play the role. An American television version of *Torchwood* (emphasizing newly immortal Rex Matheson, or even Gwen Cooper in Washington) or tie-in stories that feature other characters may effectively someday limit Captain Jack's intertextuality and character development. For the time being, however, *Doctor Who*'s and *Torchwood*'s Captain Jack Harkness provides a unique opportunity to analyze a range of television, print, and audio texts and their impact on audiences over several years.

The Cost of Intertextuality and Determinations of What Is Canon

Whether a text is free or purchased is one way to distinguish what is *Doctor Who* or its spinoffs' canon and what is not, even if the text in question is not fan created but is approved or sanctioned by the BBC. In the U.K., audiences receive official *Doctor Who* or *Torchwood* texts broadcast on BBC television or radio "free" as part of their annual license fee. Fans can choose to pay for additional "sanctioned" texts, such as novels labeled with the BBC logo. In contrast, American fans, for example, have to pay (specific premiere cable services or businesses selling *Doctor Who* or *Torchwood* merchandise) for every text, making U.S. fans less likely to make fine distinctions about what is considered canon. Because many non-canon texts — such as those novels — bear the BBC logo, non–U.K. fans often consider these materials as "real" as canon, or what the official storytellers deem is "correct" about a character.

However, using British-specific definitions of *official* and *sanctioned* are helpful in setting a definition of *canon*. In this book, *canon* refers to official BBC-produced texts broadcast free under the license agreement with citizens. Canon consists of BBC television episodes and radio plays. *Sanctioned* refers to texts British audiences would have to buy in addition to paying a license fee. Sanctioned texts may be approved by the BBC and bear its logo, but they are not canon. BBC Books' novels, for example, are sanctioned texts. Anything fan created that is neither sanctioned by nor officially from the BBC is considered *fanon*.

Most *Torchwood* fans are familiar with Captain Jack Harkness as portrayed throughout two thirteen-episode BBC television seasons; the miniseries, *Children of Earth;* and a ten-episode BBC-Starz production of *Miracle Day*. However, the television series is not the complete story, or even the complete canon. Jack also has appeared in *Doctor Who* episodes, both before and after his stint with Torchwood, and in official BBC radio plays. BBC-sanctioned, but not considered canon stories include *Doctor Who* and *Torchwood* novels, *Torchwood* comics, and audiobooks. Because hardcore fans tend to look for new or additional materials that supplement television episodes, they are more likely to purchase more texts, which then influence their interpretation of the character.

Some American Interpretations of the Intertextual Doctor

Although the U.S. boasted many *Doctor Who* fans long before 2005 ended a very long hiatus, a new generation of fans began following the series, dubbed (to the irritation of many fans) "New *Who*," as opposed to the "classic" series. Once more — to restate — *Doctor Who* is one television series that should be enjoyed by all fans. However, the designation still has been made by some critics and fans, and the increased number of young viewers who began watching the series with the Ninth (Christopher Eccleston), Tenth (David Tennant), or Eleventh (Matt Smith) Doctor makes these most recent incarnations particularly familiar to American audiences who tuned in to Syfy (back when it was still Sci-Fi) and then to BBC America. The Doctor in these guises is more likely to be co-opted by American viewers or interpreted with a peculiarly American twist. The Ninth Doctor, himself a veteran who may be suffering from PTSD, could gain sympathy from U.S. viewers in a post–9/11 world who were afraid of a global apocalypse. Episodes like "Dalek," in which the Doctor wants to destroy the last remnant of the enemy who killed the Time Lords, resonated with some viewers who wanted to hunt down terrorist organizations they held responsible for deaths on U.S. soil. The episode also allowed those who feared the War on Terror and urged caution against a black-and-white "us" versus "them" mentality to use Rose as an example of some middle ground. Rose understands that both sides — the Dalek and the Doctor — are damaged because of war. She feels shame at the way humans have imprisoned and tortured the Dalek. She questions the Doctor's judgment in preferring both he and the Dalek die, effectively destroying both races, rather than let the Dalek live.

Even when the Doctor deals with Americans, the Time Lord is easier for American viewers to relate to. Not only is he a heroic, if damaged, character, but he seems to be more of a universal character than a pro–British alien or a British icon. In other episodes, such as "The Doctor Dances"—or, in later (Tenth Doctor) episodes featuring a Margaret Thatcher-type leader or (Eleventh Doctor) dealings with Winston Churchill—the character seems quintessentially British. Americans may identify more closely with the Doctor when he is "universal" in his actions, such as when he is dealing with generic villains or aliens, rather than dealing with enemies in London or during iconic periods of British history, such as World War II.

In "Dalek," rich American collector Henry van Statten finds and imprisons the Dalek (and has plans to study the Doctor), making him a villain and hardly the way American audiences want to think of themselves. Nevertheless, the "American personality" indicated by purchasing the latest technology or gadgets (or, in this episode, aliens) and equating bigger or richer with better becomes part of this episode, even if Van Statten is not intimated to be representative of all Americans.

By 2011, the political mood of America had changed from absorption with a global War on Terror to greater economic and social concerns at home. The Eleventh Doctor, although certainly capable of tracking down an enemy (e.g., "A Good Man Goes to War"), also seemed more familiar with U.S. popular culture (e.g., Marilyn Monroe, Richard Nixon, Stetsons, convertibles) and youthful and spontaneous, especially intriguing given his advanced age. Enough episodes were filmed in the U.S. (e.g., Utah, New York City), with more public appearances by the cast, to make the U.S. seem like the Doctor's vacation home away from the U.K. Even when other Season 7 episodes were filmed outside the U.K. (i.e., in Spain), the "Western" motif seemed familiar to U.S. viewers. Whether scriptwriters or showrunners intend for U.S. audiences to interpret episodes or characters through a uniquely American perspective, they do so and decode the Doctor's (or other characters') words and actions based on an American cultural lens. The layer of cultural meaning increases the number of potential readings of any one text and makes intertextuality even more complex as an interpretive tool.

Perhaps nothing about the Doctor's most recent regenerations seems to cross cultures and attract young female viewers as much as the venerable Time Lord's love interests. Many of the "classic" Doctor's companions are female (e.g., Susan, Jo, Sarah Jane, Leela, Romana, Tegan, Ace), but Rose Tyler is the one who wins his affection through at least two regenerations. The women who have traveled most recently in the TARDIS gained a whole new audience for *Doctor Who*—one more likely to be female and young. Although sexist generalizations like "boys like the monsters, girls like romance" fail to do *Doctor Who* justice, part of the Doctor's post–2005 appeal has been his often difficult or dangerous liaisons with his companions.

In a spring 2012 interview, *Doctor Who* showrunner Steven Moffat proclaimed, "It's always [the companion's] story. It was Rose Tyler's (Billie Piper) story, it's Amy Pond's (Karen Gillan) story—the story of the time they knew the Doctor and how that began, how it developed and how it ended.... The story begins again, not so much with the new Doctor, but with the new companion. The Doctor's the hero, but they're the main character" (Potter). The Doctor's intertextuality goes beyond a new look or personality when he regenerates; even during the same regeneration, the Doctor changes in relation to the companion. Their relationship forces him to react emotionally and to base future decisions on what he learns from dealing with his (usually) very human companions. Increasingly in "New *Who*," the Doctor's love nature is an intriguing development that is explored differently through different "texts."

The Ninth Doctor frequently holds hands with Rose when the pair are in danger of imminent death, and their quarrels prompt Rose's father to assume that his daughter and the Doctor are a couple. However, the Doctor clearly does not "do domestic" and finds ways to escape spending time with Rose's mother. Even the long-awaited kiss the Doctor bestows upon Rose is given to save her life, not for romantic reasons. Although Rose initially has difficulty accepting the newly regenerated (Tenth) Doctor, she comes to love him. When they are separated in parallel universes, both the Doctor and Rose threaten the fabric of space-time in order to be reunited. A "clone" of the Doctor eventually becomes Rose's "consolation prize"—she can never have the Doctor she loves, but she can literally have part of him in the form of a mortal hybrid who loves her and agrees to stay with her for the rest of their lives.

Determined to be a loner after he no longer can be with Rose, the Doctor's next companions are Martha Jones, who suffers from unrequited love for the Doctor and finally decides to leave him for her own good, and Donna Noble, who becomes the Doctor's best friend and pseudo-sibling. Donna, too, is separated permanently from the Doctor, and her life would be in jeopardy if she ever remembers traveling with him. These losses further prompt the Doctor to travel on his own for awhile, even if his adventures lead him to some attractive women who are clearly interested in him (e.g., Astrid Peth, Lady Christina de Souza). Rose, however, is the Tenth Doctor's love relationship, and the Doctor manages to visit her one more time before he regenerates, making hers the last face he sees.

In particular, the "sexy" Eleventh Doctor received greater criticism in the U.K. than in the U.S., and his companion, "sexy Amy," attracted plenty of fanboys of all ages everywhere. However, she and her character faced backlash primarily in the U.K., who thought Amy's skirts too short or her "kiss-o-gram" history too risqué for watershed viewing. No such complaints came from the U.S., a nation whose television critics often value young women simply because they are beautiful. American audiences expect beautiful young actors in an action series, and the Doctor and Amy fulfill those roles.

In addition to his complex relationship with Amy Pond, the Eleventh Doctor is surprisingly good with children. He meets Amy when she is a young girl and completes his regeneration while she looks after him. He tracks down kidnaped, pregnant Amy, eventually finds her also-kidnaped daughter, and later, apparently, develops quite a meaningful personal relationship with River Song. The Doctor even understands baby Stormageddon and helps the child's overwhelmed father develop a bond with his son. The Eleventh Doctor is vastly removed from the emotionally awkward and far from domestic Ninth Doctor or the moody, guilt-ridden Tenth Doctor. These three incarnations are very different in appearance, certainly, but also in personality traits and ability to express their emotions, especially love. Yet because the series' premise allows the Doctor to be radically different in each regeneration, these differences can be accepted by audiences who want to get to know the latest version of the Doctor or who may compare him (favorably or not) with earlier incarnations.

Intertextuality strengthens and lengthens the Doctor's life in any medium; the mass-media texts are so numerous that I will not even begin to list the many games, Big Finish audio stories, magazine stories, and comics that are yet other important indicators of the Doctor's long-lasting popularity and multiple "versions" to interpret. Although *Doctor Who* may never become mainstream television in the U.S., its merchandising is more likely in U.S. markets — whether online or in malls, at fan conventions or in sci-fi shops — and the prevalence of print, audio, and e-books, in addition to episodes being broadcast or watched on DVD/Blu-ray, keep the Doctor making house calls throughout the U.S.

Chapter 5

Intertextuality, Captain Jack, and the Future of *Torchwood*

The Doctor as a single character is, at this point, a composite of eleven different interpretations of him at different points in his, television's, and British history; being able to be so adaptable in his evolution undoubtedly is a prime reason why *Doctor Who* has been around, in one medium or another, for nearly fifty years. The Doctor can become almost any personality when he regenerates, and fans who join the series at any point should be able to "recognize" the Doctor in his new incarnation, even if he seems very different from the personalities they otherwise have known him as. Whether the Doctor is portrayed on screen, only through audio, or in print, he has a great deal of flexibility to change while, paradoxically, remaining the same.

Unfortunately, intertextuality is more limited for Captain Jack Harkness. Despite Jack's extremely long string of serial lives, he, far more than the Doctor, must stay within expected behavioral parameters. If the character is not recognizable to audiences as "Jack Harkness," based on what they know of the character and their assumptions about reasonable variations on his personality, they may not accept him or choose to follow his further adventures.

Nevertheless, Jack as a character on *Doctor Who* or *Torchwood,* on television or in stories told through other print or electronic media, is a unique character in a study of multiple texts simply because his immortality allows writers to adapt him far more easily to a variety of situations, time periods, and settings; he quite reasonably could be anywhere in time or space, just like the Doctor. He may interact with species or characters new to science fiction, on heretofore unknown planets, and, if Jack's behavior seems plausible from what audiences already know about him, then the new story can easily become incorporated into the character's and audience's database of acceptable variations on the character of Jack Harkness. Because his character can be so malleable within the *Who* franchise, the number of texts involving Jack Harkness is extraordinarily high.

On television, he appears in three *Doctor Who* episodes with the Ninth Doctor, six *Doctor Who* episodes with the Tenth Doctor (including a cameo before the Tenth Doctor regenerates), and, to date, forty-one *Torchwood* episodes, as well as seven *Torchwood* radio plays. Most international audiences are likely to be familiar with at least some of these canon texts and less likely, unless they are dedicated fans, of understanding Jack through his role in other sanctioned media, including three novels during the Ninth Doctor's travels, two brief mentions in two novels about the Tenth Doctor, seventeen *Torchwood* novels, and six original *Torchwood* audio books, plus additional short stories and comics (some published in *Torchwood* magazine) and webcasts.

With so many texts to choose from, and even considering that Jack would change because of the experiences explicated in these many stories, audiences must find enough continuity among them to make sense of the character and find his behavior plausible in a given situation. International audiences, in particular, who may gain access to *Doctor Who* or *Torchwood* episodes after they were broadcast in the U.K.—or who may want to see older episodes or peruse non-television texts if they like the character and want to learn more about him—need continuity of character development and a clear sense of who Jack is as a character, no matter where in his timeline they pick up the story. Does intertextuality make Jack a more accessible, complex character, or do so many texts end up confusing fans about who Jack really is? Furthermore, because Captain Jack is so intimately connected with *Torchwood*, how does Jack's intertextuality affect the series' future?

Fan Surveys: The Many Roles of Jack Harkness

To discern how at least some fans interpret this character, in spring 2011 I distributed a fan survey, soliciting responses through my Facebook page as well as on *Torchwood* fan groups' pages. The survey coincided with *Miracle Day* filming and Russell T Davies' and John Barrowman's comments to the media about Jack's role in the upcoming series. One hundred Facebook fans of *Torchwood* identified Jack's most important roles in the first two seasons of *Torchwood*, then *Children of Earth*, and finally as anticipated in *Miracle Day*. The roles listed in the survey are daredevil, follower, leader, hero, lover, martyr, problem solver, sacrifice, savior, sex object, and villain. Respondents could choose more than one role as important, which is why the percentages add up to more than 100 percent for each list.

Based on the first two seasons' episodes, 91 percent thought that Jack's most important role was as Leader, followed by 77 percent choosing Hero, and 56 percent choosing Lover. Considering only *Children of Earth*, 63 percent of respondents most often chose Leader, but Sacrifice was close behind, chosen by 61 percent. Hero was chosen by only 51 percent. During *Children of Earth*, Jack was perceived as a Lover by 52 percent of these respondents, but only 7 percent viewed him as a Sex Object.

Ironically, according to these fans, in *Children of Earth* Jack is seen as a Leader or a Sacrifice more often than a Hero, although half of the group thought of him as a Hero. Sixty-four percent anticipated that in *Miracle Day* Jack would be primarily a Hero, a slightly higher percentage than the 61 percent who selected Leader.

Perhaps these shifts between Leader and Hero indicate the way Jack is perceived as Torchwood's leader. During the first two seasons, his actions were seen as those of Torchwood's leader but not necessarily as heroic. In *Miracle Day*, without Torchwood officially existing at the beginning of the story, it seems natural that fans who had not yet seen the *Miracle Day* episodes would perceive Jack as more of a loner Hero than as an organizational Leader, especially from the early publicity given to new American characters in the story. During *Children of Earth*, Jack's actions are only seen as heroic by half the respondents, but the majority view him as a Leader or Sacrifice, a very interesting finding given the nature of Jack's actions regarding the alien enemy, the 4-5-6, and the British government in this miniseries.

Where is Lover or Sex Object in these results? Reflecting on the first two seasons, 56 percent selected Lover and 25 percent selected Sex Object as an important role. During *Children of Earth*, Jack's role as Lover was perceived as slightly less important than in previous seasons (52 percent chose Lover, down from 56 percent). Only 7 percent chose Sex Object, especially interesting given that Jack is shown nude in two *Children of Earth* scenes, whereas he only briefly has been implied nude or shown bare chested in the previous two seasons. Nudity, in *Children of Earth*, may have been linked to Jack's role as Martyr or Sacrifice, given the nature of the scenes and their lack of sexual or romantic context; he is shown tortuously coming back to life (sans clothes, naturally) and escaping a military prison cell wearing only manacles.

Perhaps because of *Miracle Day*'s early promotional focus, 26 percent chose Sex Object as one of Jack's most important roles in upcoming episodes, but only 17 percent chose Lover, perhaps still a fan reaction to the loss of Jack's partner, Ianto Jones, and many fans' hope that Jack would not have a monogamous post–Ianto relationship in *Miracle Day*. In hindsight, once the episodes had been broadcast, fans were accurate in their assessment that Jack's sex life was emphasized more than his love nature, although flashbacks and references to previous relationships (especially to Angelo Colasanto) also add depth to audience's understanding of Jack's ability to form longer lasting romantic attachments.

Although there is only a 1 percent difference between perceptions of Jack as Sex Object during the first two seasons and as anticipated in *Miracle Day*, Sex Object was the eighth choice of role from the first two seasons but the sixth most popular choice of role for Jack in *Miracle Day*. Suspicion that Jack might be relegated to a role of lesser importance in *Miracle Day* matches the finding from comparisons of canon texts that the smaller Jack's role in a story, the more likely he is to be emphasized as a sex object. Although Jack is recognized as Torchwood's former leader and an increasingly valuable source of knowledge, Rex Matheson is promoted as the American leader in the newly formed "Torchwood" team shown during *Miracle Day*, and comparisons of Jack and Rex set up the characters as competing for audience attention as much as they compete to be Alpha male of Torchwood.

Studies of the intertextuality of popular series or characters can shed light on viewers' understanding of a character's complexity or their confusion about the multiplicity of depictions of a single character. In the case of Captain Jack, although writers can choose to emphasize any of a wealth of roles, they most often choose a few dramatic types, whether they are writing for a youth-oriented or adult audience. Although fans, even in my very limited survey, recognize a wide range of roles, they emphasize Jack's roles as Leader or Hero more than Lover or Sex Object in the first three seasons of *Torchwood*.

The Many Faces and Phases of Captain Jack

Because Captain Jack Harkness is a long-term, long-lived, and multiseries character who can be far more morally ambiguous than the Doctor, who must remain a family-friendly character, he encourages greater variety in storytelling more than any other SF character on television. The many texts helping audiences to discern who Captain Jack really is also are worthy of further study to analyze audiences' interpretations of the character and the ways they make sense out of sometimes contradictory multimedia texts.

Series' creator Russell T Davies suggested after 2009's *Children of Earth* that *Torchwood* could become anything because it is a "multi-purpose, multi-adaptable, shape-shifting weapon" (Ausiello, "'Torchwood' Boss"). John Barrowman reiterated that theme in a 2011 interview at the MIPTV television event at Cannes where *Miracle Day* was promoted. There he extolled the virtues of *Torchwood*'s ever-changing nature by noting that "*Torchwood* has changed every year, and this year seemed the perfect progression to add something different" (James). With the series' 2011 return as a jointly produced program from Starz and BBC, Davies and Barrowman are proved right. *Miracle Day*'s ten-episode, ten-week story arc is as dark as but more international in scope than the critically acclaimed five-part, one-week *Children of Earth*.

Just like the television series, Captain Jack seems to morph into whatever writers need him to be within a story. He has been a Time Agent, con man, World War II volunteer pilot, and Torchwood employee and leader, among his many jobs. He has been a companion to the Doctor, love interest of humans and aliens, father, and grandfather. Especially in *Children of Earth* and *Miracle Day*, new information about Jack's past may cause audiences to modify their understanding or assessment of this complex character.

In *Miracle Day*, Barrowman explained in a *Wall Street Journal* interview, Jack reverts "to his darker side than he has before and ... his con man roots" (Nishi), yet another version of the many-faceted portrayals since the character first encountered the Doctor in 2005. Yet the latest glimpse into Jack's character also reveals that he returned to Earth from intergalactic self-exile to help ensure that his remaining Torchwood teammate, Gwen Cooper, stays safe. When a "miracle" (i.e., immortality for everyone but Jack living on Earth) forces Jack and Gwen back into action, the larger-than-life Captain still makes a great entrance and looks dashing and heroic in a cape-like coat. He also seems more vulnerable and unsure of himself as he seeks forgiveness or redemption for events that transpired in the past miniseries but still haunt him in this one. By the end of *Miracle Day*, canon Jack has returned to "baseline" and roles very familiar to viewers who have seen him in previous seasons' episodes. This return to Jack as immortal, flamboyant, confident, and heroic is necessary if new audiences, especially in the U.S. (home of partner Starz), are to accept Jack as the lead character/hero in future *Torchwood* episodes or a movie. This return to "normal" also makes Jack more acceptable to long-time fans who feared the character would be "Americanized."

Reducing Jack to Three Typical Roles

Whether in a novel or a television episode, a radio drama or a comic, intertextuality not only helps sell the *Doctor Who* franchise or *Torchwood* texts but also reflects whatever version of Jack is easiest to "sell" to a particular audience. As such, a study of intertextuality and *Torchwood* presents some interesting problems in both keeping a franchise alive for many years and in maintaining the character's integrity so that audiences can reasonably expect what they will receive when they "buy" *Torchwood*.

Despite new information about his future or past being continually introduced in the latest episodes, Captain Jack often can be categorized in a few primary ways. Some roles or traits seem more "typical" because they are the ones to which writers return, television season after season, fictionalized millennium after millennium. Even though Jack can display a wide range of characteristics, the three "faces" which writers most often show to audiences are Sex Object, Sacrifice, and Redeemer or Redeemed.

Jack as Sex Object

At the end of *Children of Earth*, Jack departs Earth, and the last time audiences see him before *Miracle Day* is a brief scene from *Doctor Who*, just before the Tenth Doctor's regeneration. Jack is sitting at an intergalactic bar when the Doctor arrives to give him a farewell present: an introduction to Alonso Frame (a role reprised by Russell Tovey, who first played the character during the 2007 *Doctor Who* Christmas special, *Voyage of the Damned*). When Alonso begins flirting, Jack tells him he can read his mind and leeringly indicates they both have the same thought — sex (Davies, "End of Time"). After the many ways the Doctor and Jack have interacted during the many years of their association, apparently the most significant gift the Doctor can give Jack is a new boyfriend. Many writers seem to have taken this image to heart, whether in canon or sanctioned texts, and sometimes Jack's main contribution to a scene is to sex it up.

The Starz *Torchwood* website described the Captain Jack of *Miracle Day* in this way: "Jack looks like a hero. But he's so much more than that.... He's American, handsome, with a killer smile and a classic coat. But you don't expect heroes to be this much fun. He's witty, fast, subversive and there's a reason for that glint in his eye — he'll sleep with women, he'll sleep with men; if aliens invade, he'll sleep with them too.... The only thing that could call Jack Harkness back is his unstated love for Gwen Cooper" (Starz). This teaser misled (and upset) some fans of the Jack-Ianto (Janto) relationship that developed in *Torchwood*'s first two seasons and seemed well established within the context of the radio dramas in 2009 and 2011 but was abruptly ended with Ianto's death in *Children of Earth*. The attraction between Jack and Gwen has been a point of contention in fandom, with many fans of the Janto relationship decidedly against Gwack. (The naming of relationships in the media by combining the names of the happy couple to create one entity also takes place in fandom: Jack + Ianto = Janto, and Gwen + Jack = Gwack.) Although Jack and Gwen are close in *Miracle Day* and there is more than one hint of what might have been, Gwen's heart belongs to husband Rhys and their baby daughter, Anwen.

The introduction of sexy Jack was designed to appeal to new audiences. Because *Miracle Day*'s publicity emphasized this role, U.S. audiences accustomed to adult sexuality depicted in "original Starz" series (a label given to *Torchwood*) would expect Jack to equate romance with sex. Viewers were not disappointed, as Jack gained one-night-only and longer-term partners by the end of *Miracle Day*.

After the Starz character description was published online, a casting call named one of Jack's conquests — Brad, a 20-something Washington, D.C., bartender. Those being considered for the role were advised to be ready for "intimate scenes between two men" (Jensen). When the third episode of *Miracle Day*, "Dead of Night," was broadcast, viewers could understand why. The homosexual sex scene, intercut with a heterosexual one-night stand, helped establish Jack Harkness and Rex Matheson, respectively, as highly sexual characters easily able to attract a partner for an evening's sensual adventure. Both seem unrestrained in their passion and experienced in bed. Audiences undoubtedly compare the gay and straight scenes, however, and Captain Jack becomes the "gay character" in the minds of new viewers. Comparing Jack with newcomer Rex and establishing them as "separate but equal" leaders in Torchwood is one purpose for the third episode's sex scene.

In April 2010 Barrowman reminded an *Access Hollywood* reporter that "Captain Jack will sleep with anything with a zip code" (Kiernan). He was even more explicit in the publicity leading up to *Miracle Day*'s premiere in July 2011. The oft-quoted statement is Jack "gets to have full-on boy-sex a couple of times" (Hibberd), fulfilling the promise that a U.S.-based *Torchwood* would not dilute Jack's sexuality, or Barrowman would not play the role.

Starz' initial description of Jack Harkness, especially when fans read it long before *Miracle Day*, seems much more appropriate to *Torchwood*'s early days, when aliens mostly visit Earth for sex or send sexual paraphernalia through the Rift. Back then, almost everyone saw action — Owen Harper uses alien pheromone spray to entice a couple into having sex with him; Gwen snogs an alien-possessed woman in a cell but soon afterward begins an affair with Owen; Toshiko Sato falls for alien mind reader Mary. Jack merely talks a good game, and his team questions new member Gwen about her insights into Jack's sexuality. Owen believes Jack is gay because he dresses in period military wardrobe, but Tosh thinks he's straight. Ianto, interestingly enough, doesn't care.

During *Torchwood*'s first two seasons, Jack occasionally tells stories about his sexual exploits that leave his team uncertain what to believe. He jokes about sex with tentacled aliens and alludes to threesomes with acrobat twins. All audiences know for certain is that Jack said he once was pregnant and has no desire to be so again (Davies, "Everything Changes"). Early in the second season (Davies, "Kiss Kiss, Bang Bang"), a visit from Captain John reveals that he and fellow Time Agent Jack were trapped in a five-year time loop, during which time they were "married," each arguing over who was the "wife." This reference coincides with intimations about Jack's past, as described in Jack's second *Doctor Who* episode, "The Doctor Dances" (Moffat), when Jack reminisces about sex with his would-be executioners, one male, one female. Once on board the TARDIS he seems equally besotted with Rose and the Doctor. Yet these references to Jack's past sexual escapades hardly seem to fit with Jack's behavior in *Torchwood* episodes during the first three seasons.

On Earth in the 21st century, Jack is a one-partner-at-a-time man. He sometimes flirts with Gwen or exhibits unrequited love, but he does not do anything to permanently break up her marriage. In season two, Jack and Ianto get some on-screen "couple" time, although Gwen interrupts the aftermath of their game of Naked Hide and Seek. From their frantic kissing in the hothouse, both Jack and Ianto seem to be winners (Davies and Chibnall, "Adrift").

Jack's love nature becomes more evident in covert ways — he asks Ianto for a date (Davies, "Kiss Kiss, Bang Bang"), one apparently highly romantic, if Ianto's sister's later account is anything to go by. She has been told by a friend who watched the pair at dinner in an expensive French restaurant that "no woman was getting her legs round that table, no way, no how" (*Children of Earth;* Davies, "Day One").

The radio play *The Dead Line* provides the clearest depiction of the Janto relationship, although for most of this episode Jack is in a phone call–induced trance. Ianto refuses to leave his side and, in a moving soliloquy, expresses his love for Jack, as well as his acceptance that Jack might not stick around. When Jack awakens from the trance, he assures Ianto that he is more than a "blip in time" for him (Ford), giving voice to fans' speculation that Jack and Ianto love each other equally and that theirs is a real relationship. Of all canon texts, this is the one to which fans return when they want confirmation of Jack's romantic feelings toward Ianto.

The 2011 radio play *Submission* appeals to Janto fans because of, once again, Ianto's love for Jack and his honest appraisal of what it means to love an immortal. This radio play emphasizes Jack's love nature as well as his apparent obsession with sex and innuendo. It is a version of Jack perhaps best suited to meet the expectations of long-time fans — plus a smaller radio audience of hardcore international fans more likely to be aware of Jack's past and to look for a return to elements of the original BBC television seasons' episodes.

When a woman once smitten with Ianto asks about his relationship, she assumes that he and Jack are "together" and states her evidence since they entered the submarine and descended into the Mariana Trench, the setting for *Submission.* She recalls the way Jack acted around Ianto: "little looks, little glances, where he put his hand at 30,000 feet." Ianto readily admits that he loves Jack but acknowledges that this relationship can never be normal. "I love him, but he'll never be mine.... One day he'll leave me. He has no choice" (R. Scott). As in other radio plays from 2009, Ianto's early death is heavily foreshadowed within his proclamation of love. Although descriptions of the Janto relationship typically come from Ianto in the radio plays or television episodes, *Submission* indicates that Jack feels the same way. When Ianto's friend joins the Torchwood team on their mission, Jack jealously asks if she is Ianto's "former flame." Later, when the alien infiltrating Gwen's mind describes how many of her memories revolve around Jack, he tells Ianto not to listen to the alien. *Submission* touches on every aspect of Jack's romantic love nature in the pre–*Children of Earth* time period by including references to his relationships with Gwen and Ianto.

Jack's preoccupation with sex is mentioned several times. The dialogue includes several references to Jack's penis as a "submarine" or a "sex pistol." When Gwen asks if Jack has a submarine in his pocket (naively asking whether he can provide transportation to the Mariana Trench), Ianto groans, "Gwen, you can't set him up like that!" (R. Scott). These and other lines fulfill listeners' expectations that Jack will always be equated with sexual innuendo. Within forty-five minutes of canon radio play, *Submission* ticks all the boxes about Jack's primary roles within *Torchwood*, which may be the reason why so many fans enjoyed this story more than other radio plays or many television episodes.

Other radio plays, such as the first in the *Torchwood: The Lost Files* series, *The Devil and Miss Carew*, portray Jack and Ianto sometimes after Season Two episodes but before *Children of Earth*. At this time the Janto relationship would be well established, and the banter between the lovers is evident in this radio play. The 45-minute production relies mostly on a simple story which requires Gwen to investigate Miss Carew and Jack and Ianto to track down the alien behind the electrical outages plaguing the U.K. Nevertheless, in a script that requires Jack to "talk tech" and then argue with an alien, he still has a few innuendo-laden lines, as if that aspect of Jack's personality has to be included in every canon *Torchwood* story. In *The Devil and Miss Carew*, Ianto warns Jack about their bumpy cross-country drive, to which Jack replies, "I like it when you talk dirty." When Ianto stops the SUV near some bushes, Jack tells him not to try anything. Even when the duo enter the alien's lair and find themselves in a room of technological antiques, Jack manages to find "naughty ornaments," which Ianto agrees only Jack would be expected to find amid everything else (Laight). These comments are made lightly as part of the established Janto banter, almost as if listeners expect Jack to "act sexy," especially when he is alone with Ianto.

The Devil and Miss Carew was written by Rupert Laight, a scriptwriter for *The Sarah Jane Adventures,* the series in the franchise most obviously written for young children. *Sarah Jane* stories emphasize plucky humans, often teens, saving the world from alien incursions. The theme of this *Torchwood* radio play follows in the same vein, making this Captain Jack more suitable for younger audiences, who might not be allowed to watch the much more adult *Miracle Day*. The Janto relationship is not nearly as evident in this 2011 radio play, broadcast by the BBC only a few days before *Miracle Day*'s U.K. premiere and a few days after the first episode was shown on Starz. Within this context of canon episodes available during the same week, this radio play is remarkably chaste, and anyone not knowing about the Janto relationship would not hear anything beyond Jack's usual sexual bantering; only Janto fans, especially those wanting to hear more stories from those pre–*Children of Earth* days, could apply a "couple" meaning to the dialogue.

The radio plays and first days of *Children of Earth* provide the best illustrations to date of Jack's actions in a long-term personal relationship. Although Jack hates the word "couple," he and Ianto frequently sleep together, according to *The Dead Line*, and have grown so close that by "Day One" of *Children of Earth* they finish each other's sentences. While he and Ianto are together, Jack is not shown with any other partners. Although in *Children of Earth* Jack does not tell a dying Ianto that he loves him, Jack nevertheless offers to give the 4–5–6 anything they want if Ianto is spared, and Jack's last action before dying himself is to kiss Ianto (Davies and Moran). Throughout three seasons of *Torchwood* episodes, the Janto relationship adds depth as well as specificity to Jack's love nature and provides a departure from the stereotypical portrayal of many other canon texts.

When *Torchwood* was re-introduced after a two-year hiatus to new audiences via *Miracle Day*, the first episodes were crucial in establishing Jack's character. New audiences may have read the many sexual references provided in articles online and in print, because they often were the focus of interviews with Barrowman or critics' comments about *Torchwood*'s shift in production companies. A media emphasis on Captain Jack before *Miracle Day*'s broadcast was Will he or Won't he (be portrayed as gay, have explicit sex scenes)? issues.

Captain Jack is initially portrayed as a handsome, charismatic, if anachronistically dressed man. His first meeting with new character Esther Drummond (Alexa Havins) in "The New World" (Davies), the first *Miracle Day* episode, mirrors his interaction with Gwen Cooper in "Everything Changes" (Davies), the very first *Torchwood* episode. Jack flirts with them, provides them a little information in exchange for learning more about what they know about Torchwood, and then slips them retcon, the memory-erasing drug. As shown in these episodes, Jack could easily seduce women, even if he does not act on this impulse. During a drunken phone call to Gwen a few episodes later, Jack needs reassurance that he and Gwen, his remaining link to his original team, are "good," and he wonders if they might have had a different kind of relationship (Espenson and Davies). However, Gwen abandons the phone call when the images of husband Rhys and daughter Anwen, courtesy of Skype, turn up on her laptop. Then Jack is all but forgotten.

Again, the comparison between Jack's relationship(s)—or lack of—and Gwen's committed relationship with Rhys is made especially in scenes like this, which, in "Dead of Night," follows an explicit sex scene between Jack and bartender Brad. Even when Gwen is separated from her husband, they share a child and a deep bond that transcends separation. Especially in *Miracle Day*'s scenes set in the present, Jack's relationships seem shallow and only sex based. Mortal, "safe sex" Jack, who reminds Brad they must use condoms, is shown lacking long-term companionship and finding only temporary relationships.

When Jack the Sex Object is a primary emphasis, the resulting depiction is far more likely to become stereotypical. *Miracle Day* does show Jack in more than one sexual relationship, and he alludes to Ianto more than once, but the depth of Jack's emotions—specifically his love nature, which encompasses platonic, familial, and sexual relationships with males and females—cannot be adequately expressed in only one miniseries. Thus, new viewers, particularly international audiences, are far more likely to categorize Jack as exclusively gay and highly sexualized than as a complex, multilayered character, a depiction created through three years' previous episodes.

Jack as Sacrifice

Jack as Sacrifice takes place in episodes like *Doctor Who*'s "Utopia" (Davies), when the Doctor seems rather callous about Jack entering a radioactive chamber to fix a technical problem. Of course, they both know that Jack is the only candidate to get the job done and survive, but he still suffers. Jack may even be perceived as a Martyr in *Torchwood* episodes like "End of Days" (Davies and Chibnall), in which Jack not only sacrifices his life in the confrontation with Abaddon but basically lets the beast keep draining his life force to the point that it takes him days to revive.

Although Jack is not the one being sacrificed, either by himself or another, in *Children of Earth*, he makes several sacrifices that take him to the breaking point. He loses Ianto Jones, who accompanies Jack as his right-hand man during a confrontation with the 4–5–6 demanding Earth's children (Davies and Moran). Still reeling with grief over this loss, Jack sacrifices his grandson Stephen Carter in order to rid the Earth of the 4–5–6, thus saving every other child doomed to be taken (Davies, "Day Five"). As a result, Jack sacrifices his relationship with his daughter and finds himself so overwhelmed by grief and guilt that he cannot remain on the planet. His re-appearance in *Miracle Day* two years later indicates some return to normalcy, but Jack in this story asks pedophile/murderer Oswald Danes if he has been able to find forgiveness (Espenson and Davies).

Whether as the one making or being the sacrifice, Jack often is the character who pays the price for saving the world, a role to which *Miracle Day* returns in its final episode, when Jack offers to sacrifice himself to the Blessing, a non-human force living in the heart of the Earth — and serving as the heart of the miracle's mystery. Audiences new to *Torchwood* see Jack as Sacrifice in the miniseries' climactic scene. Of course, Jack manages to survive and is returned to his immortal status, and thus Torchwood's status quo is restored. Long-time audiences should find this type of conclusion familiar from previous seasons' episodes, but this scene takes on additional importance to new viewers, especially international audiences, who come to find out that, ultimately, *Miracle Day* revolves around Jack Harkness. Furthermore, a once-again mortal Jack agrees to be humanity's sacrifice and is, by the scene's conclusion, "rewarded" with immortality. Jack saves humanity but is granted eternal life — making the character once again seem to be a savior figure in *Torchwood*'s continuing saga.

Torchwood often teases the audience with Jack's mortality. Stories tend to show the perils of immortality, but in *Miracle Day* Jack becomes mortal while everyone else on Earth gains immortality — almost like a switch flipping between immortality and mortality. This plot point allows long-time audiences to compare pre–*Torchwood* mortal Jack with post–*Children of Earth* mortal Jack. Whether an immortal who can continue to sacrifice himself again and again or a mortal who can choose whether to make the ultimate sacrifice for others, Jack Harkness' character development often hinges on the concept of sacrifice.

Jack as Redeemer or Redeemed

Jack as Redeemer also is evidenced in "End of Days" (Davies and Chibnall) when he kisses Torchwood's doctor, Owen, on the forehead and forgives him, even though earlier in the episode Owen shoots Jack to death, opens the Rift, and releases Abaddon, the destroyer. In the episode "Adam," Ianto proclaims that Jack gave him purpose, and Jack blesses him with a kiss to the forehead (Davies and Tregenna).

Post-2006 canon (i.e., after Jack becomes immortal) and fanon (e.g., fan-created fiction, art, and videos) often make Jack a victim. He is seen as a literal whipping boy for everyone from early 20th century Torchwood to

Doctor Who's The Master. He is a betrayed leader whose closest friends and lovers ultimately abandon or emotionally destroy him. He is called a "freak" (by the Master) and "wrong" (by the Doctor). He is tortured by sadistic government representatives. Thus, the basis of many canon, and consequently fanon, stories becomes whether Jack can or should be "redeemed" and absolved of his or humanity's sins. Somewhere along the way from his first *Doctor Who* episode to *Torchwood: Miracle Day*, Jack has evolved to become a pivotal character in SF who represents not only himself but, because of his immortality and his rumored future role as the Face of Boe, an extremely long-lived and ultimately self-sacrificial character, becomes a symbol of what humanity is or might become and the necessity of sacrifice in order for humanity to evolve.

Reconciling the Three Faces of One Character

Although several canon texts include one or more of Jack's roles within a single episode/radio play, few show all three. *Torchwood: The Lost Files' Submission* (R. Scott) is one such radio play, broadcast during the week when *Torchwood: Miracle Day* debuted on television but covering the time period before and shortly after *Torchwood: Children of Earth*. As mentioned previously, Jack's role as Sex Object includes dialogue both about Jack as Ianto's lover and as a sexual being who likes to flirt and insert double entendres into conversation.

Jack as Sacrifice is illustrated when he offers himself in place of Gwen to an alien wanting to take over a human body in order to "mine" their memories. This role is emphasized the least of the three, but Jack's immortality makes him an appealing sacrifice for the alien. Jack's body would not die in the transfer, but his many memories are prized more than his body. Jack's inability to stay dead is not an issue in this play, which differs from most episodes in which Jack offers to or does sacrifice himself to save someone else (or an entire population). In *Submission*, he instead is the perfect sacrifice because of his ability to live, and therefore to have a bounty of memories the alien wants.

Jack's possible redemption receives more attention when the alien and Jack discuss long life and the nature of death. The alien taunts Jack that he can never be forgiven for all the bad things he has done; his friends would not love him if they truly knew him. Jack agrees that the price of immortality is "no redemption, no absolution." Foreshadowing his suddenly mortal again status in *Miracle Day* (which fans would learn the week that this radio play was broadcast), Jack adds that only by becoming mortal would be he able to find forgiveness, a theme also underscored in *Miracle Day*. Jack has analyzed the possibility of redemption for himself, even before the events of *Children of Earth* that made him seem a much darker character, but he does not believe in any afterlife and feels that his many "sins" (although not a term he uses) from his many lives cannot truly be forgiven. Unlike the appropriately named "Redemption" background song playing during some of Jack's final scenes in *Children of Earth*, when Jack runs away from his long-time home in order to seek some kind of peace or redemption, in *Submission* he seems resigned that he will never be absolved of his past deeds. Nothing he could possibly do would redeem him. In this way, *Submission* differs from the television canon, which shows Jack in seasons three and four as longing for redemption or absolution and, especially in early *Miracle Day* episodes, living in remorse and questioning whether other "bad people" (i.e., Oswald Danes) find forgiveness.

The three "faces" of Captain Jack may not all receive the same amount of story time, as *Submission* indicates. Although a longer story, such as the ten-hour *Miracle Day*, is more likely to present a more balanced portrayal of Jack, individual episodes, even within such a miniseries, revert to showcasing only one of these three faces. Viewers who only sample a series, perhaps by watching one or two hours, may never realize that Captain Jack is a complex character who is more than the sum of the "parts" shown during individual episodes.

The Problem with Intertextuality and Captain Jack

Jack's history, as told in flashbacks as well as new episodes throughout *Torchwood's* four seasons, illustrates the wealth of his experiences and provides a rationale for his current behavior. Audiences understand why Jack acts a certain way because of events in his past. Two examples from canon texts in 2011 show, first, how Jack's attitude changes in *Miracle Day* from what might be expected, given his experience in *Children of Earth*. The second provides a repetition of Jack's action, which is similar in radio play *The House of the Dead* and *Children of Earth*. Both actions may be understandable based on Jack's previous experience, but audiences may find one more logical or easier to believe than the other, if they believe that Jack is always meant to be a hero, no matter how difficult his choices have become. This assumption is reasonable, given Jack's status as *Torchwood's* protagonist for four seasons, the way his character has been developed in many previous episodes, and Barrowman's and Davies' assertions over the years that Jack is a hero.

Jack is perhaps one of the darkest, or morally ambiguous/pragmatic characters, on television in the early 2000s. Audiences generally accept that idea, and they may find it understandable in the context of many of Jack's experiences. In *Miracle Day*, for example, Jack returns to a darker, more pragmatic nature. During "The New World," he suggests that an "undead" bombing victim's head be cut off to see if the horribly burned and mutilated body survives, despite a doctor's assessment that the person is still sentient. Jack sees the "person" only as an experiment (Davies, "The New World"). In previous *Torchwood* episodes, including the very first, "Everything Changes" (Davies), Jack is content to use a resurrection glove to bring back the dead, not for any humanitarian reason but simply to test the glove. However, audiences who watched *Children of Earth* also might recall that Jack also was blown up, his body bag of remains re-forming to come back to life. Jack's screams during this process attest to the pain and horror of the situation. Although past experience could, perhaps should, make Jack empathize with the "undead" victim in *Miracle Day*, as well as show increased empathy as a result of character development in canon stories since "Everything Changes," he is coolly detached. Audiences might assume that, although Jack might understand what the victim is going through, learning about the "miracle" and, once again, saving the world, require sacrifice, which is something Jack well understands. Long-time fans probably feel no dissonance between Jack's current action and their knowledge of his past behavior, even if they question how much events in *Children of Earth* ultimately changed his nature. New fans see enough of "dark Jack" to accept his behavior in "The New World" without question.

When Jack's current action may seem to be very, perhaps inappropriately, different from what long-time audiences may expect, they may question a series' continuity of writing and character development or disregard one text in favor of another. New audiences, including the largest American audience to date for *Torchwood*, only draw conclusions about Captain Jack based on the limited number of episodes they have seen. Without knowing of Jack's past agony of a living death or painful resurrection, new viewers may perceive Jack as emotionally detached or more scientifically interested in the miracle's victim he suggests be decapitated. They may rationalize other aspects of his "dark" nature, even within his well-established friendship with Gwen, which is clearly presented in *Miracle Day*; they may believe that Jack is a survivor who will do anything to protect himself if he is backed into a corner. However, even new viewers may have more difficulty deciding which is "normal" for Jack: his close friendship/platonic love for Gwen or his need to protect himself at all costs, even if that means killing her. Both the loving and the ruthless sides to Jack's personality are on display in *Miracle Day*, and such radically different emotions regarding one character with whom he has developed an intense bond over several years may be more difficult for fans to accept. Long-time fans perhaps have too many texts and contexts by which to evaluate Jack's behavior and decide which episodes or events are "in character." New fans may wonder if incongruous behavior within a miniseries is typical for Jack and infers his complexity, or if one behavior is "out of character" and meant to be shocking, or if the writing is inconsistent from episode to episode.

The final *Torchwood* radio drama of 2011, *The House of the Dead*, also introduces contradictory behaviors, to the point that listeners familiar with *Children of Earth* might feel far less comfortable with Jack's role as a series hero. At the end of both *The House of the Dead* and *Children of Earth*, the world is saved once again from evil aliens. In *Children of Earth*, when Jack realizes that Ianto is dying, he begs the 4-5-6 to save him. He even offers to give them the world's children if Ianto is spared, hardly the action of a hero, especially one who, a day later, feels he must sacrifice his beloved grandson in order to get rid of the aliens and spare all other children. The actions may seem incongruous with what fans know about Jack's past motivations and sacrifices in his role as a savior hero.

In *The House of the Dead*, Jack talks with Ianto's ghost six months after the young man's death (Goss). The radio play's ending is meant to give closure to Ianto or Janto fans who wanted to hear Jack tell Ianto that he loves him. Jack and Ianto finally get to say those three little words, and they share a final embrace. Both actions should be pleasing to fans who like this relationship and detested its premature end as a result of *Children of Earth*. In the play's final scene, Jack agrees to leave the world behind — to abandon his responsibility to protect Earth in favor of leaving it in the hands of an evil alien — as long as corporeal ghost Ianto can come with him. Ianto uses Jack's love and wish for more time with his partner in order to trick the Captain into leaving the House of the Dead. Then Ianto saves the world and becomes the story's hero.

In what is possibly the final Cardiff-based *Torchwood* radio play, Ianto and Jack replay familiar roles. Ianto helps save the world — again — even though he will be permanently separated from his lover. Jack suffers the loss of the only person he wants to see again (out of everyone in his long past). More important, Jack the "hero" would give up the world — again — if he can keep Ianto with him. This plot point is emphasized in *Children of Earth* and *The House of the Dead*— both which, at least at the time they were broadcast, seemed to be the final Cardiff stories in the *Torchwood* saga. Audiences who want Jack's love nature to be satisfied and who understand that Jack has sacrificed much to save those he loves as well as the world/universe many times might accept Jack's decision. When offered the one thing he most wants (i.e., a life with Ianto), he chooses love over duty, one life over many. Ianto is the exception to every rationale for Jack's behavior as established throughout the rest of the *Torchwood* canon. Some fans, however they appreciate that love should conquer all, may find Jack's behavior far less heroic. They may even find it out of character, despite their wish for a more loving coda to the Janto relationship.

The question becomes whether Jack can continue to fit audience expectations of what is "normal" for the Captain, based on previous behavior and history, while continuing to evolve as a character. Even when "bombshells" about Jack's past detonate within a story (such as in *Children of Earth* or *Miracle Day*), his characterization must both reflect a continuity of what he has been or done before and new insights gained from an exploration of the revelations. Characters can and do grow emotionally and change physically and psychologically, but they still must be recognizable to audiences. In the case of Captain Jack, long-time viewers have spent years "decoding" many canon texts and relating their insights to the sanctioned texts, as well as fan texts. They must be intrigued by something new in upcoming canon, but they also must believe that the new details mesh with what audiences have been shown in previous texts. Anything that seems too far out of character may cause audiences to dislike a story or the series' direction or to question just who Captain Jack is or should be. Audiences may also question a television series' direction (or think that it has "jumped the shark") if it strays too far from its expected premise. Because *Torchwood* is the BBC's most malleable series in the *Who* franchise, getting fans to accept *Torchwood*'s course change is a crucial task.

Portrayals of Jack in Sanctioned but Not Canon Texts

The wider (and wilder) variety of sanctioned texts does little to reconcile Jack's many roles in the *Who* franchise or to provide continuity among canon or sanctioned texts. Novels and comics, for example — which fans are encouraged to buy — may end up confusing them instead of enriching characterization.

One of the earliest non-canon texts bearing the BBC logo is the *Doctor Who* novel, *Only Human*, in which Jack as Sex Object is emphasized more than other roles. During his entrance into this story, Jack is dressed in a suggestive new wardrobe supplied by the TARDIS: "an old-fashioned Merchant Navy outfit in blue serge with white piping." When Rose sees him, she comes on to him by saying "Hello, sailor," to which Jack replies that he wondered whether she or the Doctor would use that line first. Rose next questions whether Jack's trousers could be any tighter, prompting Jack to ask whether she would like them to be (Roberts 14). Using his body to attract attention seems natural to Jack. In *Doctor Who* television episodes, Jack also dresses to attract attention, whether jauntily tilting his RAF hat, wearing what would become his trademark RAF coat, or, on board the TARDIS, wearing body-hugging t-shirts. The form-fitting clothing is more apparent when Jack travels with the Doctor and Rose, and many scenes indicate his awareness of his good looks.

Only Human plays up this tendency but takes it to the extreme with a later scene. To distract hospital staff, police, and onlookers so that the Doctor and Rose can execute their plan, Jack runs naked through a hospital. Every time a distraction is needed, Jack either removes his clothing or offers to do so. The Doctor laughingly tells Rose that isn't the biggest distraction he has ever seen (Roberts 33), a subtle play on words that likely will go over the heads of young readers but allude to penis size for those old enough to enjoy the double entendre. Despite the Doctor's mockery, Jack, the Doctor, and Rose flirt with each other, on screen and page. As Jack completes his mission in *Only Human,* he misses his friends and dreams of kissing them both when they are reunited (Roberts 237).

Innocent kisses and sexual innuendo are the limits of Jack the Sex Object in child-friendly *Doctor Who* and its slightly more "adult" novels. Everyone understands that Jack easily expresses his sexual nature, and the fluidity of his sexuality could make him a gay or bisexual role model. Yet Jack of the *Who* stories is never "adult" or R-rated in the depictions until *Torchwood*. *Doctor Who* emphasizes relationships, such as Jack is able to develop with fellow pilots, traveling companions, or even executioners. Relationships sometimes take a backseat to *Torchwood*'s more graphic dialogue or depictions of sexual activity.

Most *Torchwood* novels only fleetingly discuss Jack's current or past partners, and most do so in a similar way to that portrayed in *Torchwood* episodes. In a story entitled "Virus," within the novel *Consequences* (Moran), for example, Jack and Gwen are stricken by an incapacitating poison that leaves its victims alive and aware but immobile. The alien poison has a limited supply of antidote, which Ianto becomes determined to take from an intergalactic smuggler. After Ianto defeats the smuggler and administers the antidote, Jack still has difficulty coming back to life. Ianto tries and fails to easily recall Jack from paralysis, as Rhys is able to do with Gwen by reminding her of their marriage.

In many 2009 stories, whether canon or sanctioned, Jack and Ianto's relationship is compared with Gwen and Rhys' (e.g., *Consequences, Children of Earth*). In this novel, Rhys and Gwen are so in tune that Rhys easily can recall his wife to consciousness. "Virus" shows Ianto's initial difficulty in quickly bringing Jack back to consciousness. As an important plot point in radio drama *The Dead Line,* Ianto worries that Jack will not always remember him, a fear restated during the young man's death scene in television's *Children of Earth.* Jack's immortality and implied long list of lovers means that Ianto has more "competition" in his partner's memory and that the Janto relationship faces obstacles different from any that might threaten Gwen and Rhys' marriage.

In *Consequences,* Ianto finally comes up with such a private memory that it must be whispered. Of course, the implication is that the memory refers to a sexual situation — one that Ianto later tells Gwen she is too young to know about. Sexually explicit talk is the best way to revive Jack and return him to normal. However, Jack later asks whether Ianto would have had him put away if he could not be revived. Ianto explains that he would care for Jack until he found a way to cure him — he would never give up on his partner. In novels such as *Consequences,* both the sexual and loving components of Jack's relationship are given equal weight. Sex is equated with life, and Ianto's ability to provide such a specific, unique memory of a sexual encounter apparently is required to bring his long-lived, highly experienced partner back to the living.

The earlier-published novel *The House That Jack Built* references three of Jack's relationships, two long ago and the current one with Ianto. Around a century earlier, Jack had individual love affairs with a man and a woman who eventually marry but ultimately destroy each other. Jack's memories of making love with each partner are described in general terms suitable for younger readers, with Jack's comment, "I only wish you had been as happy inside your body as I was," being the most descriptive line (Adams).

Such subtlety is missing from *Almost Perfect,* the novel so outrageous that many fans call it "crack" and compare it to the most blatantly sexualized fanfiction. In this story Jack frequents a gay bar run by an alien duo who like to entrap participants in orgies. Jack's interest in orgies and his complete "outness" focus the novel solely on Jack as Sex Object. He has to be rescued by a jealous Ianto, who has temporarily been "bodyswapped" into a woman (Goss). The bodyswap conceit of SF is used to hook potential readers into buying this book for its titillating cover description. Ianto is temporarily turned into a woman, which gives Jack ample opportunities to have heterosexual sex and to be interested in a cross-dressing Ianto in a story-appropriate way. These variations on the Jack as Sex Object theme, while sanctioned as BBC novels, are not part of canon and sometimes stretch the bounds of "typical" portrayals within stories bearing the BBC logo.

Comic book stories also are sanctioned but not canon texts. These stories do showcase Jack as Sacrifice — he frequently and gorily is impaled, shot, and, once, killed by Tosh with a rocket launcher fired into the SUV he is driving. Despite Jack's other roles in these stories, his sexuality is constantly underscored through his or his team's dialogue. In "Broken," both Jack and Ianto comment about Jack grabbing Ianto's derriere, and after Ianto finds Jack after believing him dead, Jack promises his partner that "we can do the reunion bit later" (Abadzis).

In "Somebody Else's Problem" (Cooper), Jack is a sex object even when he is not in the story. Gwen tells the alien who grabs her, "Don't you know it's rude to take someone from behind without asking? God, I sound more like Jack every day." Even as a reference and inside joke to readers familiar with Jack's characterization, the Captain most often is associated not only with sexual innuendo but specific positions. In "Fated to Pretend," Jack comments that, unlike the alien zombies, he doesn't have "alien goo inside him"—or at least hasn't for a while (Minchin). Such specific references emphasize Jack's sexual experience with males far more often than with females of whatever species and reinforces the concept of his dominant story-based characteristic as omnisexual.

These cheap shots at Jack's sexuality reference canon but fail to explore the diversity of Jack's past relationships in the same way as it is explored in *Torchwood* episodes like "Captain Jack Harkness" (Davies and Tregenna), in which Jack tenderly dances with and kisses farewell the real Captain Jack Harkness; "Small Worlds" (Davies and Hammond), which introduces Estelle, the woman Jack loved and lost during World War II; or even *Children of Earth,* which establishes Jack and Ianto in a loving, if often combative relationship. The shorter the story or the briefer the guest role, the more likely it is that Jack will be perceived only as Sex Object.

Torchwood the Brand

In a tweet promoting one of *Torchwood*'s many "texts," the downloadable animated *Web of Lies* series, scriptwriter Jane Espenson encouraged fans to "enjoy all the *Torchwood* brands" (Espenson). During July 2011, new products included canon television episodes (*Miracle Day*), canon radio dramas broadcast on BBC Four as *The Lost Files,* and sanctioned spinoff animated web series *Web of Lies.* By the end of 2011, new sanctioned products included three paperback novelizations, which joined two CD stories read by Kai Owen (who plays Rhys Williams). Additional tie-ins were being planned for 2012 and beyond. Although *Doctor Who* still has a far greater number of products and product types to supplement canon stories, *Torchwood* notably branches out into multiple platforms which increasingly cost fans money in order to gain more insights into the lead characters, especially Captain Jack.

5. Intertextuality, Captain Jack, and the Future of Torchwood   109

Although free *Miracle Day* screenings in major U.S. markets and online during the week of this story's premiere on Starz in effect became free samples of a new product, the majority of U.S. fans who wanted to see the episodes legally when they were first broadcast had to buy Starz programming. In the months after *Miracle Day*'s Starz debut, Netflix downloads or, later still, DVD or Blu-ray sales broadened the market for the episodes. As one U.S. reporter noted, "we're getting the television we pay for" (Gray); fans of quirky, cult, controversial, or flashy television series in the U.S. are more likely to have to pay extra in order to see their favorite programs. With *Miracle Day*, *Torchwood* followed this trend in the U.S., which, while marking it as not being mainstream, also gave it status as a higher-quality cable program worth paying for, as opposed to the programming available without extra charge by mainstream American broadcast networks.

Web of Lies became available only to iPad, iPod touch, or iPhone owners who paid iTunes for the downloaded episodes, one each week that the *Miracle Day* television series was broadcast. Online teasers introduced potential buyers to the animated Captain Jack and Gwen, voiced by Barrowman and Myles, but emphasized the lead character of this spinoff, Holly Mokri (Eliza Dushku) ("Torchwood: Web of Lies"). She wants to save the *Miracle Day* world by following clues left behind by her brother, who was shot, fueling a conspiracy-laced plot. The premise is set up in these short introductions, and the first episode could be downloaded free, just like the many "samples" of *Miracle Day*. Subsequent episodes cost less than a dollar each. A game tie-in encouraged fans to interact with the story more actively.

On the day the free first episode was made available, three *Torchwood* fans first posting comments about the webisodes voiced the most commonly heard praise and complaints found on other sites online. In iTune's customer reviews, Casey425 considered the first animated episode "okay," but "[t]he mini game tie in adds a fun twist. Personally, I want to see the rest of the series in app and am willing to purchase each episode and mini game as they come out." AmandaL "loved" the app she had just purchased. However, Bluedragonsii spoke for the many *Torchwood* fans who could not access *Web of Lies* without buying additional technology: "Extremely unfortunate for us avid *Torchwood* fans that do not have an iPad or iPhone. Very disappointing!" (*Web of Lies*).

With the multiplicity of brands being offered and Captain Jack's, as well as *Torchwood*'s, ability to become whatever is necessary in the marketplace for viability, *Torchwood*, like its parent *Doctor Who*, became a model for U.S. product development and placement in conjunction with a series. Like *LOST, Heroes, Battlestar Galactica,* and other SF/fantasy television series before it, *Torchwood* both reflected and became an innovative model of audiences' desire for more tie-ins to television programming and more products available between television seasons. Although *Torchwood: Miracle Day* episodes and *Web of Lies* tie-in frustrated those fans who did not have immediate access to these texts because of price, technology, or geographic location, anyone who chose to follow news about the series learned something about these texts' content and new character developments.

In a market that values greater intertextuality (and its resulting greater profitability), has a character as complex and controversial as Captain Jack ultimately benefited from so many divergent stories targeting so many different audiences, or has he become less "real" and effective a character because of so many varied interpretations?

Looking for Another Miracle: Implications of *Miracle Day* for *Torchwood* and the *Doctor Who* Franchise

By the end of *Torchwood: Miracle Day* in September 2011, CIA operative Rex Matheson had become an American version of Jack Harkness. The two have been increasingly shown to have a great deal in common, and many of their decisions and actions in *Miracle Day* are parallel.

Although early in the miniseries Rex bitterly ridicules Jack for killing his friends, one of Rex's last acts is to hold a dying Esther Drummond in his arms and, after the plot wraps up, to attend her funeral. Like Jack, Rex is becoming accustomed to great loss and the sacrifice of those closest to him in order to save the rest of humanity.

Rex, like Jack, willingly decides to sacrifice himself in order to reverse the Blessing's "curse" of unending death for millions of global citizens, but he first asks Jack what he should do before he agrees to spill his blood to "feed" the Blessing. He comes to understand that, by sacrificing himself, the immortality "curse" will be reversed, and people will begin dying again. Thus, with his sacrifice, he ensures that Esther will die of her gunshot wound (just as Jack's death/self-sacrifice to the Blessing ensures that Gwen's father will die rather than linger because of a heart problem). Both Rex and Jack accept the fact that those close to them often must die in order for a world-threatening problem to be solved. They also accept that they are the ones who must sacrifice themselves for the greater good. In *Miracle Day*'s dramatic conclusion, the Torchwood leader and his American counterbalance become noble sacrifices — their blood flowing across the scene and their heroic deaths emphasized by close-ups and epic music. When Rex, like Jack, demonstrates his ability to gasp back to life after being shot to death, *Torchwood* in effect has created a replacement for Jack. Both characters are now immortal and have demonstrated similar decision making and willingness to sacrifice themselves, as well as their understanding of the consequences of their actions.

Immortal, dangerous, brash Rex, who has been marginally "softened" through his experience with Miracle Day and the subsequent destruction of his workplace and loss of his colleagues, is poised to lead a U.S.-based Torchwood-style organization. Rex is in the early stages of "becoming Jack," who also underwent personality changes as a result of becoming a reluctant Torchwood leader who, over decades, faces repeated loss and the destruction of his workplace/home. Rex, like Jack, has become an outlaw or outcast from the agency to which he had given his allegiance, and the American, like the time traveler, will have to decide in any future stories whether to rebuild a destroyed agency, work on his own, or create a new agency to protect the people of Earth.

These plot and character developments have serious ramifications for *Torchwood* as a *Doctor Who* spinoff. *Miracle Day*, and the episode "Bloodline" specifically, remove *Torchwood* from its traditional (alien-fighting, supernatural-themed) style of SF and emphasize its hybrid nature as crime, mystery, or medical drama with a tinge of something alien. Although the Blessing at the heart of *Miracle Day* is a foreign life form tapped into by the series' bad guys — three families trying to re-establish a world order in their immortal favor — former alien-fighter Gwen assesses the Blessing as terrestrial. Certainly the Blessing is as strange, if apparently benign on its own, as anything alien that Torchwood investigated. However, this anomaly apparently originated in the heart of the Earth and is even more inherently terrestrial than the late-arriving humans who also occupy the planet. Although SF fans could perceive the Blessing as "alien," it technically is not extraterrestrial, and the real threat throughout most of the miniseries comes not from the Blessing but from greedy, often sadistic humans motivated by self-interest, not from another species arriving from a distant world.

During many episodes within the miniseries, Captain Jack's "otherness" as a futuristic time traveler and former Doctor's companion seems out of place in a *CSI*-styled adventure. Where does such a story leave Jack? He is portrayed as a victim of circumstance (i.e., "cursed" by having his immortality reversed when the rest of humanity becomes immortal) who, by the finale, is allowed to make the ultimate sacrifice, which may help absolve him of remorse over his actions in *Children of Earth*. Instead of running away, weighed heavily by grief and loss, Jack this time chooses to sacrifice himself. When he looks into the Blessing and sees his many lives reflected back to him, he smiles and says "not bad," a crucial turning point in Jack's character development. By the late scenes in "Bloodline," Jack is able to accept all of who he is — audiences have been shown his dark side and desire for self-preservation as well as his tender love nature in some of the miniseries' most revealing and memorable scenes. Because Jack is willing to sacrifice himself for the greater good, he regains hero status. Jack seems to be emotionally and psychologically whole; he can accept a final death because he can unflinchingly face the repercussions of all his lives. Jack's willing sacrifice of his mortal life with no expectation of resurrection gains him redemption.

This redemption, theoretically, could end the necessity for Jack's further character development and leave him in a relatively good place, should he not be included in future *Torchwood* stories. Instead of emphasizing Jack's development as an about-to-be-redeemed hero, however, most of *Miracle Day*'s plot requires Jack to be a victim of others' prejudice or greed. Without his knowledge, the three families confiscate and study immortal Jack's blood for decades. He becomes the life force feeding — and thus controlling — the Blessing's ability to turn immortality on or off for humanity. The woman in charge of the Blessing's maintenance in China even calls Jack "the creator," but he has unwittingly participated in the rise of the three families and their manipulation of the Blessing.

Jack is further portrayed as a victim by being the odd man out. When others are immortal, he is mortal. When the switch is flipped again, he returns to his immortal status — but this time with a big difference. Apparently, Jack has "created" a "monster" — the immortal Rex, who agrees to have Jack's blood transfused into him as part of his plan to thwart the families' manipulation of the Blessing. Jack is even a "victim" of this creation. He has no foreknowledge of Rex's plan and only discovers Rex's immortality in the very last scene. Although Jane Espenson later explained that fans who "read" the scene as Jack's blood creating Rex's immortality are incorrect — immortality merely is a final "gift" of the Blessing — the fact remains that many viewers interpreted the scene incorrectly.

Unlike many superheroes whose difference from humans elevates them as heroes, the writers have chosen to use Jack's otherness to make him a victim or martyr who can seldom overcome the curse of immortality. Jack becomes a hero despite, not because of, his immortality; what makes him special is his brash enjoyment of life and his ability to throw himself into danger — whether that danger is a long-term love relationship or extraterrestrial warfare. Sadly, in *Miracle Day,* Jack is seldom allowed to be a dangerous man or a hero.

Although Jack's knowledge, gained more from living through long centuries on Earth than from recent intergalactic travels, comes in handy at key points in *Miracle Day*, his experiences as a Time Agent, Doctor's companion, or Torchwood leader are relatively useless in a story that doesn't focus on aliens. Any sage old man (and Jack is older than any other human character in the franchise) could guide the makeshift Torchwood team during this miniseries; alien fighters are not crucial to the problem's solution. Instead of making Jack crucial to the story, the writers seem to use him only when they need to hook the dwindling audience back into the story and bring back the Captain Jack long-time viewers know and love.

The tenuous connection between Jack and the Doctor, or *Torchwood* and *Doctor Who*, seems strained and inappropriate for new viewers, who do not need to know about *Doctor Who* or Jack's past as a time traveler in order to understand *Miracle Day*. The occasional offhand reference to the Doctor or even previous *Torchwood* characters, most notably Ianto Jones, are provided to appease long-time fans and to reassure them that *Torchwood* is still (peripherally) part of the *Doctor Who* franchise. The result is that these unexplained references may be ignored or questioned by new fans but provide "inside" jokes or payoffs for fans who know *Torchwood*'s origins. In particular, the fleeting references to the Doctor, Silurians, and UNIT — made during *Miracle Day*'s final scenes — do not provide a meaningful context for new viewers and only pay lip service to the series' (and Jack's) origins. Long-time fans are just as likely to be annoyed by these references as pleased that they are included; they have no real bearing on the series and fail to turn a crime or medical drama into the style of SF these fans enjoyed in previous *Torchwood* seasons.

With the ascension of Rex as American immortal agent, comfortable with the existence of aliens on Earth but better versed in crime-fighting methods, Captain Jack is unnecessary to a new, possibly filmed-in–America *Torchwood*— at least from a writer's perspective. Even the finale's title, "Bloodline," indicates that Jack has begat a successor; his bloodline can be traced from *Doctor Who* through the original Welsh *Torchwood* to the America-based hybrid. However, the continuing number of tweets specifically praising Captain Jack or Barrowman or beseeching Starz to continue the series with Captain Jack — especially in the hour after the finale was broadcast — indicate that Captain Jack is perceived by many fans as a crucial element in any future *Torchwood*.

Barrowman himself suggested a fan write-in campaign in the days before "Bloodline" aired in the U.S. and more than a week before the finale's broadcast in the U.K. In a *Wales Online* interview, Barrowman emphasized his continuing desire for Captain Jack to reprise his role in *Doctor Who* in an upcoming episode or at least during the 50th anniversary special. He stated his wish to work alongside Eleventh Doctor Matt Smith and underscored comments made by Russell T Davies and Steven Moffat that Jack could return to *Doctor Who* at some point. Barrowman knows his fans well, and even an offhand appeal for the BBC to receive requests for Jack's return is sure to get a fan campaign started (Byrne-Cristiano, "Video"). Barrowman chose to make the announcement during the week of *Miracle Day*'s finale, when his fans would be concerned about not seeing Captain Jack again, should *Torchwood* be canceled or return with Rex as the star. It is a shrewd move to ensure that, in addition to Barrowman's roles as television producer and presenter, concert and recording artist, stage actor, and book author, he can continue to play the role that made him an international star. Even in spring 2012, months after *Miracle Day*'s conclusion, additional questions about Jack's return to *Doctor Who* kept the issue alive in the media, and fans attending *Doctor Who* conventions in 2011–2012 discussed the possible ways that Captain Jack could be worked into anniversary celebrations.

At the conclusion of *Miracle Day*, where could *Torchwood* be headed if, indeed, Starz and the BBC decide to continue their partnership? It was a worthy experiment, but, as ratings indicated, some of *Miracle Day*'s meandering plotlines undoubtedly were the result of designing a story for two widely diverse audiences, with some writers more comfortable with an American-styled "writers' room" and others preferring British methods of writing and revising. Of course, the British-American differences were played up throughout the miniseries' development and early episodes, and even final Twitter comments from fans suggest that dissatisfaction with *Miracle Day* is the result of "Americanization." However, differences between expectations for "American" and "British" television series, as discussed in earlier chapters, cannot account for all problems in plot or character development.

One problem is that viewers never warmed to Rex Matheson, no matter how many fans like Mekhi Phifer. Even when Rex is portrayed as less sure of himself and more concerned with his teammates, most noticeably during "Bloodline" than in previous episodes, the impression of Rex as a callous, attention-seeking, self-centered workaholic created during his very first scene in "The New World" is difficult to overcome. Many viewers who watched the entire miniseries just do not like Rex as a character and might not follow a series built entirely around him. Whether Rex could become a sympathetic series lead (or only series lead) is questionable at the end of *Miracle Day*. A blogger on ScienceFiction.com wrote favorably about Barrowman's continuing involvement in *Torchwood*, although she was worried in light of his role in an American TV series pilot in 2012. "While I wish Barrowman much success, I'm hoping that if there is a revival of 'Torchwood,' the producers will find a way to work around his schedule. Heaven forbid they decide to go forward without him and make Rex the new Captain Jack!" (Kay).

Viewers have also been desensitized to the number of deaths taking place not only in *Miracle Day* but the final episodes of *Torchwood*'s second season and *Children of Earth*. By now, long-time fans have likely lost the characters they followed. Although love for Captain Jack or Barrowman may be enough to keep a core following faithful to *Torchwood*, the fact remains that fans of actors Burn Gorman (Owen Harper), Naoko Mori (Toshiko Sato), Gareth David-Lloyd (Ianto Jones), Arlene Tur (Vera Juarez), or Alexa Havins (Esther Drummond) feel cheated by character deaths and question whether they should give their loyalty to a series that, before final credits roll on a story arc, likely will kill off their favorite character. Even immortal Jack is regularly shown being murdered rather gruesomely.

The violence in *Miracle Day*, which caused the BBC to issue an age warning of 15 for the DVD and Blu-ray sets and to schedule episodes post-watershed, is an expected part of a cable miniseries broadcast in the U.S. Starz, in particular, achieved a reputation for graphic depictions of violence and sex that would not be suitable for network broadcast. The people who pay for Starz programming often do so because of original series' graphic content. Although *Torchwood* has long been called an "adult" series, especially for the *Doctor Who* franchise, the level of violence and sex shown in *Miracle Day* is a vast departure from typical BBC programming. Even the number of edits made to the British-broadcast versions did not appease at least a few hundred who sent protest letters to the BBC after particularly graphic episodes (most notably, "Immortal Sins"). Different expectations about what is acceptable for broadcast is more of a cable versus network problem, rather than one purely reflecting national cultural differences.

A third problem is the dichotomy between fans highly familiar with *Torchwood* in its purely BBC incarnation — whether during the first two seasons of largely stand-alone episodes or the more global *Children of Earth* miniseries — and fans who heard about *Torchwood* from its pervasive press in the aftermath of *Children of Earth* and during production of *Miracle Day*. *Doctor Who* or *Torchwood*'s history was largely absent from the marketing for *Miracle Day*, and such a connection between past and present was not necessary for the miniseries' story. As tweets and blogs indicated throughout *Miracle Day*, the viewers enjoying the series most likely were new to *Torchwood*. They were not only a target audience but the group easiest to please because *Torchwood* did not have to live up or down to the expectations of long-time or one-time fans.

However, by jettisoning much of the connection with *Doctor Who* or alien-infused SF, the series lost much of its sparkle, particularly by keeping Captain Jack on the sidelines and not allowing him to shine in all of his fabulous glory. Replacing out-of-this-world adventure and coat-swishing heroics with the real-world horrors of overpopulation or lack of resources, coupled with images of government-controlled death camps, understandably took much of the fun out of *Miracle Day*. New fans liked the drama and conspiracy-fueled plotlines, but Captain Jack fans, in particular, complained that his scenes were few and far between. Even black humor or irreverent bantering was lost to increasingly long exposition and characters' (especially Gwen's) impassioned speeches. The confusing plot developments, stretched into ten episodes, allowed viewers time to pick apart plot holes. Favorite scenes rather than a cohesive long-form story compelled fans to return episode after episode. Whereas new audiences were more likely to stick with the miniseries, longtime fans often gave up in frustration.

Perhaps the most divisive issue is whether *Torchwood* should tell global stories, not always requiring human-alien interaction. The quirky, often cheesy stories of a small, dysfunctional family of alien fighters living in an underground bunker in Cardiff are difficult to reconcile with an expensively produced, international, above-ground conspiracy drama that reflects current real-life concerns about government or private sector control over the lives of ordinary citizens. *Torchwood* has never succeeded in being completely a serious drama *or* a campy adventure; its episodes, even across a miniseries, often jump between extremes. If *Torchwood* is going to continue, it needs to have a clear identity, albeit one that allows a range of possible stories and an expansion of its original premise. It simply needs to decide what it wants to be when it grows up. *Torchwood* has had a rocky adolescence, but, if it is given future stories in any medium — print, radio drama, television episodes, or film — it must establish its identity in order to regain its audience. Much of that future identity rests with the decisions of Russell T Davies, and even whether he can or will continue the series.

As members of the media are fond of noting, against all odds, Captain Jack has come back from the dead many times before. Even a huge leap not only in the nature of the production shift from the U.K. to primarily the U.S., but the very concept of the show, has not doomed the series thus far, and a movie or television series' finale is not out of the question, even in light of *Miracle Day's* less than stellar performance.

In late March 2012, Starz' CEO hoped for a break in Davies' schedules (Hinman), Eve Myles (*Torchwood*'s Gwen Cooper) stated her wish for one final story, and fans were encouraged to "vote" for a new 2013 story (Hardbarger). Periodic *Torchwood* speculation or interviews with the series' stars are one way to remind audiences about the currently off-air program.

Meanwhile, new novels — again set in Wales as well as Washington, DC, feature Andy Davidson and Gwen Cooper. Joseph Lidster, who has written many BBC tie-in books and audio stories, including those for *Torchwood*, presents Captain Jack in *Torchwood: Red Skies,* an audio adventure produced by AudioGo, In it, Jack "wants to get away from Torchwood, away from the human race" and therefore ventures to another planet where, according to the promotional website, Jack's past catches up to him when he is arrested for murder ("AudioGo").

A fan review of this audio story adds insightful interpretation of what other fan reviewers dubbed a "story for fandom" because it is only about Jack and builds on the complete *Torchwood* television canon through *Miracle Day*. Although fans often look for stories with Ianto still in them, *Red Skies* indicates that some writers, obviously aware of fandom's continuing interest in Janto, may be turning the short-lived love story into a longer-lived catalyst for Jack's character development. Part of Jack's character development throughout *Torchwood* has been his guilt, whether it is over his failure to protect his younger brother during an invasion, being unable to stop the New Year's Eve massacre of his colleagues, or the very personal loss of those he loves (e.g., former lovers Estelle and Ianto, his grandson Stephen). The reviewer cautions those "fans about to squee that Jack is still so upset" about Ianto's death years later, because the implication of Jack's inability to overcome his grief and guilt is the warping of a love relationship and the reinterpretation of a character long missing from the television episodes. The reviewer explains, "In that long line of deaths, Ianto and Esther's remain the freshest. Worryingly, Ianto is now Jack's personification for guilt and any deaths he feels responsible for causing. The second he mentions to someone he didn't need another death like Esther's, Ianto's name is right after.... Jack is turning Ianto into a representation of something darker, and more depressing.... Jack's lost lovers before, and the thing that makes Ianto unique right now is that he's becoming Jack's symbol of guilt" (Firesnap).

The review was linked to fan sites like the Torchwood Three fanfiction forum. Comments from fans in the U.K. and U.S. about the review or *Red Skies* indicate not only how much they look forward to new canon or sanctioned texts but how much they interact with them. In response to the reviewer's interpretation of Ianto as a symbol of Jack's guilt, other fans agreed that this is an important development (even if it is one they did not like to see occurring) and further discussed the evolution of both Jack and Ianto. Ironically, the latter character has been absent from the series since 2009 and should not be able to be developed further. (The radio plays *The Lost Files* is a notable exception, by returning *Torchwood* to a time or scenario in which Ianto could be actively involved as a current character.) That fans look for any mention of Ianto in a canon or sanctioned text and discuss the ramifications of the reference has interesting implications for intertextuality, too. The stories that fans anticipate — or that they avoid after reading a review — often hinge on portrayal of Jack and his ongoing character development, especially in light of his past relationship with Ianto.

Even if Captain Jack does not return to television soon, character development still continues, and fans are paying attention (as well as paying for these CD stories). Some fans simply like the stories that feature Jack, without

Torchwood or other characters from the television series. Another *Red Skies* reviewer wrote "Captain Jack IS Torchwood!" and added that this new text is "without doubt one of the best *Torchwood* spin-offs in any format. More like this please!" ("Audio Review"). Intertextuality, especially when it includes well-received sanctioned texts, may prolong Jack's life beyond television canon and keep him a more active player in the *Doctor Who* franchise.

That the books and CDs — as well as online audio for BBC Four radio dramas — are available in the U.S. makes *Miracle Day* and *Torchwood* likely to stay on fans' radar, even if the audience of casual viewers may not seek out these non-television texts. Although Captain Jack is not featured on the 2012-published print novels' cover or mentioned in their promotional blurbs, he is front and center on *Red Skies'* CD cover and has gained positive attention from consumers for his starring role in this off–Earth adventure. He also graces the cover of a CD in 2012, *Mr. Invincible,* which pictures him in front of the Millennium Centre in Cardiff. These tie-in texts may indicate yet another shift in Jack's intertextual development, but emphasis on other continuing characters introduced during *Torchwood*'s first season — characters that have a strong connection to Wales — can strengthen the series' overall intertextuality by providing a broader fan base for the series and allowing other characters also to be developed.

Captain Jack Harkness is a unique character. Not only has he been played by the same actor in two television series and several radio plays, but his lifetime spans a great deal of time and space, as well as styles of SF and texts developed for a variety of audiences. Even more than the Doctor, who can appreciably change within the structure established by the regeneration concept inherent to *Doctor Who*'s success, Captain Jack poses special problems for the intertextuality needed for successful spinoffs in the *Who* franchise. If, indeed, *Torchwood* or Captain Jack continues for the next several years, further study of the way his character is presented and perceived can also shed light on the significance of intertextuality in the development, or regression, of a long-term character.

Chapter 6

"You Don't Kill Sarah Jane!"

So proclaimed *The Sarah Jane Adventure*'s script editor Gary Russell at a Gallifrey One convention panel in February 2012 (Russell and Ford). Although the death of actress Elisabeth Sladen meant that her television series would end prematurely in 2011, Sarah Jane Smith continues in the Whoniverse. Russell explained that the character lives on, as illustrated by the montage at the conclusion of "The Man Who Never Was" (Roberts). The series' frequent scriptwriter Phil Ford reiterated at Gallifrey One that he believes there can be no better television ending for the series, or the adventures of Sarah Jane, than to show how pleased she is to have traveled the universe with the Doctor but, eventually, to find her greatest happiness back on Earth. She is surprised and gratified that her greatest adventure is in having a family. The final episode leaves *Who* fans with Sladen's voice saying that the adventure goes on.

The U.K. children's series could not have a more positive ending, letting young viewers who do not know that Sladen died think that the actor, as well as the character, continue somewhere — just not on screen. Although she no longer will be part of any new *Who* episodes, the character lives on — audiences merely are not able to see any further adventures. The idea that Sarah Jane's adventures continue is especially appropriate given Sladen's long association with the role. She played Sarah Jane Smith longer than any other British actor had ever played the same character in a drama (not a soap opera), returning to the role periodically throughout her acting career and making Sarah Jane an important character in the series' and the Doctor's long history.

The Sarah Jane Adventures' Struggle in the U.S. Marketplace

Before Sarah Jane Smith was the leading character in fifty-three episodes of *The Sarah Jane Adventures,* she was a fan-favorite companion, traveling first with the Third and Fourth Doctors (Jon Pertwee, Tom Baker). Introduced in "The Time Warrior" on December 15, 1973, Sarah Jane became an integral part of the series through her final episode, "The Hand of Fear," whose four-part serialized story ended in late October 1976. Sladen may have thought that her *Doctor Who* journey ended there, but Sarah Jane became destined for a much longer life. "The Five Doctors" brought her back in 1983, ending her run of eighty-one now-"classic" episodes, but the character continued to return in a variety of specials and spinoffs.

Sladen was featured in "making of" and commemorative programs, including television documentary *Sidekick Stories* (2010) and mini-documentary *Doctor Who Greatest Moments* (2009), segments of *Doctor Who Confidential* between 2005 and 2009, video documentaries about episodes, such as one made in 2007 about "The Time Warrior," and several other similar pieces about SF or specifically *Doctor Who*. *The Sarah Jane Adventures Comic Relief Special* was broadcast in 2009, and Sladen participated in a Children in Need special in 1985. Then there was the less fortunate attempt at a spinoff, 1981's *K-9 and Company* television movie that, perhaps thankfully for all, did not become a series. Although Sladen and Sarah Jane were in the public eye in the U.K. long after their time in the TARDIS, neither the actor nor the character was as well known in America.

Who fans who grew up watching episodes on PBS well remember Sarah Jane; the highly popular Tom Baker episodes were often repeated on PBS stations, and many U.S. fans first became aware of *Doctor Who* during the Baker era and, thus, met Sarah Jane. Younger or newer fans may have first encountered her during the tenure of another highly popular Doctor — the Tenth, played by David Tennant. "School Reunion" re-introduced Sarah Jane to U.S. audiences and, because of its popularity, led to the character's further appearances in later Tennant-era episodes, "The Stolen Earth" and "Journey's End," and practically only a cameo during Tennant's farewell episode, "The End of Time," before the debut of her own series, also created by *Doctor Who* showrunner Russell T Davies.

The Sarah Jane Adventures has been compared to "classic" *Who*: it has serialized cliffhangers similar to those in *Doctor Who*'s pre-hiatus past (although *Sarah Jane* "serials" are only two parts, whereas *Who* serials include three or more parts); it mixes adventure and character moments in a fairly straightforward story; it features Sarah Jane Smith. As Gary Russell proudly noted during the Gallifrey One panel, *The Sarah Jane Adventures* often was the highest rated U.K. children's television program — and repeated episodes leading up to the series' finale, shown after Sladen's death, were the top rated broadcasts of the week. Children, as well as their parents or grandparents who grew up during the Sarah Jane years of *Doctor Who*, enjoyed *The Sarah Jane*

Adventures. Live-action children's programming is especially rare nowadays, and *The Sarah Jane Adventures* provides interesting episodes with likeable characters. The emphasis is on the family, even if it is not a traditional one, and addresses the typical problems of preteens and teens trying to grow up and fit in. That aliens usually interfere in their lives is an added story bonus.

Because *The Sarah Jane Adventures* offered a much closer structure to the "classic" *Who* episodes with which long-time American fans were familiar, many of these fans expected the new series to be well received when it made the transatlantic crossing. However, the *Who* franchise by then included *Torchwood*, which is very different in tone and style from its parent and sibling, and the revamped version of *Doctor Who*, with a faster pace, more expensive production values, and more stand-alone episodes. Although *The Sarah Jane Adventures* presented Sladen and Sarah Jane in a comfortably traditional *Doctor Who* format, that "traditional" format had changed in 2005, making *The Sarah Jane Adventures* seem more old fashioned; fans of "new *Who*" who tuned into Sladen's series likely could not appreciate similarities between this children's series and the classic episodes of *Who*. American audiences new to both series likely had no understanding of *The Sarah Jane Adventures*' many links with the past, and the pace and story structure of a children's show made it much easier for them to abandon the series after a quick sampling.

Gillian Hanhart, a reference librarian at London's Westminster Reference Library and devoted *Doctor Who* fan, suggests reasons why *The Sarah Jane Adventures* failed to find an American audience and, indeed, why it needed to attract a new, younger audience even in the U.K. Although long-time *Who* fans would remember Sarah Jane Smith, children (or some parents) are far less likely to be familiar with her. Parents who grew up during the years without *Doctor Who* may have just "met" Sarah Jane during "School Reunion." When *The Sarah Jane Adventures* went too far into the past—or too much into its character connection with "classic" *Who*—the audience was likely to become bored with the digression.

Even *SFX*'s special Doctor Who the Fanzine edition, which called the series "the big success of children's television of recent years" (Lewin 108), added that even in a highly promoted episode, in which Katy Manning's Jo Grant returned to the Whoniverse, the pace could lag and ostensibly lose the audience. When Sarah Jane Smith and Jo Grant begin discussing their travels with the Doctor (during the "classic" series), "younger viewers perhaps twitch in their seats and hope there'll be something exciting happening shortly" (110). What did attract children to the series was attractive young actors doing the things typical British middle-class teenagers do, as well as having atypically adventurous lives.

Hanhart further explained that the DVD commentaries regarding

"School Reunion" noted "this double-sided thing, where ... some of the audience can remember Sarah Jane, seeing [her reunion with the Doctor] from her point of view and the Doctor's, because he remembers Sarah Jane, whereas the youngsters see Sarah Jane from Rose's point of view as this woman who has traveled with the Doctor in the past and initially looks upon her as something of a threat. Sarah Jane is a stranger to a whole generation."

Hanhart understands what is most British about *The Sarah Jane Adventures* and thinks that the cultural differences are more distinct in this spinoff than in *Doctor Who*. "*Sarah Jane* worked over here, not in America, because it is very British. The children around Sarah Jane.... Luke and the two different girls, depending on which series you're watching, and Clyde, are ordinary British [young people] and they're doing things that are very very British, so I think it's the culture. [British children], even if they weren't at the same type of school [as Luke and the others] ... were at a British school, so they got the [series'] cultural references.... American kids won't get what they're talking about. [Some references don't] necessarily travel well, particularly when [Luke et al.] talk about the soaps that they watch. [American children] are not going to want to watch [an episode] where people are talking about something they don't understand. So I suspect that's why *Sarah Jane* didn't transfer well."

Unlike *Doctor Who*, in which time periods or locations alien to all viewers will not seem so culture specific (even if they are used as metaphors for current real-world situations), *The Sarah Jane Adventures* is very specific to English culture. Although *Torchwood*, especially in its first two seasons, also is culture specific to Wales, it is an adult series, and adults are more likely than children to want to watch a series simply because of its cultural differences. Probably fewer American children than their parents are Anglophiles.

When *The Sarah Jane Adventures* was launched in 2007, many longtime American fans of Sladen and Sarah Jane assumed that the series would be shown, even belatedly, in the U.S. The Sci-Fi/Syfy Channel showed *Doctor Who* episodes beginning with the re-launched 2005 series and continued broadcasting them on Friday nights (with multiple showings throughout the schedule) through 2010, when they decided not to renew their contract with the BBC, possibly in favor of developing original series. By then, BBC America had become home to new *Doctor Who* episodes, and the ability for U.S. audiences to watch episodes shortly after their U.K. broadcast made Syfy's longer broadcast lag more noticeable. (Not all BBC-originating series go directly to BBC America. In 2011–12, *Merlin*, for example, continued to be broadcast only on Syfy in the U.S., and its episodes were shown a few weeks after the British run of latest episodes. Although it began its U.S. television life on mainstream NBC during summer 2009, its less-than-spectacular ratings relegated it to NBC Universal-owned Syfy after its first-season episodes had been broadcast [*Merlin*].) With the Syfy Channel's track record of showing BBC series like *Doctor Who* and *Merlin* on Friday nights, viewers assumed that *The Sarah Jane Adventures* would become part of the schedule.

The assumption that, because *The Sarah Jane Adventures* is British SF and a *Doctor Who* spinoff, it would mesh seamlessly with Syfy's Friday night lineup was based on a false premise that the series is adult SF. Granted, fantasy series *Merlin* combines elements of romance and comedy that could appeal to teens, tweens, or adult viewers, but it also regularly features poisonings, enchantments, and battles that end in favorite characters' severe injuries or even death. *Merlin*, like *Doctor Who*, is broadcast by the BBC during watershed (family-viewing) times but is designed to appeal to a wider audience.

The Sarah Jane Adventures was always meant to be purely a children's show, and the level of violence is far less than anything shown or implied in its parent series. Episodes were originally broadcast on CBBC — the children's network of the BBC — after school or early on Saturdays when children are primarily the audience. Plugging a children's show into Syfy's Friday night lineup of adult SF shows failed to attract the desired audience. Children may have been unaware of the series or their parents may have thought, because of its inclusion on Syfy, it was not exclusively a children's show. Adults who tuned in to see a *Doctor Who* spinoff or the latest British SF show may not have been inclined to watch a children's program or, if they were not as familiar with the Sarah Jane character, may not have been enticed to watch in the first place. Whatever the reasons, Sarah Jane did not get the reception in the U.S. that she received at home, and after only one season, Syfy canceled the series. Since then, U.S. fans have had to wait for DVD sets to go on sale, because no U.S. network carried the remaining four seasons' episodes.

During the Gallifrey One panel about *The Sarah Jane Adventures*, I asked Gary Russell if there was a split in viewer response between the U.S. and British audiences. Russell noted that this is a difficult question to answer, in part because he (and others associated with the series) mostly had contact with American fans over the years and "our only reaction to American opinion tends to be formed at conventions." Russell mentioned that he knew "Syfy showed series one, and they showed it late, I think eight o'clock at night" but added that "it wasn't even treated as a kid's show. It was treated as a *Doctor Who* spinoff." Phil Ford had heard the series had been edited quite a bit, to which Russell only half-jokingly questioned how anyone could "cut Sarah Jane." The session's audience heartily agreed. Ford remembered that, at an earlier Gallifrey One, he discovered an American fandom eager to see more episodes: "We've always been delighted by it, but [it was] actually quite unexpected. We didn't realize that everyone here had seen *Sarah Jane*. It was kind of like we assumed after that first series being shown and then never shown again [that] it's a curiosity that half a dozen people at Gallifrey might have downloaded. We were wrong, thank God."

Intertextuality and Sarah Jane

In addition to the lack of U.S. network support, the series faced a further, if understandable, challenge in finding an audience: it lacked merchandise. Considering how much *Doctor Who* or even *Torchwood* merchandise has been generated since 2005 alone, *The Sarah Jane Adventures* showrunners and fans are understandably surprised that little was ever produced for this spinoff. Even *Torchwood*'s Captain John Hart, who played a memorable but brief role in three second-season episodes ("Kiss Kiss, Bang Bang" and "Exit Wounds," and was uncredited in "Fragments"), earned a place in the series' line of merchandise. An action figure of Captain John was sold alongside, and marketed even before, action figures of some of the series' regulars. Of course, James Marsters, who played Hart, also has a devoted cult following from other SF roles, most notably as vampire Spike from *Buffy the Vampire Slayer* and *Angel*. Nevertheless, the lack of merchandising for *The Sarah Jane Adventures* presents something of a mystery.

During Gallifrey One, Russell commented upon the series' lack of merchandise, calling it his "greatest disappointment" with such a good show. He explained that Character Options introduced a few toys at the beginning of the series' run, but they did not sell well. Penguin similarly produced a few novelizations that failed to find an audience. American fans tend to purchase *Doctor Who* merchandise related to the parent and spinoffs — possibly because it has been difficult for vendors to import merchandise from Britain, and the BBC has not licensed American manufacturers or vendors for their series' merchandise, creating a greater demand for products in the U.S. Thus, Russell and many American fans are surprised and dismayed by the poor response to merchandise introduced in the U.K., much of which never made it to the States and, possibly, a niche group of buyers. Because *The Sarah Jane Adventures* is a *Doctor Who* spinoff, Russell thought that this fact alone would make the merchandise desirable, but, unfortunately for the series, it did not bring in as much revenue as *Doctor Who* or *Torchwood*.

The lack of merchandise limited Sarah Jane's continuing intertextuality, which likely kept the character from being well known outside the U.K. From 2002 to 2006, Big Finish, which also renewed the Eighth Doctor's life in a series of audio adventures starring Paul McGann, presented an audio series that explains what happened between the time Sarah Jane leaves the TARDIS and when she again meets the Doctor in "School Reunion." In these stories, "intrepid journalist Sarah Jane Smith fights corruption and crime" (Big Finish). The ninth and final story, *Dreamland,* was released shortly before Sarah Jane reappears on television in *Doctor Who.*

As a way for *Doctor Who* fans to follow Sarah Jane, the CDs tell more of her story between television adventures; they also provide more backstory to help new fans of *Doctor Who* or *The Sarah Jane Adventures* get up to speed with more recent television episodes. However, not all fans — especially those new to *Doctor Who*— may turn to Big Finish audios for more *Doctor Who.* Whereas the BBC-sanctioned stories have filled in the gaps left by the series' hiatus or have allowed characters to be developed beyond the boundaries of their television or movie exploits, they are less widely marketed in the U.S., and fewer American fans not specifically looking for Sarah Jane texts might not be aware of them. Fans who attend conventions typically see the dozens of available CDs furthering their favorite Doctors' or characters' story lines, but audiences who only watch the television series may be unaware of other available multimedia texts, especially those featuring actors and characters introduced long before the 2005 reboot.

Sladen herself bemoaned the lack of "Sarah Jane" merchandise as far back as the 1980s, when she visited Los Angeles as a convention guest. She failed to bring photos or *Who* memorabilia to sell, not realizing that American fans typically buy actors' as well as series' merchandise. In her autobiography, Sladen recalled that "we really missed a trick there. Americans, I soon learned, were so far ahead of Brits in this area" (Sladen 249). Considering the BBC's prolific merchandising of *Doctor Who* in the 2000s, this idea seems strange. Nevertheless, Sarah Jane Smith, whether by accident or design, never benefited, in the U.S. or even U.K., from intertextuality as much as the Doctor or Captain Jack.

As discussed in previous chapters, the Doctor and Captain Jack have benefited from intertextuality. In contrast, Sarah Jane has been limited to a linear time span and far fewer texts. Her television travels with the Doctor largely take place when she is a young journalist. The Big Finish stories allow the character to be an indeterminate age, because the actor/character is never seen, only heard. How Sladen — or Sarah Jane —"looks" is therefore up to the individual listening to the story. Only when Sarah Jane returns to television in "School Reunion" does the character appreciably change. She has aged and realizes that she no longer is the Doctor's young female companion — Rose has taken that role.

In subsequent reunions with the Doctor, whether on *Doctor Who* or *The Sarah Jane Adventures,* she is an older career woman who, later in life, becomes a mother. Motherhood and her role as a protector of Earth present new dimensions to the character. However, Sarah Jane's career as an investigative journalist remains the same.

Sladen herself mentioned that Sarah Jane changes very little over time, although, during an interview in the 1990s (long before the return of *Doctor Who,* much less of Sarah Jane), she indicated that the character should remain in the "time capsule" created by her journeys in the TARDIS. She recalled that the original "Time Warrior" script provided few clues about Sarah Jane's backstory or character: "they wanted her to stand up for herself and not be a wimp. I think Women's Lib was mentioned as well" (Russell 13). Although the actor thought that Sarah Jane was never as strong in subsequent episodes, the character at least started out that way. By the end of her time as companion, Sladen did not want Sarah Jane "to be married off, nor did I want a whole story about my leaving.... [T]he series wasn't about her" (Russell 15). ("Companion" Sladen took a very different view of the companion's role from that held by current showrunner Steven Moffat, who emphasizes the companion as the primary character.) The 1992 issue of *Doctor Who* magazine in which Sladen's interview was published concluded with her "final words" about the character: "*Doctor Who* gave me a ... good character, and I really liked her. I *still* really like her, although I could never play her again because she's in a time warp — she's of a certain age, of *that* time, and I don't think you could, or *should,* change her" (51).

A decade later, Sladen voiced new Sarah Jane CD adventures for Big Finish. In another *Doctor Who Magazine* interview (in 2006), she discussed Big Finish's revival of her character: "that was a challenge — to see how you could make her work, all these years down the line, also minus the Doctor." Talking about Sarah Jane in "High School Reunion," Sladen noted that she is "essentially the same character wherever she's put.... It's the situations that define how she behaves" (Cook 14–15). Although Sarah Jane, fifteen years after the 1992 interview, would return as the lead in a children's series, the character did not appreciably change her personality and interests in any of these texts, despite growing older and gaining a family. She still investigates alien incursions and helps the Doctor save the planet; she still is determined and can "stand up for herself."

This continuity makes her a far less controversial or mercuric character than Captain Jack or the Doctor. Although she still is featured in multimedia, including television, books, and audios, Sarah Jane Smith has fewer texts and fewer differences in character among these texts than is typical for *Doctor Who* or other spinoffs. Lack of specific merchandise, and lack of additional texts to supplement television appearances, limited Sladen's and Sarah Jane's popularity in the U.S.

Sarah Jane and American Conventions

Perhaps two quotations from Sladen's autobiography sum up her relationship with fandom. Comparing herself to Jon Pertwee near the end of their time together filming *Doctor Who*, Sladen remembered that Pertwee felt comfortable being around fans, whereas, although she loved meeting people, "there's something unnerving about having a conversation with someone who knows so much about you when you don't even know their name — especially when you've just popped out to buy a pint of milk" (132). Nevertheless, when Sladen and Pertwee met fans at an exhibition in Blackpool, shortly before Pertwee's Third Doctor would regenerate into Tom Baker's Fourth, Sladen felt overwhelmed by fan love. Writing about the event years later, she praised *Who* fans as "the best in the world; if you're good to them, they're magnificent to you" (148).

In 1980, when Sladen visited the U.S. for a *Doctor Who* fan convention in Los Angeles, she was surprised at fans' recognition of her work. PBS channels frequently showed the episodes with Sarah Jane, and videocassette recorders made sharing episodes far easier — and so Sarah Jane was known by more U.S. fans than ever before, even though it had been a few years since Sladen had played the role. She discerned differences between U.S. and U.K. fans, noting primarily that American fans "didn't have the benefit of the same historic relationship" with the series because it arrived later in the U.S. Although British and American fans all were polite, knowledgeable about the series, and respectful to the actors, in the U.S. "everything was so much bigger and louder and more extreme" (249). (Sladen's experience differed from that of *Torchwood*'s Kai Owen, who, more than thirty years later, told me that U.K. fans were a bit more outgoing than their U.S. counterparts. Although Americans are generally perceived as louder and more extroverted than the British, perhaps Sladen, as a "classic" companion revered for decades, was, then and now, put on a pedestal more than the stars of recent spinoffs and who, through social media, have more "everyday" interaction with their fans.)

Although Sladen herself never seemed to completely understand why fans would be so interested in her, she could not deny that Sarah Jane attracted a lot of positive attention from fans everywhere, beginning in the 1970s and continuing through the rest of her life. *The Sarah Jane Adventures* has been well received at U.S. conventions, despite all its challenges to find an American audience (e.g., lack of a broadcast home, lack of available merchandise). At recent *Who* conventions in the U.S., such as the 2010 Chicago TARDIS, the series' teenaged co-star, Tommy Knight (Sarah Jane's son Luke), gathered his own youthful following of fangirls (and their mothers) who watch the series on DVD. Like Sladen, Knight appeared in the *Doctor Who* episodes "The Stolen Earth," "Journey's End," and "The End of Time," but his role was smaller, and American viewers in particular may not have realized that Luke Smith has a far larger role, in Sarah Jane's life as well as *The Sarah Jane Adventures,* because they had less access to the latter series. In the U.S., convention appearances helped make more *Doctor Who* fans aware of the spinoff. Knight's engaging personality and enjoyment of meeting fans not only endeared him to a wider *Doctor Who* fandom who otherwise may not have met him but also encouraged them, after watching his panel interviews or meeting him during autograph or photo sessions, to buy the series' DVDs. Although Russell's and Ford's 2012 Gallifrey One presentation seemed to signal a formal conclusion to panels about the series, fans of *The Sarah Jane Adventures* undoubtedly will continue to discuss episodes and invite the series' young stars to future conventions.

Once a Companion, Always a Companion: Sarah Jane and the Doctor

Like Captain Jack, Sarah Jane was once the Doctor's companion, but instead of being abandoned like Jack, she was returned to her home nation when the (Fourth) Doctor was summoned to Gallifrey. She found it difficult to return to a "normal" life, a fact emphasized when she reconnects with the (Tenth) Doctor when he and she are separately investigating the same alien incursion ("School Reunion"). Both Tennant and Eleventh Doctor Matt Smith guested in episodes of *The Sarah Jane Adventures,* making Sarah Jane Smith a companion who meets the Doctor in more "guises" than other companions. In addition to "The Five Doctors," which brought together many Doctors and companions, Sarah Jane significantly interacted with the Third, Fourth, Tenth, and Eleventh Doctors.

Because "School Reunion" led to her own series, and likely because Tennant is a tremendous fan both of Sladen and Sarah Jane (he authored the Foreword to Sladen's posthumously published autobiography), it seems fitting that the last time Tennant filmed his role as the Tenth Doctor was on *The Sarah Jane Adventures* ("The Wedding of Sarah Jane Smith"). The episode ends with a rather sentimental send-off from Sarah Jane, echoing the Fourth Doctor's farewell line not to forget him. Just as Sarah Jane assures him that he will be remembered, so too will Sarah Jane, and Sladen, be fondly remembered in *Who* fandom.

Remembering Sarah Jane: Tributes to Sladen

In April 2011, Sladen died after a brief battle with cancer. The announcement of her death surprised and saddened Whovians, including those who had worked closely with her. The BBC's official statement on April 19 began, "It is with much sadness that we can announce Elisabeth Sladen, the much-loved actress best known for her role as Sarah Jane Smith in *Doctor Who* and CBBC's *The Sarah Jane Adventures*, passed away this morning." The press release mentioned the actor's impact on British television and fandom: "*The Sarah Jane Adventures* brought Lis a whole new generation of fans who grew up to love her alien-busting adventures. The series was hugely popular with fans young and old and won this year's [Royal Television Society] RTS Award for best children's drama."

Numerous BBC executives, showrunners, writers, directors, and co-stars immediately sent their condolences and paid tribute to Sladen, most commenting on their experiences while working with her on *Doctor Who* or *The Sarah Jane Adventures*. Among them were Matt Smith, David Tennant, and Russell T Davies. Steven Moffat wrote that "Sarah Jane Smith was everybody's hero when I was younger, and as brave and funny and brilliant as people only ever are in stories." Moffat's impression of the character was verified when he met the actor years later. "Lis Sladen ... was exactly as any child ever have wanted her to be. Kind and gentle and clever; and a ferociously talented actress, of course, but in that perfectly English unassuming way" (BBC Press Office).

Only a few days after her death, a memorial was broadcast on CBBC (*The Sarah Jane Adventures* network) immediately following the BBC's broadcast of *Doctor Who*'s sixth season premiere. The BBC's announcement of the special, entitled *My Sarah Jane: A Tribute to Elisabeth Sladen,* described Sladen as the creator who "brought the feisty, compassionate journalist to life, creating a figure that was adored by audiences of all ages — truly a heroine whose appeal had no boundaries" (BBC).

Sladen's loss was more publicly mourned in the U.K. Not only were there many in-press reminiscences and tributes in the days after her death, but Sarah Jane's recent reunion with another former companion, Jo Grant (played by Katy Manning), was brought to the forefront of publicity. The *Sarah Jane Adventures* episode, "Death of the Doctor," which also featured Matt Smith, became a highlight of the series, much as "The Wedding of Sarah Jane Smith"— attended by David Tennant's Doctor — also proved a publicity high point of a previous season. Furthermore, because only a few episodes of the next season of *The Sarah Jane Adventures* had been filmed, no one was surprised a few months later when the BBC announced the series' end, although the episodes that had been filmed would be shown nearly a year later, in late 2011.

The brief retrospective was not broadcast in the U.S., where *Doctor Who* also premiered only a few hours later than in the U.K. Perhaps the BBC anticipated that only "old timers" in *Who* fandom would remember Sladen — the

U.S. fandom is often perceived as a largely new audience, drawn to BBC America after extensive media campaigns to draw attention to the Matt Smith episodes. Posts in response to *Entertainment Weekly*'s tribute to Sladen, for example, devolved into online "arguments" about whether *Doctor Who* is a children's show. U.S. fans who posted their own tributes between April 19 and 21 often noted that not everyone would understand Sladen's significance to *Doctor Who* fans (Collis, "Doctor Who Actress"). Unlike in the U.K., where Sladen's recent performances had endeared her to new generations of fans, as well as continued to receive long-time fans' devotion, American fans often needed to explain Sladen's role in the series and the reasons why they were so sad at her passing. The U.S. memorials posted to media sites like *Entertainment Weekly* (as opposed to *Doctor Who* fan forums populated by an international fan base) had a significantly different tone and content than fan postings (which included those by *Doctor Who* and BBC insiders who were also Sladen fans) generated in the U.K.

A number of Sladen's long-time American fans typically held their own mini-memorials online or with friends. During *Doctor Who* panels at the U.S. Popular Culture Association, held in San Antonio, Texas, on the weekend of *Doctor Who*'s sixth season premiere, scholar/fans stopped for a moment of silence during more than one panel in remembrance of Sladen and Sarah Jane. Online fans debated why BBC America did not see fit to include the Sladen tribute after the U.S. broadcast of "The Impossible Astronaut." During the 2011 Emmy Awards later in the year, Sladen's photograph was missing during the annual "In Memoriam" segment of actors who had died during the previous year. Although American *Who* fans' reaction to Sladen's passing was just as intense as that of *Who* fans in the U.K., the U.S. memorials were personal and private instead of national and television-worthy.

After *The Sarah Jane Adventures*

By the end of 2011, Russell T Davies had returned to the U.K. Despite comments earlier in the year regarding *Torchwood*'s future that he might move away from SF or that he was taking a break from television, news came in January 2012 that he and Phil Ford were working on a new children's series, *Wizards vs. Aliens*. The series was described as "the story of a 16-year-old boy who is secretly from a family of wizards. When alien race the Nekross arrive from the moon, he and his friend Benny are all that stands in the way of the Earth's destruction" ("Russell T Davies Announces"). The series has been described as a mixture of SF, fantasy, and adventure. Some critics have suggested that it was created primarily to fill the gap left by *The Sarah Jane Adven-*

tures, but Davies, Ford, Russell, and others affiliated with *The Sarah Jane Adventures* seem excited by the new series and tout its differences. Script editor Derek Ritchie was quoted as describing the new series as "similar to *The Sarah Jane Adventures* only in the respect of being an adventure show with strong character-driven narratives, and big moral themes. But this is a new universe, and the conflict between science and magic ... is already inspiring very different stories from *SJA*, and giving us a lot of scope in a very, very rich fictional universe!" (Peat).

Twitter has become a way to interest fans in the development of a television series, and *Wizards vs. Aliens'* creators used it well in March 2012 to alert potential viewers about the series' progress. Russell asked Ford about the first read-through of the script, and tweets abounded on the first day of filming in early April (*Wizards Vs. Aliens* blog). Notably, many former *Sarah Jane Adventures* creators, writers, and directors came on board the new series, enticing potential audiences with the promise of the same award-winning quality found in the earlier children's series.

Family-oriented themes and a child-friendly premise reminiscent of *The Sarah Jane Adventures* may help the new series retain the former's U.K. audience. Without a specific link to internationally marketed *Doctor Who*, and because it is designed specifically for CBBC, the new series seems unlikely to be marketed to the U.S. With the premature end to *The Sarah Jane Adventures*, the children's television part of the *Who* franchise seems to be over.

Although the series attained a passionate niche in American fandom, it, more so than *Doctor Who* and *Torchwood*, never became a ratings leader in children's (or any other) programming in the U.S. Nevertheless, within *Who* fandom, Elisabeth Sladen and Sarah Jane Smith will be remembered fondly through their long association with the Doctor.

Chapter 7

Tweet Success: Social Media and Television Marketing

Want to send thanks or congratulations on a fine performance or a well-written script? Or how about just saying hello and asking *Doctor Who*'s or *Torchwood*'s actors, showrunners, writers, or directors how they are doing today? Thanks to Twitter, and the increasing number of cast and crew signing up for social media, fans can far more easily send messages to the series' insiders at much less risk of warranting a restraining order. Their messages also are likely to make entertainment news. According to a February 2012 article, Steven Moffat (showrunner), Mark Gatiss (writer), Arthur Darvill (Rory Williams), John Barrowman (Captain Jack Harkness), Murray Gold (composer), James Moran (writer), Noel Clarke (Mickey Smith), John Simm (The Master), and Billie Piper (Rose Tyler) are only a few of the famous who now have Twitter accounts (McAlpine). Although Moffat's and Gatiss' tweets about either *Doctor Who* or *Sherlock* tend to be retweeted most often, *Torchwood*'s use of Twitter to connect with fans during *Miracle Day* became a worthwhile study in the art of marketing a series via social media.

Tweets and twitpics are the way to a fan's heart. In the months leading up to *Torchwood: Miracle Day*'s debut in July 2011, fans posted photos and observations of filming in Wales and the U.S., but, in addition, scriptwriter Jane Espenson, cast members Kai Owen, Tom Price, and John Barrowman, and various crew members kept fans aware of on-set developments. They enthusiastically tweeted behind-the-scenes news, such as casting updates or reports of the day's action, to keep fans aware of the stages of production; these messages were immediately retweeted or reposted on fan websites and *Torchwood* or *Doctor Who* forums. *Torchwood*'s increasing reliance on unofficial online networks to get out the latest (and most positive) announcements indicates the importance of word-of-mouth publicity. In *Torchwood*'s case, Espenson's tweets during episode broadcasts not only helped fans better understand the series but also went a long way toward ameliorating discontent with everything from scheduling to storytelling.

Social media, including but not limited to Twitter, are changing the way fans discuss television. A news article entitled "Even *Doctor Who* Can't Time Shift Social Media" notes that fans of a television series often discuss in real time an episode in progress. Twitter can provide a forum for communal viewing among fans, no matter where they live in the world, but it also increases the number of spoilers for those living in a time zone or country where the episode has not yet been shown. The social media article attributed illegal downloads of *Doctor Who* episodes to fans reading spoiler tweets and wanting an episode immediately, instead of days later. According to this article, BBC America responded by showing *Doctor Who* episodes only a few hours after their broadcast in the U.K., making American fans much happier — and less likely to illegally download episodes. BBC America gained its largest audience for any show when the sixth season of *Doctor Who* began in April 2011. The article predicts that "as more success stories like these emerge, syndication delays and time zones will be tested" (Bergman). Apparently the moral of this success story is that those fans who tweet often and loudly enough will be heard by the BBC.

Torchwood did not need to be told twice. When the *Miracle Day* marketing campaign kicked into high gear in spring 2011, social media was at the top of the to-do list. Online news articles discussed how "Starz is preparing the masses by getting social on several different platforms [e.g., Facebook, Twitter, Four Square, Glue] to get people talking about the show" (Ferguson).

In its 2010–2011 annual report, BBC Worldwide listed its intention to more effectively use social media as part of its marketing strategy. It launched the *Doctor Who* Facebook page in December 2010, and "in just a few months it had 800,000 fans. Via this, we engage daily with fans, give them the most up-to-date news, and provide a single destination for all things *Doctor Who*. The page has also proved a valuable marketing tool, delivering 12.6 percent of traffic to the BBC's *Doctor Who* website to date." Furthermore, *Doctor Who*'s recent ratings spike and high iTune sales in the U.S. were "largely driven by our highest-ever level of marketing investment — including social media engagement" (BBC Worldwide).

Part of that "media engagement" could be used to make fans feel appreciated and to encourage them to keep an open mind about new *Torchwood* episodes. Starz' and the BBC's unique partnership to bring *Torchwood* back for a fourth season already had many fans worried how the show would change. The discussions on fan forums seemed split between extremes, although undoubtedly only the most vocal fans, those either very much for the new episodes or those very much opposed to a format change, share their thoughts online. One group consisted of former fans who no longer liked the direction *Torchwood* took with the 2009 miniseries *Children of Earth* and did not plan to watch *Miracle Day*. At the other extreme, new viewers or returning fans enthusiastically posted messages to social media sites that they were counting down the days until *Miracle Day*'s premiere, just like the Starz official countdown clock that fans could download from the network's website. Of course, fans who watched but did not like everything about *Children of Earth* took the middle ground, writing that they at least wanted to check out the first episode or two before deciding whether to continue viewing.

For many reasons, whether to make more people aware of *Torchwood*'s premiere or to reassure former fans that the new series would be worthwhile and respectful of its origins, Starz and the BBC frequently tweeted series news. On the respective days of *Miracle Day*'s premiere in the U.S. (July 8) and U.K. (July 14), fans who signed up for Starz updates received email reminders about when to tune in, and tweets celebrated *Miracle Day*. More important, however, is the way that the show's "insiders"—current and former *Torchwood* scriptwriters, actors, and cast members' family or managers—also tweeted to fans and each other about the premiere episode.

Tweets by *Torchwood* Insiders

On July 14, *Miracle Day*'s first episode was broadcast in the U.K. Throughout the day, BBC America sent tweets tagged #Torchwood and #TorchwoodMiracleDay, which were then retweeted by fans at related links, such as #/@Team_Barrowman (John Barrowman and family's official Twitter account). During the broadcast, scriptwriter Espenson, watching a recording in Los Angeles, followed the first episode along with fans watching in the U.K. and tweeted her insights into the production.

Espenson's running commentary did more than give some new information to fans following the Twitter feed. Because U.K. citizens received the first episode almost a week after it had been broadcast in North America and Australia, Espenson's tweets were directed specifically to British fans who might have been left feeling less than special. Because *Torchwood* shifted much of its production to the U.S. from Wales for the latest episodes, plus the fact that British fans were unhappy about the delayed broadcast, Espenson's tweets became a friendly bonus directed to U.K. viewers.

As well, John Barrowman, his sister Carole, and his nephew Trevor all tweeted during the broadcast. Carole retweeted some fans' comments to the rest of the team, making these fans, whether in the U.K. or U.S., feel special to be singled out for their messages to presumably be read by Captain Jack himself (or at least I did; she retweeted two of my comments). Having the U.K.'s BBC star watch from Glasgow and become part of fans' communal viewing experience made the first episode seem like a huge global slumber party.

During the hour of the first episode's U.K. broadcast, I searched for #Torchwood as a keyword, although many other possible keywords could have been used. I also followed Jane Espenson, Tom Price, Kai Owen, Team Barrowman, and Barrowman Crime (Carole Barrowman's official account). I counted the number of messages during the *Miracle Day* episode's broadcast. During the hour *Torchwood* debuted in the U.K, several types of comments were posted: what was being seen on screen, what had happened behind the scenes, and what the person writing the message was doing during the episode's broadcast.

Espenson logged the most messages about the episode: 16, plus a couple of messages about technical difficulties. John Barrowman posted 5, but one was a birthday message to Espenson, whose birthday coincided with *Miracle Day*'s U.K. premiere. Espenson's comments about what she was watching sometimes reflected her American sensibilities and knowledge of American or Welsh culture. During *Miracle Day*'s promotion by the press, cultural differences often became newsworthy, because the joint Welsh-American production, featuring an international cast, often poked fun at both cultures and the differences between them. In addition, some early *Miracle Day* episodes made humorous comparisons between American and Welsh cultural expectations and linguistic differences. On Twitter, Espenson's comments reflected a genuine fondness for Welsh accents. She noted that "the Welsh accents always sound like tunes to me!" and later commented, "I wrote a draft of one of my eps in which they [characters Gwen Cooper and Rhys Williams] actually spoke in Welsh. But it didn't make it to the screen."

Perhaps Espenson's "insider" comments also offered fans following on Twitter some unique, spontaneous insights that had not been revealed during press interviews. In addition to the comment about one of her scripts, Espenson explained one line of dialogue: "'Nice for some' is a Brit expression—I should've helped get that out of script. My bad. But fun." During a scene in which reporters announce the "miracle" of the end of death, Espenson wrote "I like this news montage. One of those guys is a reporter on local LA news." Although the fact that Espenson spent an hour on Twitter, on her birthday, no less, to bond with British fans is a good way to generate goodwill, the content of her messages also let those who followed her tweets learn something more about the scripts as well as Espenson's favorite moments from this episode.

A former *Torchwood* scriptwriter, James Moran, posted a positive comment about Wales, similar to Espenson's, at the beginning of the broadcast: "Isn't Wales gorgeous? Aren't all the Welsh gorgeous? With their faces and accents and everything!" Whereas Espenson's comment could be perceived as appreciation of Wales and the Welsh cast by an American member of the new production team, Moran's tweet reinforced the ideas that Wales and the Welsh are special and should remain an integral part of *Torchwood* in future episodes. These positive comments from Espenson and Moran could help reassure fans who love *Torchwood* because of its very Welsh roots and who feared that the series' shift to the U.S. would turn *Torchwood* only into an American *CSI*-type show.

John Barrowman's comments were less personal, except for the birthday message to Espenson. Just before the return of Captain Jack into the new season of *Torchwood*, Barrowman tweeted "Spoiler ... here he comes!! Get ready!" and then "Captain Jack is BACK!!" Because of Barrowman's love of playing Captain Jack, a fact repeated in countless interviews, fans might expect his tweets to be focused solely on Captain Jack. The use of several exclamation points also represented in print the actor's outgoing personality and enthusiasm for the role.

The actor's fans often turn to Twitter to read personal messages. At times Barrowman even enlists fans' help in pranks, something the extroverted entertainer also is known for. In August 2011, for example, Barrowman tweeted the location of his partner, Scott Gill, as he went sightseeing while the actor was away at rehearsals. Barrowman asked fans to approach Gill, have their picture taken with him, and then post the photographs. The initially unsuspecting Gill finally created a new Twitter account under a fake name just to keep tabs on what his partner was tweeting. Such playfulness via Twitter seems to endear Barrowman to his fans and to make them part of his extended family.

Barrowman typically posts messages online around birthdays or special events after fans have sent hundreds if not thousands of good wishes. During these moments when fans "discover" him online in real time, he answers questions or posts personal messages about what he is doing at home (e.g., playing with the dogs, having dinner with his partner). His fans have come to expect the actor to share an inordinate amount of personal information.

Thus, his tweets during *Miracle Day* and his later comments about watching the show with manager and business partner Gavin Barker were not surprising to fans but continued to meet their expectation that Barrowman will share both his work and personal life with fans, creating a sense of camaraderie between the actor and his *Torchwood* fan base. Fans know which tweets Barrowman writes himself, as opposed to other messages coming from Team Barrowman, because he adds his initials at the end of the message. During the *Miracle Day* broadcast, Barrowman's initials appeared after each comment, reminding fans that the actor himself was watching with them.

Although cast member Kai Owen did not comment during the episode, earlier in the day he tweeted that *Torchwood* was finally returning home, a comment that could be construed by U.K. fans in a number of ways. First, it may be perceived as recognition that the series belongs in and to Wales in particular and the U.K. (or even BBC) more generally. It could also be read as a commentary about British fans receiving the first episode later, or even merely noting that *Torchwood* was at last back on the air after two years.

Former *Torchwood* scriptwriter and novelist Phil Ford simply tweeted "Happy Miracle Day," marking the day as special because of *Torchwood*'s premiere, making it seem that July 14 was a *Torchwood* holiday. However, his parenthetical addition — "apart from everyone in the rest of the world who has already seen it!" — was a barb aimed at the BBC. Tweets with specific or implied criticism of BBC's scheduling of premiere episode "The New World" united fans critical of the BBC's handling of *Torchwood* with those *Torchwood* insiders who also complained about the delay. The messages helped further align high-profile writers and actors with fans instead of with Starz or the BBC. Even when fans are upset at the networks, they may feel less likely to criticize their "friends" — such as the actors or writers who make such tweets and make an effort to include them in a conversation about *Torchwood* that goes beyond advertising the series.

Although Tom Price, who plays police constable Andy Davidson, worked as a comedian the night of *Torchwood*'s return, even he managed to send a humorous message en route. He wrote that, as he walked past a household watching *Miracle Day* on a big plasma TV screen, he was tempted to bang on the window. Fans got a laugh imagining the family's shock at having "Andy Davidson" outside their home while he was on screen in the episode.

Price in particular is developing a greater fan following because of his online bantering with castmates and his humorous, often ribald Twitter messages. Because Andy is on screen less than other returning characters, Price's use of Twitter helps fans get to know him and better associate him with his character, now one in an internationally promoted series.

Out of all these many tweets, perhaps the greatest surprise is James Moran's many posts directed to fan groups #Torchwood and #TorchwoodMiracleDay. In July 2009, shortly after fan-favored character Ianto Jones was killed in an episode co-written by Moran, a few angry fans threatened him online. The fan messages became so nasty, even including death threats, that Moran stopped posting his blogs about *Torchwood*, which had provided fans with lots of behind-the-scenes information prior to *Children of Earth*'s broadcast. Gareth David-Lloyd (Ianto Jones) appealed to fans to stop these actions on his character's behalf, and, indeed, the majority of Ianto fans found positive outlets for their grief— including raising money for charity. Some fans posted apologies to Moran, even though they were not the ones who sent negative messages to his website (Mutster101; Walker; Wilkes). In the two years since *Children of Earth*, Moran began appearing at fan conventions in Wales and England, posting blogs about new projects, and tweeting more frequently.

Thus, when he posted several exuberant messages about the return of *Torchwood* in 2011, he reached out to the fan community and re-established his bond with *Torchwood*. Moran also has written "shipper" stories published in *Torchwood* magazine and the novel *Consequences*, and many stories, such as the one in *Consequences*, illustrate the depth of the Janto relationship. If Moran had positive comments to make about *Miracle Day*, at least some *Torchwood* fans were willing to read them and, perhaps, be influenced by Moran's "insider" perspective.

Moran's tweets during *Miracle Day* were not personal, but they reflected his "we're in this together" attitude. With exclamations like "Woohoo!" and "Yay!" Moran reminded fans of the broadcast time and then wished them a happy viewing. He added that he liked the first episode and thought fans would, too. He posted primarily before and after the broadcast, at one time asking those who were tweeting during the episode how they could watch and comment at the same time without missing important parts of the story. As soon as the first episode was over, however, Moran began tweeting more frequently.

The writer brings up a good point. Although tweeting creates a fan community of episode watchers, it also splits audience attention between two screens. Presumably the people associated with *Torchwood* both want fans to feel like a community but also to pay attention to the story. Barrowman's "spoiler" alert about Captain Jack's entrance into the story is a good example of a way to direct online fans' attention back to the television story — they likely followed Barrowman's directive to watch the upcoming scene.

Espenson's comments, however, reference a scene being shown at the time the tweet was sent. Her running commentary became a "show" all its own. The assumption behind her tweets is that tech-savvy fans who come to Twitter during an episode know how to multitask. Nevertheless, they are far more likely to be distracted from the episode because they are reading or reacting to tweets as much as to plot developments. The question becomes whether Twitter fans were online at that time in order to capture the attention of other fans and, perhaps more important, the famous people also online at the same time or whether they really wanted to share the *Torchwood* viewing experience.

Torchwood Insiders' Tweets During the U.S. Premiere

The Twitter experience during the U.S. premiere of *Miracle Day* was quite different, in part because many *Torchwood* insiders, including Barrowman, Owen, Price, Ford, and Moran, were in the U.K. when the premiere episode was broadcast in the U.S. on July 8. Because U.S. fans were able to view the episode first, they did not need to be reassured that *Torchwood*'s American viewers were more important or that the series had not become solely an American production. For several practical reasons, then, the "insider tweets" targeting U.S. fans could be expected to have a distinctly different tone and content.

The actors and writers behind *Torchwood* posted general "today's the day" messages on July 8, but they did not watch the episode with fans. Espenson wrote an excited message early in the day: "It's Miracle Day!!!! *Torchwood* premieres tonight on Starz! Eeeeeee!" On the day before, she had reminded fans that the *Web of Lies* online animated series, for which she wrote the first episode, was available on iTunes. Her limited messages were slightly more personal than those sent by Starz but did not provide any of the insights written during the U.K. premiere on July 14.

Barrowman tweeted specifically "To my USA fans," encouraging them to "Have a blast watching *Torchwood* tonight." He did not write that he also would be watching, because by that time he was busy at work in the U.K. on his purely BBC series *Tonight's the Night*, which would debut the next evening. However, his message further indicated that his U.S. fan base knows him well. He added the following comment: "Popcorn and a Grey Goose and tonic. Bliss." Barrowman's fans know from previous publications and interviews just what Barrowman likes to drink. This post started a round of tweets among the actor, family, and friends about what they would be drinking to celebrate *Miracle Day*'s U.S. debut. Clearly, Barrowman was writing "to my USA fans" who know him so well and often feel themselves part of his extended family, not to the larger Starz *Torchwood* audience. The tweets, while perhaps interesting to *Torchwood*—but not specifically Barrowman—fans, did not really invite them into what essentially was a private conversation made public.

Later interviews and tweets expressed Barrowman's anticipation of San Diego Comic-Con. His promotional appearance there, which required him to make two international flights within a few days between his show-hosting duties in the U.K., became a more personal way to meet his American fans and *Torchwood* fans and share his enthusiasm for *Miracle Day*. Nevertheless, the content and number of tweets sent by *Torchwood* insiders on the respective *Miracle Day* premiere days indicated an international audience separated not only by time and geography but by cultural association with *Torchwood* and their concerns about or reasons for watching the series. The tweets from series' insiders therefore became obviously targeted to different readers in the U.K. and U.S.

Mass Tweets from Starz or the BBC

These previously discussed tweets are far more personable than the messages sent by corporate entities Starz or the BBC, which promoted the series through messages as simple as "Watch tonight" or announced extra materials, such as trailers or the web-based game series, *Torchwood: Web of Lies*. Corporate tweets are far more likely to be standardized supplements to traditional advertisements found in magazines, newspapers, official websites, or email reminders.

Starz, tweeting through #Torchwood_Starz, offered fans an exclusive Captain Jack sticker if they registered at Glue. The network encouraged viewers to tweet the "play-by-play" during the episode. Comparing a television drama with a sports event underscored the special "event" nature of Starz' promotional messages. The tone and language in Starz' tweets followed along the lines of the network website's countdown clock and television countdown clock shown on screen until the episode began.

The "play-by-play" tweet also provides a different vocabulary for a communal viewing experience. It encourages a separation between viewer and the story by asking fans to immediately comment on their response to elements like plot or special effects, or even to their feelings toward a character or actor. Such responses lack any reflection or development because they are spontaneous in reaction to what has just been seen. Of course, most tweets are anything but philosophic treatises, but a play-by-play account only reports what is being seen and how the viewer feels about it. The linear, real-time conversation cannot provide an adequate interpretation of a scene in light of the whole episode's story arc or the development of a character or performance. By encouraging fans to create a play-by-play account of the episode, Starz was also encouraging fans to react immediately to individual scenes or characters instead of giving the story their undivided attention, simply enjoying the episode, or even waiting until the episode had ended before critiquing it. Perhaps inadvertently, Starz emphasized the communal viewing experience as it happened instead of inviting analysis or reflection on a completed episode. The act of watching television became more important than analysis or criticism of the episode as a whole unit.

Fan Tweets

Fans who joined the Twitter conversation during the U.K. broadcast targeted some messages directly to individuals, primarily Barrowman or Espenson (evidenced by the use of the @ symbol instead of the # before the keyword, which sends a message directly to the target person/group instead of to a general collection of people searching by the # keyword). These fans wrote as if they were writing to other friends, a further indication that Twitter helps establish a bond — even if it is online, carefully managed, and ultimately superficial — between those behind a production and those who watch it.

The majority of comments indicated what fans were seeing at the time and how they felt about a scene, actor, or the entire episode. The comments were mostly positive, but some fans unfavorably compared the current season with previous ones. Still, they were watching the premiere and had not boycotted *Miracle Day*— a plus for the Twitter promotion.

Getting Tweet on Fans

Twitter announcements were not limited to promotion of the first episode on the day it was broadcast. Kai Owen hosted a live Twitter party on the day that he wrapped filming on *Miracle Day*. While waiting for pizza to arrive at his California home, he tweeted fans that he would take their questions for an hour. The conversation was fast and funny, endearing Owen to *Torchwood* fans and keeping them updated on his feelings about the end of filming. Fans just as quickly sent their congratulations and offered to buy him a drink, something known to happen at fan conventions.

Although Owen maintains a firm line between being friendly with fans and inviting them to become his new BFFs, his online communication helps make his fans feel like they matter to him. During my interview with him in August 2011, Owen explained that tweeting "is a good way" to interact with fans. "I'm also enjoying Twitter to get general news and speak to friends. I think it's a good way of promoting yourself. I enjoy interacting with fans and doing Q&A. I'm quite fan friendly."

Fans would certainly agree. Owen's brief notes about the filming of his scenes and some non-spoilery highlights also created more excitement among fans interested in *Miracle Day*. The tweets not only made fans feel like they had insider insights to the current production but that they were important enough for Owen to write to them periodically.

Price and Owen bantered online via Twitter, their comments funny and sometimes a bit risqué. Price's tweets let fans know not only about his *Torchwood* scenes but current and forthcoming appearances at comedy clubs. Like Owen, Price's online persona is brash and funny, which probably encourages more fans to come see his standup act in the U.K.

These tweets also help fans separate the actors from their roles, which are somewhat limited in *Torchwood*. Viewers who keep up with *Torchwood* via Twitter are far more likely to become aware of the actors and to pay attention to their screen time, but they also are more likely to follow them to other performances. Self-promotion via Twitter is especially important to actors who may not yet get as much publicity as the series' stars or have as broad a fan base. By communicating with fans via Twitter or Facebook, they may gain more fans or win greater devotion — they have to promote themselves beyond the often-nominal official publicity given to actors (or writers) who are not household names.

Jane Espenson and the Infamous Episode, "Immortal Sins"

By the time of the broadcast of "Immortal Sins," *Miracle Day*'s seventh episode, the second to feature explicit sex scenes starring Captain Jack, and one seemingly designed to court controversy in the U.K., Espenson was the lone *Torchwood* insider still tweeting during episodes. She continued this practice week after week, watching an episode on her computer in California while U.K. fans watched in real time on the BBC. Just as U.S. viewers may have spoiled other scenes throughout *Miracle Day*, they referenced the seven-minute sex scene in "Immortal Sins" in posts made days before U.K. audiences had the opportunity to watch the episode. American viewers seemed split on the episode's merit, half liking Jack's backstory (and probably his backside, both which are prominently featured in the episode), and half disliking the regression in any forward momentum *Miracle Day* was building. The discussion was kept mostly to fan forums or social media that U.K. fans could avoid if they chose.

Apparently the BBC was kept busy during and after the broadcast of "Immortal Sins" when it received more than 500 complaints about the sex scene (which likely had been edited, given the precedent of editing the second episode's far shorter but more sexually graphic sex scene). Those who complained called "Immortal Sins" everything from "gratuitous sex" to "softcore porn." Espenson did not respond to the complaints or articles indicating British viewers' displeasure with the episode she wrote. She did acknowledge her monitoring of tweets during the episode and commented that different people posted negative messages about either violence or explicit sex, but not both. She even warned, "shouting" in all caps, squeamish viewers to cover their eyes or turn away during the most graphic scenes of Jack being repeatedly slashed to death. She encouraged them to come back a few minutes later.

Espenson wrote even more tweets during this episode's broadcast than she did during the premiere, and at the beginning and end of the broadcast she praised *Torchwood* fans, first, specifically saying hello to British fans and then writing that "*Torchwood* fans are the best!" shortly after the broadcast ended. As with previous broadcasts, she provided insider information about the script, comments about the scene being shown, and personal preferences about a performance or line.

An episode like "Immortal Sins" seems more appropriate for Starz than the BBC. Espenson acknowledged but did not apologize for or explain the necessity of the episode's greater emphasis on sex or violence. Her matter-of-fact tone, even when she saw negative comments online, kept the tweets focused more on the story in progress and may have minimized damage from British viewers who complained to the BBC. Espenson's tone, number of tweets, and comments about fans' tweets did not differ significantly from her responses during the other Twitter viewing parties she hosted. She responded to fans' comments sent directly to her during the hour and was upbeat, making "Immortal Sins" seem just like another episode instead of turning it into Captain Jack's shocking sex show, as some viewers seemed to think of it. As an interesting aside, the press reported the primary complaint of disgruntled BBC viewers was the depiction of a homosexual sex scene rather than the repeated brutal murder of its lead character. On Twitter, the number of negative comments was more evenly split.

As criticism for *Miracle Day* mounted, Espenson became the only continuing online presence and fan contact, especially for fans in the U.K. Her insights (some different from her tweets) were part of a weekly feature on the AfterElton web site, for example, and interviews about *Miracle Day* were published in *Doctor Who* magazine and the British press around the time of "Immortal Sins"' broadcast. These published interviews, however, are not as spontaneous as Espenson's tweets, and they seem to promote the production rather than reach out to fans and make her seem "one of them." By continuing to tweet during the U.K. broadcasts, Espenson maintained her support of the increasingly criticized series and underscored her commitment to U.K. fans, whereas other cast members had returned to using Twitter as they previously had done—to communicate with their specific fans or promote projects, not necessarily *Torchwood*. Espenson's tweets increasingly became important to maintain a "business as usual" stance throughout the series and to remind

British fans that they were receiving insights during each episode that American viewers had not received when they watched the program nearly a week earlier.

Tweets with and Without a Context

Both the Starz-based U.S. Twitter conversation and the one bringing together *Torchwood* insiders and fans can be interpreted in different ways, depending on the context of the messages. Tweets read as a transcript long after the messages were originally posted, or posts isolated and later reprinted or retweeted, encourage different interpretations of the message. Fans who later read what amounts to a transcript of others' tweets collected in chronological order by keyword search (e.g., #Torchwood) may interpret fans' comments about the premiere episode very differently than readers who come across single, out-of-context tweets reposted on Facebook or another social media site. The separation of one retweeted message from a thread of hundreds gives more weight to the single message. If the message happens to be negative, fans reading it out of context may have a different perception of an episode or even *Torchwood*. For example, one U.K. reader who only followed American fans' tweets posted under #Torchwood questioned whether he wanted to view the finale when it was broadcast. Although *Torchwood* often benefited from fan tweets, especially early in the miniseries, seeing an incomplete "conversation" about an episode might lead later readers—such as U.K. fans—to give more weight to American fans' perceptions than to the comments made by Espenson days later during the same episode's broadcast on the BBC.

To be fair, an analysis of tweets allows academic researchers to read far more into a single, isolated message or even a series of messages than probably was meant by the people who spontaneously tweeted within the context of a conversation. However, because Twitter is being used more extensively to promote television series, including *Doctor Who* and *Torchwood*, showrunners, writers, and actors also are inviting more analysis of their messages. If *Torchwood* insiders use Twitter to promote their series or themselves, then Twitter analysts are going to scrutinize their messages long after they were written, because Twitter makes conversations a public record.

Twitter (like Facebook) is one way for those affiliated with a television series to maintain a superficially close relationship with fans, who feel they get to know the performers through the messages they post. The immediacy and uncensored nature of tweeting creates a sense of getting to know the real person, not the public persona carefully building an image through interviews or roles. Although most professionals who value good PR are careful what they tweet, the fans who read the messages may not question whether the tweets are anything but spontaneous and unedited.

Social media and fan websites are at least as important as the official promotional outlets, for example, network upfronts or Cannes television-marketing events that were also used in 2011 to promote *Torchwood*. The Starz and BBC official websites receive fewer daily hits than fan sites or retweets on social media sites, perhaps because these official sites often are updated after fans have already learned and passed on information gleaned from Twitter or first-hand observations posted to fan sites. "Insider" information during production helped make fans feel like they were part of the process of getting *Torchwood* back on television before an eagerly awaiting audience, whereas official websites merely document news or provide additional content, such as trailers, photographs, or other promotional materials.

Beyond Television: Fan Response to Multimedia *Torchwood*

In addition to promoting the television episodes, official network websites, as well as social media, are used to make *Torchwood* fans aware of stories being told through other media. As Espenson tweeted shortly before *Miracle Day* wrapped production in mid–May, "Enjoy all the *Torchwood* brands." These brands include novels, radio plays, television episodes, and a web-only interactive series offered to consumers around the time that *Miracle Day* debuted.

Almost immediately after the radio plays were broadcast on consecutive days in July 2011, just before *Miracle Day* premiered in the U.K., *Torchwood* fans provided online summaries and comments, either on fan forums as each episode was broadcast (similar to the Twitter commentary during *Miracle Day*'s premiere) or as blogged reviews written in the days after a broadcast. Many fans who had not yet heard the plays through BBC broadcasts or downloads first warned and later complained about spoilery comments on Facebook or Live Journal forums as excited fans posted their sometimes not-so-cryptic or generic appraisals online.

Few entertainment reporters or critics mentioned the radio plays, except to announce their broadcast dates or briefly tease the plots. In-depth analyses were instead provided by fans, who debated the merits of the radio plays as thoroughly as they scrutinized television episodes. Fans typically debated the structural problems with story or character development. They critically evaluated the accents of the actors (which sometimes varied from English to American) and noted leaps of logic in the 45-minute plots' development. They compared their knowledge of characters, as presented in television episodes and previous radio plays, with what was presented in this latest batch of radio stories.

The consensus among fans is that the BBC radio plays were written specifically for long-time fans, particularly Janto fans, who had been extremely vocal in their displeasure over the death of Ianto Jones and the lack of positive closure to the Janto relationship. In the final radio play, Jack and Ianto declare their love for each other, Jack offers (again) to sacrifice the world in order to keep Ianto with him, and Ianto (again) saves the world by sacrificing himself. The fact that this group of *Torchwood* stories was set prior to (in two plays) or six months after (in the final play) the events of *Children of Earth* seemed to rewind the ongoing *Torchwood* story to a much earlier time than the beginning of *Miracle Day*. The radio plays also reunited the four *Torchwood* cast members from *Children of Earth* and earlier episodes and allowed Ianto fans to hear, one more time, Gareth David-Lloyd in that role, more than two years after the character's death and nearly three years since David-Lloyd had filmed *Children of Earth*.

During interviews in July 2009, Russell T Davies was adamant that the number of fans unhappy with Ianto's death was small and unimportant. During the 2011 publicity for *Miracle Day*, Davies, as well as Barrowman, indicated that fans should move on and enjoy the new season, that the choices to kill Ianto and allow Jack to sacrifice his grandson in *Children of Earth* were the right decisions (Paddon). The 2011 radio plays, however, seemed a way to appease the vocal online fans and possibly get them excited about more *Torchwood* stories.

BBC radio plays seldom get the attention granted to television series, and U.S. audiences initially could only listen to the stories through a BBC website. (CDs of the plays could be purchased months later.) Messages promoting and critiquing the plays mostly came from *Torchwood* fan forums, the majority on Live Journal, via Facebook, or linked through tweets or Facebook status statements to individual fans' blogs. After each day's play—or even throughout a broadcast—fans posted their reviews or reactions. Most were positive, especially about David-Lloyd, Ianto, or the Janto relationship, but others more critically evaluated the plot and noted plot holes or discrepancies between a scriptwriter's interpretation of characters and differing depictions from television episodes. The discussions, however, were lively and indicated fans' commitment to this version of *Torchwood*—one set prior to *Miracle Day*. The tw_classic forum's reaction post for the July 12, 2011, radio play gathered 195 comments; many included links to other sites where fans could hear the plays or read the running commentary as fans had live-blogged. *Torchwood*'s longer-term fandom assumed that they were the target audience and that the plays' very existence might be attributed to appeasing fans of the former series so that they would also tune in to *Miracle Day*.

Online fandom could still make or break *Torchwood*, which relies on an international audience for its survival. *Torchwood* fandom has been particularly vocal about either its pleasure or displeasure with story and character developments, especially those associated with 2009's *Children of Earth* and 2011's *Miracle Day*. Word of mouth often translates into higher viewing numbers, and *Torchwood* needed to sustain high enough ratings both in the U.S. and U.K. in order to continue. The series' ability to court audiences on different continents, who may view first-run episodes days or weeks apart and who have different cultural expectations for the series, relies on social media to generate interest and create communities of viewers. With special content only available on the internet, such as *Web of Lies*, *Torchwood* branched out into new media and solidified several "brands," as Espenson calls them, with products available in various markets and media. Although other series also offer multimedia content and try to gain feedback and promote programming through social media, *Torchwood* is an interesting case study because of its unique fan controversy and history, bi-national production partnership, and sometimes conflicting cultural expectations of what the series should be. For series like *Torchwood* to survive, much less thrive, television "insiders" need to mingle online with their fans. As *Torchwood*'s publicity and marketing strategies indicate, renewal requires tweet success.

Chapter 8

Friday Is Fez Day: The Popularity of Conventions

When the Eleventh Doctor proudly proclaimed that fezzes are cool, fans took notice, and then promptly started donning them. During each day of the 2010 Chicago TARDIS convention, fans were encouraged to follow the theme of the day. Friday's Fez Day was a highlight, and the hallways became a sea of red as fans roamed from event to event on the packed schedule. Participating in fandom often is a solitary activity, one pursued at home watching episodes or posting messages on forums. Conventions provide a way for fans to congregate and share their love of the *Doctor Who* franchise, to make fandom communal and face to face, which is one reason why many participants travel cross country year after year to attend conventions. They renew old friendships and make new acquaintances; they share critiques and news; they celebrate skill in art, music, poetry, storytelling, costuming, and role playing; they revel in being part of a group. They often raise money for charity and teach others not only about fandom but more generalized skills (e.g., how to write a short story, make a video, sew a costume). They also get to meet actors, writers, directors, and designers who work in television or film; have their photo taken with or get the autograph of a famous person; and learn behind-the-scenes information. However, the community experience is most highly prized. Wearing a fez is only part of the fun.

Among the many fan conventions held around the world each year, at least three in the U.S. are specifically *Doctor Who* conventions: Gallifrey One, held in Los Angeles in February; Chicago TARDIS, a staple of Thanksgiving weekend; and newcomer Hurricane Who, in Orlando, inviting guests to sunny Florida in autumn. In addition, dozens more SF, fantasy, or general television conventions take place annually, whether from companies specializing in big events (e.g., Wizard World, Creation Entertainment) or fan volunteers united in their desire to celebrate their favorite series; they often host actors affiliated with the *Doctor Who* franchise. In recent years, Atlanta's DragonCon, held during Labor Day weekend, and midsummer's San Diego Comic-Con have attracted actors and showrunners from British television, especially SF. *Doctor Who* and *Torchwood* have been in high demand at more than one Comic-Con, and DragonCon's many sessions include a specific British television track that, in recent years, invited *Torchwood*'s Gareth David-Lloyd, Kai Owen, and Eve Myles and *Doctor Who*'s Peter Davison and Sylvester McCoy (DragonCon). Add to that local *Doctor Who* fan clubs and viewing groups around the U.S., and the conclusion is apparent: face-to-face fandom is alive and well — and thriving — in the U.S.

Thriving seems to be the operative word with *Doctor Who* conventions. Gallifrey One, heading into its twenty-fourth year in 2013, reported in a 2012 convention overview session that, by the first day of the three-day convention, 2002 people had pre-registered, and more fans lined up for same-day tickets each morning. Breaking the previous year's attendance (2190) was not difficult. When fans who pre-registered for the 2013 convention during the 2012 event were notified that the block of hotel rooms was open for reservation, the entire block sold out within one hour — a first for Gallifrey One. The convention staff quickly worked with the hotel to make additional convention-discounted rooms available, but many people planning to attend the convention snapped up rooms at nearby hotels, just so they would be ensured a room close to the convention venue. Such seems to be the trend in *Doctor Who* fandom in the U.S.

U.S. Conventions

Gallifrey One is not alone in facing an increased number of convention attendees. Jennifer Adams Kelley, programming director of Chicago TARDIS, noted that the convention had 1183 attendees in 2011, its "biggest number of attendees ever" and "nearly 300 more than in 2010 and 2009 (each)." Since 2000, Chicago TARDIS has provided fans with a series of panels spotlighting actors and other professionals affiliated with *Doctor Who*; fans can ask questions of the famous guests and later meet them during photo ops or autograph sessions.

Orlando's Hurricane Who convention is much younger, holding its second convention in 2012. A 2010 convention brought in 561 attendees, and convention chairman Jarrod Cooper has seen the number of pre-registered attendees increase before the second convention, which he attributes to "the rise of *Doctor Who*'s popularity in the States."

Kelley adds that the increased attendance at conventions can be the result of other factors, namely, "The series going back into production [in 2005] and becoming easily accessible to American viewers via BBC America. Also, the rise of social media has made it much easier to get the word out that the convention exists." Furthermore, the growth in interest in *Doctor Who* in the past couple of years reminds her

> very much of *DW* fandom when I first entered it way back in the early 1980s. Fanfic and art, cosplay (or as we called it back then, 'hall costuming'), more and more conventions and fan groups popping up everywhere in cities big and medium, references in other pop culture artifacts ... it's all happened before. Now, though, it's on a larger scale, since news and information about the show (as well as copies of it) travel instantaneously across the country instead of via the post office.

Some guests like to talk with fans informally, which, when a convention remains small, often creates a collegial atmosphere that fans and guests equally enjoy. In contrast to extremely large events like a Comic-Con or Wizard World, conventions run by fan volunteers have often provided a better experience for both the star-guests and fans, simply because the pace is more relaxed and guests can informally interact with respectful fans without the need for bodyguards or security staff to ensure their safety.

To date, these fan-operated conventions have not had to limit attendance, and so they, unlike some large conventions run by corporations, have not been compelled to turn people away at the door if they choose to walk in on the day of the event. If attendance increases exponentially, however, some *Doctor Who* events may become large enough either to compel organizers to limit attendance or to find bigger venues to accommodate the number of fans who want to attend.

Gallifrey One, Chicago TARDIS, and Hurricane Who all plan special events to commemorate *Doctor Who*'s 50th anniversary, although, in the months before them, convention staff tended to keep quiet about specifics in order to maintain surprise. Because Chicago TARDIS holds its annual convention during the U.S. Thanksgiving holiday in late November, the 2013 event will take place close to the series' true anniversary date; as well, 2013 is a special year for Chicago-area *Who* fandom. Kelley adds that "we're mindful that not only are we celebrating 50 years of *Doctor Who*, we're celebrating 30 years of a Thanksgiving weekend *Doctor Who* convention in Chicago. We hope to mark the lasting impact our fair city has had on *Doctor Who* fandom, both in the early days (the 1980s) as well as today."

Putting together a convention created and staffed by volunteers is long, hard work, even if the payoff is an event enjoyed and praised by guests and attendees. New episodes of *Doctor Who*, involving dozens of lead and supporting actors, plus the creative minds behind the production, as well as multiple series (*Doctor Who, Torchwood, The Sarah Jane Adventures*) being in production recently, would seem to indicate that convention planners would have an easier time in getting guests to headline the event. Unfortunately, contracting guests continues to be a tricky, time-consuming business.

Kelley explains that one of the challenges of programming a convention today is "getting 'new series' guests to appear — especially actors. They're all quite active, so it's really hard to a) book them and b) hold onto them once they're booked. It's one thing to pop around to a city 2 hours away in the midst of filming something, and another beast entirely to pop across the ocean for 4–5 days." Cooper's challenge is in "finding something for everyone," including fans of the "classic" or "new" series, plus spinoffs, but "making sure everyone is represented in some way" is one of his objectives for Hurricane Who.

Booking guests may be particularly difficult for U.S. conventions — especially those run by and for fans. Whereas companies that specialize in several large events each year as their primary business can afford to offer more money or special perks to guests, fan conventions face limitations in clout and budget. However, because a well-run annual convention, especially one with a track record of happy guests, can build a reputation for excellence over the years, some guests prefer fan conventions because they provide that personal touch and are smaller, less stressful events. The geographic distance from many actors in the *Doctor Who* franchise, who are usually based in the U.K., means that American conventions are more likely to require far more planning and incentives for international travel.

Some British guests simply like the "vibe" at American conventions and find them "more laidback" than U.K. conventions (C. Cooper). Although Kelley has not seen any major differences between U.S. and U.K. fans attending Chicago TARDIS, her British guests expressed an opinion that "American fans are more demonstrative." Cooper also has experienced the less pleasant side of fandom, however, from "some U.S. fans [who] feel more of a sense of entitlement of attending conventions without putting a cost to it. They feel that they should just be able to come and get everything for free." All fans, according to these convention planners, share the same enthusiasm for and appreciation of *Doctor Who*, and the volunteers behind the increasingly popular U.S. *Doctor Who* conventions develop and promote these highly anticipated events for love, not money.

The BBC theoretically can run a much larger and more lucrative convention. After all, it employs the creative cast and crew members of *Doctor Who* and have access to sets and props available to no one else. Until 2012, however, the BBC had not operated a convention since the arrival of "new Who." With the anniversary year approaching and the nearby Doctor Who

Experience soon open for business, spring in Cardiff seemed like the time and place for an official event, one that could be a test run for a larger or different event during the anniversary year. The way the official convention was initially presented to fans, however, left many offended, but, in the end, the event was deemed a success, not only by convention planners but the 3000 fans who attended from around the world. Before the convention, however, fans debated online the BBC's approach to the convention business and how it reflected on *Doctor Who*.

Doctor Who as "Cash Cow": Fans and Controversial BBC/BBC Worldwide Decisions

"Exciting news! We are launching the Official Doctor Who Convention to be held in Cardiff. Be quick to not miss out." The tweet from DW_Experience (the BBC's Doctor Who Experience) not only announced the first official convention in nearly thirty years but indicates the event's exclusivity. As fans soon found out, only 3000 tickets would be sold: 1500 for each day of programming. What the BBC likely expected would be cause for celebration instead managed to underscore a growing gap between what the BBC thinks its audiences want and what the fans of a television series expect to receive.

To those reading the press release outside the U.K., BBC Worldwide's idea did not seem startling or controversial. What may be surprising to American fans, then, is the response to BBC Worldwide's announcement of an official Doctor Who Convention to be held in Cardiff in spring 2012. The official announcement, immediately circulating in the media at such SF-related sites as *SFX*, described the convention as the "ultimate event for *Doctor Who* enthusiasts. With unparalleled access to the cast and crew, this event offers fans a one-off chance to immerse themselves behind the scenes" ("No One Gets You Closer") and limited ticket sales to 1500 for each of the two days of programming. Steven Moffat and Matt Smith were the first announced guests, with effects professionals, writers, and directors added to the list a few days later. The statement from BBC Worldwide's press office proclaimed the event as the "greatest gathering of *Doctor Who* cast and creators ever!"

Several newspapers included enthusiastic comments from both Moffat and Smith. Moffat sounded like a fan himself: "A whole weekend dedicated to all things *Doctor Who*, brilliant! We're going to be celebrating the whole team behind the show, people who bring to life the Doctor's craziest adventures and letting fans into some of our trade secrets. If you want to get under the skin of *Doctor Who* this is an unmissable event!" Smith praised the choice of Cardiff, where the series is filmed, for the event and added that he was looking forward to meeting fans (Golder, "Official BBC Doctor Who Convention"). The local *Wales Online* began its article with the optimistic claim that "it's the news that *Doctor Who* fans throughout the UK have been waiting for — an interactive Doctor Who Convention is coming to the Wales Millennium Centre in Cardiff" ("Cardiff to Host"). The optimism and support indicated by the media upon receiving the press release failed to generate the same level of positive response among fans.

Fan Response to BBC Worldwide's Convention Announcement

One comment on the Radio Free Skaro podcast of November 13, 2011, seemed to summarize much of the fan discontent: "There's a lot of thought that *didn't* seem to go into this thing." Nevertheless, the hosts reminded fans that the BBC has far greater access to the people who put together *Doctor Who* (and are under contract to the BBC) and has content that no fan-run convention or professional event-management company can hope to match. The dilemma of participating in an official convention offering different types of programming than fans can usually find at unofficial conventions versus attending a less expensive fan-run event became part of a cost/benefit analysis on forums throughout the weekend before tickets went on sale.

One blogger eloquently summed up many fans' discontent: "[J]ust because some people are daft enough to pay £120—almost an entire year's License Fee — to meet an actor or writer and get their autograph, doesn't mean it's right to charge it. The event threatens to dent the goodwill of legions of fans and risks badly backfiring on the BBC. Part of me hopes that it does exactly that — there's more than a whiff of greed in the air" (Hoscik).

The price for tickets caused quite a stir: £99 for a ticket, plus another £20–30 per autograph or photo opportunity with Matt Smith or Steven Moffat. (Karen Gillan, Arthur Darvill, and other actors, directors, and design specialists eventually were added, with the showrunner and current stars becoming part of the autograph and photograph events. However, at the time tickets went on sale, Smith and Moffat were the key guests.)

The cost may seem in line for such an event, if U.S. ticket prices are used as a comparison. U.S. fans paid $400 for the best access seating (i.e., closest to the stage, first in line for autographs) for the four-day Chicago TARDIS 2011 fan convention (with ticket prices as low as $50 for a one-day adult ticket) and $80 (the pre-registration price through December 31, 2011) for the four-day Gallifrey One in Los Angeles in February 2012. In the U.K., the SFX Weekender (which has included *Doctor Who* or *Torchwood* guests in the past) held in North Wales in early February 2012 was a two-day event with a pre-convention kickoff party. A low-end Silver ticket was sold for £189, with a signing pass to ensure getting an autograph fetching another £30—however, the Silver ticket also included accommodation at the host hotel. With currency conversion rates favoring the pound at the time tickets were first sold for the BBC's convention, the £99 ticket would cost around $160 U.S. dollars. Conversely, with a currency conversion going the other way, on the same date, the $400 top-priced Chicago TARDIS ticket would cost approximately £249.

For a full day of programming, including Q&A sessions with Eleventh Doctor Matt Smith, companions Karen Gillan (Amy Pond) and Arthur Darvill (Rory Williams) and explanations of technical wizardry behind the scenes, surely the Official Convention would be a bargain. Not so, unhappy fans argued. Unlike other conventions that offer discounted children's ticket prices or even allow children under 12 years old to attend free, as long as they are accompanied by at least one adult, the BBC's convention had only one ticket price, making the event out of the price range of many families who wanted to attend the event together. The one-price-fits-all approach also seemed to discourage the presence of children, who should be a major part of the Doctor's fan base (and the BBC's target audience for this television series). Several fans posted comments about the FAQ list's statements that the convention was not designed for children, which would seem to be at cross purposes with the television series' target audience. Having a *Doctor Who* convention where children are not recommended to attend seemed designed to annoy children and their parents.

Another reason why U.K. fans may have reacted differently from U.S. fans is the fact that many of the series' actors live and work in Britain. Because Cardiff is in many ways a small town compared with New York, Toronto, or Los Angeles, where actors or location filming are more difficult to track down on a given day, *Doctor Who* cast sightings reported in the professional media (e.g., *Wales Online*) or by fans' tweets of seeing an actor in public are more numerous. As well, many BBC stars, including David Tennant and John Barrowman, frequently appear on stage or in concert, making stage-door fan encounters or run-ins with actors around the theater more likely for U.K. fans than for U.S. fans, even those living in LA, where more accessibility to television actors might be expected. When the BBC limits access—even to maintain order at a convention or to ensure that as many people as possible get through an autograph line—the limitations upset fans who feel they should be allowed at least a moment with a guest without having to pay an additional fee or be shut out altogether from having a personal moment with a cast or crew member.

Yet another complaint about the official convention stemmed from the convention's Cardiff location. Although those fans living near Cardiff appreciated the fact that, for once, a convention was being held nearby instead of a more typical convention city like London, even U.K. residents living a few hours away complained about the travel time and need for overnight accommodation that would add to their expenses. Comments from U.S. fans contrasted these posts by noting that Americans often think little about driving long distances or flying cross country to attend a special event, but few Americans indicated they would fly to Cardiff for the Official Convention (DoctorWhoTV forum).

Although these concerns became vocal points of debate about the convention, beneath the complaint about pricing was a deeper issue: Should *Doctor Who* be BBC Worldwide's cash cow? Unlike other types of "merchandise," the convention was perceived as an attempt by the BBC to rip off the Doctor's loyal fans and make *Doctor Who* merely a product to be sold, not family entertainment made freely available in the U.K. by rights of paying the annual television licensing fee. The BBC was accused in some fan forums of trying to pit fans against each other; the "haves" with plenty of disposable income can meet the Doctor, but the equally loyal "have nots" cannot gain such access to an actor in a public television series paid for by the license-paying citizens.

U.S. fans had more difficulty understanding the "Should we boycott the convention?" rhetoric, in part because fan conventions in the U.S.—whether operated by fans themselves or a for-profit company like Creation Entertainment (or *SFX*, in the U.K.)—are becoming higher priced or, if the entry price is low, premium prices are additionally charged for items like better or reserved seating, autographs, or photo opportunities. Meet-and-greet events such as parties or brunches also are a popular way for a limited number of fans to pay a higher price in order to meet a celebrity. To many U.S. fans, the BBC was only following a common practice: it has a marketable product in its television series and the performers currently under contract, and it can charge what the market will bear to those willing to buy this product.

In the well-respected and moderated Gallifrey Base fan forum, the comments appearing in the thread about the Official Convention quickly changed in tone and content from a discussion of how to read the confusing ticket information (e.g., How many autographs were going to be permitted? Could one person attend both days, even if the Saturday program was repeated on Sunday?) to a discussion of pricing and concern (including some flippant remarks) over where the money was going. Within two days of the BBC's convention announcement, the forum's thread was heavily weighted against the convention, largely because of price. Even the marketing of the convention and timing of its announcement were perceived as designed to maximize profit and pit fans against each other in order to secure a seat at the convention. Some representative comments are these:

> Good old BBC — subtle as ever when it comes to profiteering [Mr. BHT of Rassilon].
>
> They're trying to get people to book early by 1. Announcing the event before tickets are on sale, thereby trying to generate a rush once the box office opens to maximise revenue early on. 2. Limiting autographs/photographs....They're also not allowing photographs etc. outside of the "official ones." (In a (later post, this fan further complained that "This is not a child-friendly event. Or, indeed, a fan-friendly event. IMO it's an exercise in making money, run on behalf of BBC Worldwide by an 'event company' who know bugger all about Doctor Who.") [The Coordinator of Rassilon].
>
> To put things into perspective It was pointed out on Twitter by Gary Gillat, that in the 1980's at the Longleat convention it was £4.50 (£16.60 after inflation) and you got 4 Doctor's autographs for free!!. Really shocked by the prices I have to say...Oh but wait! ... you get a souvenir ticket [Morethanatimelord of Rassilon].
>
> Very sad day this, our favourite show selling its soul for money. Thought they were better than this? [Danny].

Interestingly, the people whose posts identified them by location (at least in this galaxy) and who found fault with the BBC convention's pricing or policies were all from the U.K. and therefore the BBC's primary market for programming as well as merchandise. U.S. fans either did not plan to attend a one-day convention in Wales or kept their opinions to themselves.

Larger Issues Revealed by Fan Comments

Two other big concerns were raised in regard not to the BBC's handling of *Doctor Who* fandom but of its approach to the series and possible repercussions. One person noted that fan-friendly Moffat, who signed *Doctor Who*- or *Sherlock*-related merchandise at venues ranging from London's Waterstone bookstore to SF mecca Forbidden Planet in autumn 2011, might find BBC Worldwide's handling of the convention bothersome. Another fan alluded to rumors of in-house dissent between Moffat and the BBC's press department and described the current BBC as an uncontrollable hydra with its different divisions not knowing what each other was doing or why. The unflattering description led other fans to wonder if the BBC was running a test event in 2012 for a much larger (and potentially more profitable) anniversary event in Cardiff (The Coordinator of Rassilon) — the perfect time and place to unveil the new BBC Wales studios and Doctor Who Experience, in addition to celebrating the Doctor's 50th anniversary. More detrimental to the franchise was the concern that the BBC did not know how to work with fans and would alienate them — or worse yet, Moffat — and force the series into decline at a time when it should be peaking in popularity.

The wording of the FAQ list on the Doctor Who Official Convention site provided further material for analysis. For example, some of the first answers in the FAQ list spelled out limitations of fan-celebrity interaction. The first question addressed one of the main reasons why many fans would want to attend — to meet the actors and have a special moment talking with them. The response to the question about opportunities to meet the cast emphasized the difference between the Official Convention and other signing events or an actor's special appearances. The purpose of this convention is to give fans "the opportunity to immerse themselves in the making of *Doctor Who* with interactive demonstrations from the production and prosthetics crew" (Doctor Who Official Convention), although fans could participate in Q&A sessions. To many who read the responses to questions, the language seemed abrupt and designed to limit fans' interactions with what would be demonstrated or shown or with the actors themselves. Confusing language or lack of complete explanation also put off fans:

How many photo/autograph opportunities can I purchase?

Due to the popularity of photo and autograph opportunities with our special guests, only a limited number are available to purchase each day, with a maximum of one per guest (one photo or one autograph) [Doctor Who Official Convention].

Fans questioned whether the total per day was one autograph or photo opportunity, or one autograph or photo per guest. The definition of "limited" also worried readers looking forward to meet-the-actor events, even if they cost an additional fee.

Other topics, such as booking a nonrefundable ticket months in advance of the convention (even though the Official Convention's stated policies are similar to those followed at other conventions), were also perceived negatively because they forced potential ticket buyers to commit to the event in November or risk losing out. Later FAQ questions dealt with the problem of ticket buying:

Can I buy a ticket on the day?

All tickets are to be sold in advance and no tickets will be available on the day.

Will you refund tickets if I buy them in advance and find out I can't go?

No refunds will be offered under these circumstances.

If I find I cannot go, can I transfer my ticket to another name?

All tickets are non-transferrable [Official Convention].

A final FAQ item indicated that no further events were being planned for Cardiff, implying that those who wanted to attend an official *Doctor Who* event should buy tickets right away, because another opportunity to attend a similar event in Cardiff or elsewhere was unlikely. This answer went against much of the fan discussion that the BBC was trying out a large-scale event in Cardiff in order to better plan anniversary celebrations in 2013.

Unfortunately for the BBC, fan interpretations of the FAQ list's answers were simplified as No in subsequent forum posts. Anything that the fans wanted to do was not allowed; anything the BBC was willing to permit would result in a higher price. A Yes in fan-spoofed FAQ lists was given only with the stipulation that the attendee had to pay more money. In contrast to the official responses given in the FAQ list on the Doctor Who Official Convention site, one fan's "translation" of the FAQ list became popular. In a list labeled "highlights from the official FAQ, in a more to-the-point form" (MinkyKnights), fans' biggest complaints were indicated by the content of the answers and the abrupt, negative tone, which is mimicked in this fan's FAQ:

Do you offer a family ticket?
No. In fact, we recommend that you don't bring kids.
Is there an age limit on attendance?
No. But, again, we recommend that you don't bring kids.
Will I have opportunity to meet the cast throughout the day?
If you pay extra per guest, yes (note: tickets are limited). Otherwise, no.

Confusion about an accurate interpretation of the official FAQ responses regarding photo ops and autographs was translated in "fan speak" as the following:

How many photo/autograph opportunities can I purchase?
One, of some description. (Per type? Per guest? Per entry ticket? Who knows?)

Other questions receiving only No responses, with no elaboration, involved organized activities during the evening, after the convention ended; the availability of a tour of the BBC Wales studios; the availability of same-day tickets; and the possibility of getting a refund if fans were unable to attend. The final line, "etc., etc.," underscored the fan's frustration with the length of "rules" attached to the Official Convention (MinkyKnights). Whether the convention promoters' intention was brevity and clarity, the resulting official FAQ messages seemed abrupt and oppressive to fans who were questioning whether an official convention would be worth the price of admission, much less the additional travel costs or "incidentals" like souvenirs.

Once again, *Doctor Who* or one of its spinoffs created a fan controversy. No matter if the BBC in general or a high-level employee in particular discounts such fan comments as unworthy of consideration, the fans (internationally) who actively and vociferously debate everything from episode content to media coverage to BBC policies once again perceived there to be an "us" (fans, fan-friendly cast or crew) against "them" (the BBC). Although the BBC has the power to decide how or if beloved series will be funded, fans — while recognizing their lack of political decision-making power — still choose to make the world aware of their concerns in two potentially powerful ways: by Internet discussion or with consumer buying power.

Unfortunately for fandom, buying power may be minimal, given the costs of producing a television series versus the lack of revenue from a single event, such as a convention. If the "product" is perceived as being unmarketable, it may not be further produced; if *Doctor Who* or *Torchwood*, for example, fails to bring in viewers who watch Starz' commercials or subscribe to its channel, or if *Doctor Who* fails to sell merchandise bearing its logo, they may no longer be available.

The Internet, however, can cause a bigger problem for a network like the BBC. Even if individual fans are perceived or described in the media as being unrepresentative of the typical, larger fan base, media outlets tend to pick up on the discontent and make the world more aware of dissent among the fan ranks. Fandom, in this case, can become an "issue" to be dealt with.

As one person posting a message in the Gallifrey Base forum noted, Twitter became a fast way for fans to voice their opinion, and retweeted criticism again became the focus of later blogs, Facebook posts, and forum messages. As noted in an earlier chapter, Twitter in particular has become a fast, readily accessible, and far-reaching method for fans to vent their anger or publish their opinions spontaneously. A flurry of tweets, especially those written by upset fans, typically makes the news more often than longer posts or blogs made hours or days later; trending topics often make pop culture or entertainment news. A topic may seem more controversial than it really is, simply because of the number of tweets with the same hash tag. However, once a topic is perceived as controversial or at least worth publicizing because it creates a Twitter trend, the world — and perhaps even the BBC — notices fans' comments, whether or not they truly represent the range of fan opinions. Blogs or days of forum posts, which require more time to write or may invite entire conversations instead of sporadic tweets, may instead provide a better measure of long-lasting fan discontent.

In the case of the Official Convention's ticket sales, furor over price and the conditions of sale slowly died out. Although fans eager to participate in the first official convention in decades bought tickets right away, the event was not sold out within a few hours or even a few days. In the week leading up to the convention, some tickets remained for specific items (e.g., autographs or photo ops) as well as for certain types of tickets (by day and schedule of events). The convention eventually sold out, and media and individual fan reports indicated a high level of satisfaction with the actual event. A BBC-posted message on the official convention website after the event indicated that such a convention might take place in the future, and fans were encouraged to sign up for a newsletter that would announce upcoming events.

Not only does the controversy surrounding the BBC's convention policies illustrate a growing divide between its series' fans and the BBC, but it also indicates a difference between U.S. fans' assumption that *Doctor Who* is a product to be consumed and the U.K. fans' assumption that it is public entertainment paid for by licensing fees. American fans may expect the BBC to treat *Doctor Who* as a cash cow, but U.K. fans, or at least those posting in forums during November 2011, thought they had already bought the cow and should be getting at least a little free milk.

As some fans noted, however, the very fact that BBC Worldwide scheduled a convention for 2012 is a plus for *Doctor Who* and indicates that the BBC is firmly behind the series. However, the way the convention was presented to fans, and the amount and type of fan discussion surrounding the announcement, suggest that the BBC really does not know what to do with *Doctor Who* fans, who may think of themselves differently from fans of other SF television series. What would work for a *Star Wars* or *Star Trek* convention may not be as popular with *Doctor Who* fans.

Several *Doctor Who* fans also emphasized online the difference between their fandom and other SF fandoms. One wrote a letter on the Gallifrey Base forum: "Dear Mr. BBC, We are not *Star Trek* or *Star Wars* fans! Our fan base is much smaller ... and not as inclined to spend half as much money on merchandise.... Please stop trying to milk us for everything we got, yes we know you have never really had a franchise you could make money off before but please stop looking at other people's work and trying to force the template on a fan base that can't support it!" (Humphries).

In addition to the ongoing perception that the BBC is out to exploit fans is the comparison of *Doctor Who* fandom with other SF fandoms, including such blockbuster franchises as *Star Wars* or *Star Trek*. Both of these U.S.-based franchises have diligently developed merchandise on every available platform, but they operate from different marketing models. Although the *Star Wars* franchise includes animated spinoffs, as well as other types of texts (e.g., novels, videogames), it primarily is a movie franchise that emphasizes special effects and periodic pop culture events (i.e., the release of a new film). Although *Star Trek* originated as a television series only a few years after *Doctor Who* debuted, at one time it specialized in spinoff series (e.g., *Deep Space Nine, Star Trek: The Next Generation, Voyager*), some more successful than others, that encouraged niche fandoms within the larger "whole" of the *Star Trek* mythology. With the introduction of J. J. Abrams' *Star Trek* film in 2009, the franchise was rebooted and modernized as a *Star Wars*-style blockbuster event far more successful than the majority of the *Star Trek* films produced in earlier decades.

Doctor Who has remained a television staple, albeit with some lengthy hiatuses. Its primary "product" is far more accessible within a shorter time frame because it consists of television episodes and occasional specials, such as those at Christmas each year. The series does not have the production budget or marketing power of an international summer blockbuster movie. *Doctor Who* fans still largely operate as a cult television fandom devoted to a program financed by public broadcast entity BBC, not the fandom periodically invigorated with big movie events backed by a U.S. studio. Although "science fiction" might be the common genre, *Star Wars, Star Trek,* and *Doctor Who* have different mythologies and premises, different expectations set by their producers and audiences, and different fandoms.

Although it may have invited fan discussion and dissent, the Official Doctor Who Convention was successful. All tickets were eventually sold, and the fans who attended reported their satisfaction on a variety of forums and blogs. A convention report by fan "John Smith" described a special effects demonstration, followed by a Q&A "Meet the Stars" session with Matt Smith, Karen Gillan, Arthur Darvill, Steven Moffat, and new producer Caroline Skinner. After talks with directors and specialists who work with costumes and props, the fan concluded his day by watching a trailer for the upcoming season's episodes. Between sessions, "John Smith" ventured outside to the front of the Millennium Centre, "where the free cast signings were taking place.... Nick Briggs, voice of the Daleks, and Raquel Cassidy, Foreman Cleaves from this year's 'The Rebel Flesh,' ... were welcoming and allowed me to chat to them for a good five minutes each." Such encounters, as much as the Q&A sessions or behind-the-scenes revelations, make a *Doctor Who* convention worthwhile, no matter who hosts it.

Is Bigger Better?

The limited number of tickets (3000) and the limited interaction with cast and crew signal a shift from the way conventions have been run. Perhaps the big conventions, such as San Diego Comic-Con, have removed lots of potential attendees from the convention experience because it is difficult, if not impossible, for everyone to get in, much less see actors or get an autograph. Comic-Con's online and on-the-phone ticket sales have become so popular that fans crashed the system for the 2011 convention as soon as registration opened. No one wanted to be left out. Lines for advance ticket purchase for the next year's convention are so long that fans line up the night before the doors open, just to have a chance to wait in line for hours in hopes of getting a ticket.

San Diego Comic-Con has become such a popular venue for television series and films to introduce their products and schedule advance screenings that the event has become as famous for the number of hours required to queue as it has for the impressive line-up of famous attendees. Some fans attending Comic-Con do no more than stand in long lines for hours, only to be turned away when even the largest rooms fill to capacity before everyone who wants to see a panel can get in the door.

In 2011, as we stood in line for more than four hours for a *Doctor Who* panel starring Matt Smith and Karen Gillan, two fans standing in front of me confided that they had not seen anything during the convention, because they went from one long line to another without successfully getting into a panel session. I heard that story from many people at this convention, but my experience was better, perhaps because I often attended smaller sessions instead of main hall events. Although I stood in line for four hours and was admitted to the *Torchwood* panel, I later chose to talk with Anthony Head at the BBC America booth, where he represented *Merlin* (but he also had a role in the *Doctor Who* episode "School Reunion"). If I had decided against the BBC America line, I could have queued hours earlier for the *Doctor Who* panel and maybe gained a place inside the hall. I lost my opportunity to see Matt Smith from afar (that is, the back of a huge auditorium), but I enjoyed meeting Anthony Head. Doing everything one hopes to do during Comic-Con, or any large convention, becomes impossible. Being able to do a lot becomes a matter of difficult choices and luck, because long lines and overcrowding are very much part of the modern convention experience. Fan-run conventions are catching up to the problems of rapid ticket sales or hotel overload, as Gallifrey One's initial hotel-block sales indicate.

Smaller fan conventions may not be able to compete with larger conventions or professional event companies in attracting big-name guests, but they can offer a more interactive fan experience. In 2011, for example, Orlando-based Hurricane Who held a weekend convention starring *Doctor Who* companion Rory Williams (actor Arthur Darvill, making his North American convention debut) and *Torchwood*'s Toshiko Sato (actor Naoko Mori). Fans were able to buy, for an additional cost, autograph and photograph tickets, but the convention's lower cost for the three-day event (two days featuring the *Doctor Who*/*Torchwood* guests) and the Q&A sessions gave more fans the opportunity to see or hear the actors without having to spend additional money. The auditorium was large enough to provide a seat for a crowd of approximately 450, should the majority of people in the venue want to see the same presentation. Similarly, Chicago TARDIS and Gallifrey One, which bring more guests than Hurricane Who but also attract more fans to provide the revenue for them, has main events in an auditorium large enough for everyone to attend.

In 2011–12, the number of *Doctor Who* conventions and events featuring cast or crew from the *Doctor Who* franchise, held in the U.K. and U.S., was higher than ever and encompassed a greater variety of hosts: fan-run groups, professional event-management companies, and the BBC. Such events illustrate that, despite a recession in the 2010s, *Doctor Who* fandom is not only alive but healthy and willing to spend money on tickets. *Doctor Who* may, practically speaking, be the BBC's fattest cash cow for now. Whether the franchise is milked — or fans feel they are being bilked — by the BBC may ultimately turn fans of the television entertainment into foes of BBC Worldwide's marketing its international product.

Chapter 9

The Cosmos Is Their Oyster

The November 21, 1963, *Radio Times* described the premiere episode of *Doctor Who* as the story of "how the Doctor finds himself visiting the Britain of today: Susan ... has become a pupil at an ordinary British school, where her incredible breadth of knowledge has whetted the curiosity of two of her teachers ... [which] leads them to become inextricably involved in the Doctor's strange travels.... [They can travel] absolutely anywhere in time.... The cosmos in fact is their oyster" (7). William Hartnell was introduced as a well-known film actor making his first appearance on BBC television. The serialized format was mentioned, and Australian author Anthony Coburn was credited with the script.

This announcement does more than summarize the first episode's and series' premise; it emphasizes its Britishness. Although the Doctor is alien (which is implied but not mentioned in the description), he visits modern Britain where Susan (who, as it turns out, is the Doctor's granddaughter) attends "an ordinary British school." Making the ordinary extraordinary within the context of everyday British life set the tone for the series.

When *Doctor Who* episodes made their way to PBS around a decade later, the choice of PBS as venue clearly identified the series as Made in Britain. A staple of PBS, during that time and since, has been British imports, from the original *Upstairs, Downstairs* to Agatha Christie or Poirot mysteries to *Prime Suspect* to the recent *Downton Abbey* or *Sherlock*. Decades before BBC America, PBS provided the only way for most Americans to see British programming, whether it was current or several years old. Although *Doctor Who* never made it to primetime PBS but was available through individual local stations, who decided when and how it would broadcast episodes, the Doctor's continuing association with local PBS affiliates helped "cult"ivate an audience. Its limited availability in the U.S. also limited its fan base, but its sense of exclusivity as a British import — and thus perceived as being of higher, or at least different, cultural quality — made it more desirable. Once audiences sampled the SF import, they found other reasons to make *Doctor Who* appointment viewing.

Making *Doctor Who* in America seemed to make the series less desirable for some viewers, and the 1996 television movie Fox hoped to use to relaunch the series still generates controversy. Even during a Gallifrey One panel in 2012, Paul McGann questioned whether fans truly accept the Eighth Doctor and consider him part of the canon. Several U.S. fans attending the session quickly spoke up, reminding everyone that Russell T Davies' counting Christopher Eccleston as the Ninth Doctor clearly validated McGann's Eighth as a "real" Doctor, and Big Finish's series of audio adventures fleshes out what the television movie only broadly sketched. Nevertheless, criticism of the 1996 movie links Fox's film with the worst of American television, as scathingly described in a British Film Institute-published book about *Doctor Who*:

> With the production values of mid-range, shot-in–Canada, American television come dumb ideas that overwrite the basics in unhelpful ways. This Doctor had a human mother (like Mr. Spock!), these Time Lords have diplomatic relations with Skaro and the Dalek legal system (?!) to dispose of the Master, and the TARDIS is powered with the equivalent of a colossally unstable nuclear reactor that can destroy a solar system as a side-effect if a random Earthling puts his or her eyes into a beam of light [Newman 111].

The author concludes that "*Doctor Who* (1996) is stuck with half-formed notions of what might work in a transatlantic incarnation of the programme that never eventuated" (Newman 111), fortunately, it would seem, to this writer and many television critics at the time.

When Davies resuscitated the Doctor in 2005, the character's "alienness" remained, but he retained his affinity for British culture and, in episodes like "The Doctor Dances," spouts extremely patriotic dialogue praising British pluck. By the time the Ninth Doctor regenerated into the Tenth in 2006, Davies had a right to boast to the *Radio Times* that 2005 was a banner year for the Time Lord. He attributed the Doctor's increased popularity to the audience's welcoming response to "that rarest of things, a genuine TV hero. The Tardis *came home* (emphasis added). Christopher Eccleston and Billie Piper burnt their way across the screen, reinventing the concept of Doctor and companion.... With David Tennant now at the helm of the Tardis, bringing a wholly different dynamic to the show, we decided to make the story even more epic" (38–39). The idea that *Doctor Who* or a spinoff should be "epic" is a theme to which Davies returned when he described *Torchwood* as "bigger and better" during its transition into an international marketplace.

Tennant himself became something of a national television hero through his role as the Time Lord. The story lines became more "heroic" or "epic" (although, by 2010 the Tenth Doctor's story lines had grown very dark, and audiences questioned if the Time Lord could still be considered a hero). Throughout the 2000s, the Doctor is quintessentially British, comfortably adopting the U.K. as home. The Tenth Doctor's Britishness might seem less patriotic than the Ninth's, but bits of British culture slipped into episodes on a regular basis.

London reference librarian and long-time *Doctor Who* fan Gillian Hanhart notes that, during *The Christmas Invasion*, the Doctor only needs a cup of tea after a grueling regeneration — a very British cure-all. Brit Movie Tours *Doctor Who* guide Helen Thomas explains a few other "insider" jokes to American visitors, such as Lady Christina's mention of her Lobster card (*Planet of the Dead*). London travelers can use their Oyster card on public transportation, a fact that not all non–U.K. residents may know. As well, the Tenth Doctor refers to ASBOs, or Anti-Social Behavior Orders, when he describes his low expectations of some students at Deffry Vale school, where he is masquerading as a teacher ("School Reunion"). The Doctor's Britishness is inherent in the character, and nothing American television does to him — whether relegating him to late nights on local PBS channels or holding him hostage until U.S. fans contribute to public television, much less trying, as Fox did, to take over production — has been able to "Americanize" him.

Not all of the *Doctor Who* franchise has been able to retain its cultural identity so completely. Far more fans argue that *Torchwood* can easily become "globalized" (i.e., turned into an American hybrid). Perhaps what needs to be distinguished is a difference between "Americanizing" a television series, as described in previous chapters, and an American influence on an international television marketplace. Thus, a series like *Torchwood* may be more heavily influenced by Starz, which shared *Miracle Day* production with the BBC. Such arrangements are far more likely to become commonplace; PBS's Rebecca Eaton, who helms *Masterpiece Mystery!* and *Masterpiece Theatre* and is an executive producer on *Sherlock* and *Downton Abbey,* announced to *Sherlock* fans attending a special screening in May 2012 that PBS would be partnering Hartswood Films and the BBC to make the third season of episodes. Other BBC dramas filmed in 2011 and scheduled for international audiences' viewing in 2012 include *Parade's End,* which brought together British BBC, American HBO, and Flemish VRT to co-produce the television movie. *Doctor Who* comes from BBC Wales and, although location filming has taken place internationally, recent events (such as the 2011 announcement of a *Doctor Who* movie backed by BBC Worldwide in Los Angeles, which was later denied by the BBC and Steven Moffat) indicate that this series, perhaps more than other BBC dramas, is likely to be financed (for better or worse) at home. That's not to say that showrunners like Davies and Moffat are not well aware of an international audience clamoring for more *Doctor Who;* they can be aware of and market to an international audience without pandering to it.

Although Eaton was discussing *Sherlock* in particular, her comments about the popularity of British programming on PBS also has implications for *Doctor Who,* which is no longer a PBS station-by-station acquisition but a syndicated series broadcast by BBC America and promoted by BBC Worldwide. According to Eaton, British programming has "never been unpopular, but shows like *Sherlock* and *Downton Abbey* ... are proving to be American and international sensations, rather than the smaller cult followings our favorite BBC and other across-the-pond productions tended to build in the past." The comparison can be made that, decades ago, *Doctor Who* could be included in Eaton's description. Although British programming has always had a following in the U.S., there has "been a sea change and surge of interest that coincided with the rise of social media and online accessibility to shows streaming at all hours" (Hale-Stern).

To what extent television showrunners and producers are truly influenced by fans' comments or complaints likely depends on the individual. This social media "sea change," however, applies to *Doctor Who, Torchwood,* and *The Sarah Jane Adventures,* as well as to current PBS imports, and has made the voices of fans, through social media and websites, heard more loudly.

In the case of *Torchwood: Miracle Day,* fan tweets during episode broadcasts, forum and website comments and reviews after broadcasts, and fluctuations in ratings may have more influence on the future of this series than of *Doctor Who.* Because so many characters involved in *Miracle Day* are American — and not all were popular with fans or critics — and the majority of U.S. filming locations gave the series a distinctly American tone, the implications of an international, or even specifically American influence may have more weight in decisions about the series' future. In the past few years, when *Doctor Who* visited the U.S. to film episodes, audiences expected the Doctor to return to the U.K. after location filming wrapped. Production and plot details in *Miracle Day,* in contrast, indicate to fans and critics that *Torchwood* may prefer to retain its "international" designation rather than be exclusively associated with one country or culture.

A Franchise in Transition: Facing the Doctor's Future

Just as the Time Lord must deal with temporal and spatial changes, so too must *Doctor Who* confront the challenges of changing times and an international marketplace. At the Official Doctor Who Convention in March 2012, current showrunner Steven Moffat told fans that he doubts there will be another spinoff television series — at least in the foreseeable future. Claiming his busy schedule would not permit it, Moffat explained that he is "not against it. Spinoff shows happen because you think 'That is so good, you should spin it off'" (Knight). Whereas a few years ago a fan-favored character like Rory Williams might have earned himself a spinoff (Rory the Roman?), that possibility is far less likely today. Instead, Moffat's eye seemed firmly focused on the 2012–13 season. With eight episodes from the seventh season being shown during the anniversary year (and, Moffat suggested in early 2012, more than that being filmed and shown in 2013 [Jeffery, "Jenna-Louise Coleman"]), a new companion (Jenna-Louise Coleman) arriving in the 2012 Christmas episode, and possibly a new Doctor after the anniversary, the series seems once again poised for more changes.

Since the Doctor's return in 2005, *Doctor Who* has undergone several shifts owing to choices made by Russell T Davies and a new direction taken by Moffat. Davies not only re-invigorated the series but turned it into a modern television franchise. Although *Doctor Who* had attempted other spinoffs during the "classic" era (e.g., *K9 and Company* on television and a 1960s movie with Peter Cushing), only *Torchwood* and *The Sarah Jane Adventures* succeeded as continuing spinoff series. Each gained respectable ratings during multiple seasons and took the Doctor in directions not possible within his own series. Whereas *Torchwood*, during Davies' tenure, became more firmly attached to *Doctor Who* through the character of Captain Jack, when the Doctor was not around, *Torchwood* could involve over-the-top, alien-hunting stories or offer groundbreaking, GLAAD-approved story lines. It was designed to attract an adult audience. At the other end of the audience spectrum, *The Sarah Jane Adventures* attracted a much younger audience appropriate for CBBC. Creating successful spinoffs that, among them, provided a wide audience base in the U.K. is one of the major shifts initiated by Davies in the early 2000s, although even he reportedly thought that spinning off one more series (featuring Rose Tyler as defender of the Earth) would be taking the concept a bit too far (Knight).

When Davies spread his wings to fly to the U.S., buoyed by the success of *Torchwood: Children of Earth*, he left the Doctor behind and, unfortunately, much of the momentum and success generated by his career in the U.K. Although Davies was a veteran of U.K.–U.S. television through, for example, *Queer as Folk*, *Torchwood*'s transatlantic flight was far bumpier. To make *Miracle Day* something different for an international audience perhaps not familiar with the Doctor, *Torchwood* took on a new identity — one that, in some episodes, vainly tried to please everyone with obscure references to previous *Torchwood* characters and the Doctor that were inconsequential to the plot; it also expanded the plot to make it international in scope and as much science as SF. Not everyone liked the combination, and the series has languished post–*Miracle Day*, its actors moving on to other television series and projects. Although Davies had previously announced his next series would be *Cucumber* on Showtime, he instead developed *Wizards vs. Aliens*. In 2012, the great American experiment with *Torchwood*—and with Davies' based in LA—seemed to be over. The presumed next phase in the *Doctor Who* franchise, one significantly emphasizing U.S. television production, was far less successful than Davies' reboot of *Doctor Who* and development of a franchise through three series aimed at different audiences.

Another shift in the franchise can be attributed to Moffat, whose young, often-erratic Doctor sees the universe through incredibly old eyes. Moffat combines his vision for a 21st century television series with elements of "classic" Doctors. Creating multiple-episode story arcs, interspersed with standalone episodes, recalls the famed multi-part serials of *Doctor Who*'s past; fragments of early Doctors (e.g., Patrick Troughton's performance) find their way into Matt Smith's interpretation of the role; and scary monsters instead of emotion-laden subplots that leave the Doctor brooding and reflective (as in the Tennant years) indeed seem to be foundations of Moffat's *Doctor Who*. The showrunner's plans through the anniversary year seem to include more of the same — story arcs combined with standalone episodes and no development of spinoffs. *Doctor Who* once again is a single "product" presented through a variety of media platforms marketed to the "family" audience of children and adults.

Although *Doctor Who*, unlike spinoff *Torchwood*, has retained its Britishness, it nonetheless operates in the world of BBC Worldwide, which increasingly strives to attain a larger share of the American audience. The "American influence" may be interpreted in subtle ways — a Western motif in first episodes of the seventh season, with a teaser trailer unveiled during the Official Doctor Who Convention and then placed on the web. That trailer, because it was made available months before the new season's episodes — when fans are eagerly awaiting news and spoilers, receives far more attention than trailers and previews played once the episodes are shown. Just as "The Impossible Astronaut," actually filmed in the American West, received a great deal of publicity and started the sixth season's episodes off with a specific international flair, so too does the 2012 trailer continue that Western (or "American") theme (even if location filming took place in Spain). Additionally, Amy Pond's and Rory Williams' final episode was filmed in New York, closing their story not only with a U.S. location but returning filming to North America once again, part of a trend toward international filming locations.

Shortly before Steven Moffat began filming the New York City episode, he emphasized that *Doctor Who* is not being Americanized and, furthermore, that U.S. fans do not want to see that happen. (Especially since 2010, when rumors of an American series circulated, as well as in late 2011, when a U.S.-filmed movie was announced [then later declaimed], even U.S. fans express dismay online about an Americanized *Who*, although my brief surveys indicated that in mid-2011 the fans who responded to my questions did not think that was happening.) BBC America reiterated the fact that *Doctor Who* was the series most often downloaded in America on iTunes, indicating the show's continuing popularity in the States. Using iconic New York City landmarks (e.g., the city skyline, Central Park) may seem to be one response to the show's increasing popularity and to be catering to the American audience.

Moffat replied that the location filming was not, as the reporter suggested, to give U.S. viewers a greater sense of familiarity with the setting, because he does not think "the American fans care whether we set shows in America. It's not like they're starved for shows set in America.... It's just that it's a different backdrop for the story.... It's not to appeal to the American audience particularly. I don't think they come to *Doctor Who* to see themselves. They come to *Doctor Who* to see others" (Byrne-Cristiano, "It's Up to Fans").

Certainly, many U.S. fans, like those anywhere, identify with characters because of a universal experience, such as Rose falling in love with the Doctor and doing everything in her power to be reunited with him. Even if fans cannot literally share that experience, they empathize with Rose because they understand the power of love and may have similarly felt such love for a romantic partner. They may project themselves into the story and live vicariously as Rose. They may cosplay as Rose to act out her relationship with the Doctor. Beyond that universal experience of love, however, some American audiences or critics may relate more specifically to *Doctor Who* by putting it into an American cultural frame of reference — just as British fans automatically do. Americans may not watch *Doctor Who* to see themselves, but they may interpret the Doctor's actions or themes within the series differently in order to integrate the Doctor's world into their everyday world.

Even when Moffat made the offhand comment that he thought the Weeping Angels (within the New York City-set story) would be appropriate in NYC, Americans most likely will automatically infer a reference to 9/11, especially because the *Doctor Who* filming coincided with real-world news reports about the new tower rising from Ground Zero surpassing the World Trade Center towers' height. Although the implication is that Moffat meant for the reference to indicate 9/11, he could have had a completely different meaning, but Americans in particular are likely to interpret the statement to fit within their cultural frame of reference. Similarly, seeing the Doctor in a fez may be intriguing because it is different, but seeing him in a Stetson, lounging against a convertible in the American West, is going to have a greater cultural meaning to Americans than to others. Cultural interpretations of iconic images are likely to differ, but the reasons behind selecting cultural images is the real determiner if *Doctor Who* is being Americanized. An increasing American influence on the show, however, can be interpreted by fans in many, many ways.

Moffat — or perhaps more accurately, BBC Worldwide — continues to increase the series' international appeal and strives to make the Doctor more marketable to a wider audience. Although the Doctor likely will never become mainstream in the U.S., the number of American viewers is increasing, thanks to BBC America's publicity and BBC Worldwide's marketing strategies. Through all these ways, the Moffat era might be described as retaining the best elements of "classic" *Doctor Who* while addressing modern marketing realities.

A New Companion in 2012

Although Amy Pond often was a controversial companion who stirred up some British viewers' concerns about appropriate "watershed" family content, she also attracted a great deal of attention. Near the end of her time on the TARDIS, Amy was described by one critic as an "entitled space hipster" who, despite the character's evolution, is still often thought of as spoiled or ungrateful, a woman who "decided to flounce around, complaining incessantly, or belittling the unbelievably old, wise and wonderful man who was generous enough to drag her American Apparel clad and admittedly fine arse from adventure to adventure" (Verhoeven). By the time her travels with the Doctor ended, she nevertheless had become a significant character in the show's mythology, not only as a companion but as the mother of River Song, who develops a most meaningful relationship with the Doctor and leads Amy to decry at least once that she is the Doctor's "mother-in-law." At the time of her casting, Karen Gillan was relatively unknown to British television audiences, but Americans were even less familiar with her. However, for many new viewers who began watching the series on BBC America, Amy was their first companion, the one who explained the Doctor to them and who became their entry point into the series. Seeing her leave and a new companion arrive is a first for these newbies, although long-time fans expect companions to come and go.

The new girl on the block, or in the TARDIS, is Jenna-Louise Coleman. The announcement of a new *Doctor Who* companion brought out the press in London and generated a lot of excitement. Although the event, as should be expected, received a great deal of coverage in the U.K. press, it received little to no attention in the U.S., outside of *Doctor Who* fandom. Coleman is likely to be recognized by British audiences from her work on the television series *Emmerdale*, which has not been imported to the U.S., although Americans may have heard of it. Similarly, her role in ITV's drama *Titanic* gained her much more attention in the U.K. than abroad. If not a household name in the U.K. yet, Coleman certainly will be by Christmas, when her character will be revealed in the popular Christmas episode. Again, the impact of her selection and her popularity outside of the U.K. is limited and is a good indicator of the Doctor's lack of mainstream pop culture acceptance in the U.S. When former Time Lord Tennant was asked if he had advice for Coleman, he commented that she will face an incredible amount of publicity with this role and she might want to "watch her back" (Digital Spy). Although among *Doctor Who* fans and, as the series is promoted in the U.S. in 2012 by BBC Worldwide and, specifically, BBC America, Coleman will receive greater recognition than she has so far gained with her acting career, her level of popularity likely will still be far less in North America than in Britain, where she should become a household name because of her role on the series.

Can a British Series Really Be "Americanized"?

British television series undoubtedly have been influenced by U.S. television imports, their structure and pace, and the expectations global audiences now have for a "successful" television series. As discussed in previous chapters, as well as in previous sections in this chapter, the differences between U.S. and U.K. television series may be most strongly seen in the development of *Torchwood: Miracle Day*, but they also have had an impact on the evolution of *Doctor Who*, as well as the lack of success of *The Sarah Jane Adventures* as a U.S. import. An academic paper about the influence of U.S. television series on the development of British television summarizes the impact of American imports: "The narrative in the new series [of *Doctor Who*] also demonstrates the influence of the U.S. drama series.... The narrative in the new series was consciously developed to follow the U.S. scheduling model" with the inclusion of special event or multi-part stories during ratings sweeps periods and a blockbuster season finale. The writers "are very deliberate in the 'importing' of U.S. techniques. The show has a long history on British television yet the writers are firmly engaged with the generic conventions and methods developed by the U.S. models. By doing so the show has become highly successful, finding new audiences as well as retaining old ones" (Dobson).

Less successfully, perhaps, with *Miracle Day*, the use of "American" television techniques has become a part of *Doctor Who*'s production, although the series is even more heavily influenced by British (specifically the BBC's) way of doing things, as evidenced in the writers' room "culture shock" when Davies encountered U.S.-based writers (e.g., Jane Espenson, Doris Egan) who were familiar with a very different way of planning and writing a series of episodes (Torchwood). The most popular U.S. television series are imported by the U.K., and audiences begin to alter their expectations for dramatic television series based on what they see arriving from the U.S. The style of U.S. TV shows has had some influence on *Doctor Who*, which is glossier and faster paced in recent years. The more potent influence, however, seems to be less about production and more about marketing the completed product.

From a marketing perspective, ultimately, the answer to the "Americanization" question is no, even if the U.S. audience is a huge market the BBC wants to continue to tap and one that will continue to influence the amount and type of programs made in Britain and exported internationally. The fact is that, despite its America-friendly marketing and recent filming locations, *Doctor Who* cannot be Americanized. Its cultural roots are not even in Gallifrey, but in Britain. Since 2005, *Doctor Who* has become specifically identified (especially by cinematic tourists) with Cardiff and Wales as much as London and England. However, the American influence is being increasingly felt as BBC Worldwide expands network product lines and emphasizes exports to English-speaking countries, including but not limited to the U.S. The coveted cult status of *Doctor Who* is still operative in the U.S., but not in the U.K. (although someday it might return to cult-only status). Perhaps the best way to illustrate marketing changes is not to say that British series are being Americanized per se, but that they are being globalized for wider sale. They may be British exports, but they are created with an eye toward ever wider markets. However, iconic British characters, like the Doctor, will always remain clearly identified with their country of origin.

American fandom may still be playing catch up — the fans who came on board during the PBS years and had to search diligently in order to find episodes in order to learn more about the Doctor had a more vibrant underground forged from a mutual lack of *Who* and sense of accomplishment at sharing gems with other fans. Although British fans of the classic series often had to fight the "uncool" stigma of being *Doctor Who* fans before the series gained mainstream popularity, they at least had a bit more access to the complete series of episodes or more merchandise. They could see episodes sometimes years before their overseas counterparts. Today, the new (or new *Who*) fans have almost the same access to episodes (legally or not) as British fans, although merchandise may be more difficult to come by in the U.S.

Whereas the U.K. television market still may have that gloss of "prestige" that U.S. cable emulates more often than U.S. network offerings do, the whole of British television is not the consistent quality that American viewers might anticipate. British fans visiting Gallifrey One, for example, reminded their American friends that the majority of British television programming these days consists of reality shows that are not always great. Americans see the "good stuff"— the high-quality dramas, period miniseries, and iconic characters like the Doctor and Sherlock Holmes.

Of course, because it is, by definition, "foreign," many Anglophiles will love *Doctor Who* even more than other SF offerings because of its long association with British television and the series' cultural entrenchment. Nevertheless, the Doctor more likely fits with "American sensibilities" and preference for dramatic content, as a *Salon* writer hypothesized after the announcement that U.S. network NBC would be re-making British series *Prime Suspect* (and similar arguments were offered on other media outlets a few weeks later at the announcement that CBS would re-make Sherlock Holmes as an American-set series, *Elementary*). The article postulated an important difference between the content of much British and U.S. television drama: "American TV is averse to letting race, class, politics and other touchy elements drive stories because it might make viewers and sponsors skittish. That's why the American crime show's favorite bad guy is the serial killer, a mythologically exaggerated monster whose existence lets filmmakers titillate and terrify while declining to engage with society at large" (Seitz).

Doctor Who fits into the comfortable dramatic model Seitz suggests, not because it is afraid to tackle modern problems, but because it can do so more acceptably within the realm of SF. Science fiction provides a safe space for controversial ideas, because when the Doctor or another alien suggests a controversial idea or points out a human flaw, it is done from an outsider's (otherworldly) perspective. Controversial issues involving genocide, racism, religion, or any hot topic seem less controversial and more philosophical when broached through SF rather than modern day drama. If Amy Pond sees the destruction of a space whale, the last of its kind, she may learn important lessons about the sovereignty of species and the fragile interrelationship between humans and their environment, but the "lesson" is taught via aliens in a galaxy far, far away. When the Doctor and Amy visit Vincent Van Gogh, the "lesson" may involve insights into depression and the tragedy of suicide, but it is presented as history, although correlations to modern problems with treating depression can certainly be made. *Doctor Who* can safely deal with "otherness" and current issues because of its narrative distance from "reality"— it is SF, not fact-based modern drama. As such, it can benefit by being "just a sci-fi" show instead of being perceived as hardcore drama.

In contrast, *Torchwood: Miracle Day* introduced social, medical, and political horrors into a modern day "real" setting and far more graphically illustrated death camps, for example. Although it too is SF, *Children of Earth* and *Miracle Day* removed the series from its original "alien-fighting" premise to deal with thinly disguised human problems dealing with government cover-ups, political machinations behind mass killings, and potential real-world problems of overpopulation and lack of resources to deal with a burgeoning population. *Torchwood* seemed more likely to "get away" with being an atypical U.S. drama not only because it was marketed in 2011 as an edgier series but because it became associated with Starz, noted for its adult content. *Torchwood: Miracle Day*, based on the framework Seitz suggests, may have made viewers too uncomfortable; elements of the plot (e.g., a global medical disaster, government agencies becoming dictatorial in a crisis) may have seemed too plausible when set on Earth in the present time. The combination of plot and setting often did not seem to be SF, especially in early episodes of the miniseries. American viewers, even those familiar with Starz' often explicit programs, might have been surprised and uncomfortable with the subject matter of *Miracle Day* because it included too many "touchy elements."

Despite cultural differences and expectations for programming, as well as the logistics of selling British television series or finding partners to help produce them, the U.S. market is enticing, and BBC Worldwide's greater presence in the U.S. undoubtedly will have an effect on *Who*'s marketing strategy and possible filming locations.

But Will There Be Another Movie?

On the day tickets went on sale for the Official Doctor Who Convention, fans received another surprise. *Variety* broke the story that David Yates, best known for directing four films in the *Harry Potter* franchise, was working with the BBC on what they hoped would become a *Doctor Who* film franchise. Although the proposed film was described as being at least three years away, and as far from casting as possible at that stage, speculation — including enthusiasm as well as concerns — began to be voiced online immediately. Yates fueled controversy right away by stating the films would be completely different from the television series: "Russell T. Davies and then Steven Moffat have done their own transformations, which were fantastic, but we have to put that aside and start from scratch" (Dawtry). Predictably, fans complained about the loss of canon, the series' strong points that would be lost with a cinematic do-over, and comparisons with the Peter Cushing vs. Daleks film from the 1960s.

Another complaint was the connection between Yates and based-in–LA Jane Tranter of BBC Worldwide. One British fan tweeted "Not made by

Americans!" after *Variety*'s story went online. Other unfavorable comments included comparisons between an American-made feature and the one-shot 1996 Fox telemovie/pilot that failed to relaunch the Doctor on television (or to successfully introduce him to primetime American audiences). Twitter comments like these made #DavidYates trend on Twitter on November 14, and tweets directed at Jane Tranter, David Yates, the BBC and BBC Worldwide, as well as anything tagged Doctor Who encompassed every emotion from joy to rage, disbelief to anticipation.

Yates yet again did not help his cause with Whovians when he suggested, "We want a British sensibility, but having said that, Steve Kloves wrote the Potter films and captured that British sensibility perfectly, so we are looking at American writers too" (Dawtry). The same was said of *Torchwood: Miracle Day*'s writers' room, which included American and British scriptwriters but which ended up producing an often confounding mixture of plot and character development within scripts for the ten-episode story arc. Online consensus was that, presumably, a *Doctor Who* movie would not be written by committee, and either a British or an American writer would be in charge of the shooting script.

The Telegraph identified the film version of *Doctor Who* as part of a trend of turning television series into movies and compared it with recent film versions of purely American series like *Bewitched, Sex and the City,* and *The A-Team* ("Doctor Who Joins Top Hollywood Spinoffs"). However, the other television shows in this comparison are no longer being made and have not been around for many years. It seemed that Yates' perception of the American audience was that they may remember PBS broadcasts of the Tom Baker years, but he was ignoring the current fan base additionally generated by the post–2005 series. While referencing Davies and Moffat in his interview, Yates nonetheless explained that his version would be very different. He emphasized that the series' concept is excellent, but he seemed to want to introduce the Doctor to an international audience as an American-made blockbuster.

As noted in several articles and blogs in response to the *Variety* announcement, television series remade into films have a patchy success record, whether they are made in America or Britain. With the lackluster result of the Starz-BBC partnership in *Miracle Day*, fans might understandably be worried about a future *Doctor Who* film franchise, even one helmed by veterans of *Doctor Who* television (BBC Worldwide's Tranter) and *Harry Potter* films (director Yates), no matter who ultimately would write a script. As *Wales Online* thoughtfully summarized, the question on the minds of proponents or opponents was this: "The Doctor might well be able to travel through time, but will be able to travel across the Atlantic?" Yet, even as fans warmed up their arguments for or against a future film, the BBC itself backed off the "done deal" tone of the *Variety* announcement. As *Wales Online* updated the report a few days later, the BBC "has made it clear that the film idea is only 'in development' and not yet confirmed as a definite release" (Pascoe).

By April Fool's Day 2012, the Yates announcement had become nothing more than a joke, with Sciencefiction.com running the headline "David Yates 'Doctor Who' Reboot Movie Coming to the Big Screen December 2013." The proposed new Doctor would be a woman, and Eva Longoria, Pamela Anderson, Lindsey Lohan, and Kate Upton were suggested for the role. The reporter commented that "although I like the idea of a female Time Lord, I can't help but notice that all the actresses mentioned are all American ... leading me to believe [Yates'] version of the Doctor will not only be female but also non–British" (Kay). Knowing that this type of article would push fans' buttons just as surely as the original film announcement had, the writer reminded "those who may be upset about the news" that "you can't always believe what you read!"

The Doctor in Another Fifty Years

Doctor Who—the television series—is influenced by the U.S. market more than American fandom. In the U.S., the Doctor has a powerful niche market, and anniversary-year celebrations are something that Americans can do very well—not because they necessarily recognize fifty years of British television but because they know how to plan big events and to celebrate. They may not be as invested as British fans in the early days or classic series, but they can appreciate the show's current pop culture impact and its newer "cool" factor. The Eleventh Doctor may tease what is cool, but he has redefined cool SF for U.K. and U.S. audiences. If he became mainstream in the U.S., he likely would not be so cool.

During the Official Doctor Who Convention in 2012, showrunner Steven Moffat was asked where he thinks *Doctor Who* will be fifty years from now, on the series' 100th anniversary (S. Brown). His reply was simple: "On television." And fans everywhere will be watching.

Bibliography

Abadzis, Nick. "Broken." Part 1. *Torchwood Comic #1*. Artist Paul Grist. Aug. 2010. Print.
_____. "Broken." Part 2. *Torchwood Comic #2*. Artist Paul Grist. Sept. 2010. Print.
Adams, Guy. *Torchwood: The House That Jack Built*. London: Random House UK, 2009. Print.
Ainsworth, John. "Welcome." *Doctor Who Insider*, 1 (May 2011), 3. Print.
Andreeva, Nellie. "Starz Signs Multi-year Production Deal with BBC Worldwide Prods." *Deadline Hollywood*. 8 Aug. 2011. Web. 10 Mar. 2012. <http://www.deadline.com/2011/08/starz-signs-multi-year-production-deal-with-bbc-worldwide-prods/>
Ariens, Chris. "Morning Show Ratings: Week of May 9." *TVNewser*. 20 May 2011. Web. 21 May 2011. <http://www.mediabistro.com/tvnewser/morning-show-ratings-week-of-may-9_b67322>
"Audio Review: Torchwood — Red Skies." Cambridge First. 3 May 2012. Web. <http://www.cambridgefirst.co.uk/what-s-on/audio_review_torchwood_red_skies_1_1367600>
"AudioGo Announces New Doctor Who and Torchwood Adventures." 12 Apr. 2012. Web. 12 Apr. 2012. <http://www.seenit.co.uk/audiogo-announces-new-doctor-who-and-torchwood-adventures/0418799/>
Ausiello, Michael. "Ratings: Was *Torchwood*'s Return Miraculous?" TVLine. 11 July 2011. Web. 11 July 2011.<http://www.tvline.com/2011/07/ratings-torchwood-miracle/>
_____. "'Torchwood' Boss to Angry Fans: Go Watch 'Supernatural.'" *Entertainment Weekly*. 24 July 2009. Web. 24 July 2009. <http://insidetv.ew.com/2009/07/24/backlash-shmacklash-thats-torchwood-creator-russell-t-davies-reaction-to-the-outcry-over-the-death-of-gareth-david-lloyds/>
BBC. "*My Sarah Jane: A Tribute to Elisabeth Sladen.*" 20 Apr. 2011. Web. 20 Apr. 2011. <http://www.bbc.co.uk/doctorwho/dw/news/bulletin_110420_02/My_Sarah_Jane_A_Tribute_to_Elisabeth_Sladen>
_____. Promotional clip. "Rendition." June 2011. Television.
BBC America. "About the Show." *Doctor Who*. Web. <http://www.bbcamerica.com/doctor-who/about-the-show/>
_____. "Characters: The Doctor." *Doctor Who*. Web. <http://www.bbcamerica.com/doctor-who/characters/the-doctor/>
BBC America Shop. "Doctor Who Insider Magazine." Web. <http://www.bbcamericashop.com/magazines/doctor-who-insider-magazine-16311.html>
BBC Press Office. "Elisabeth Sladen." 19 Apr. 2011. Web. 19 Apr. 2011. <http://www.bbc.co.uk/doctorwho/dw/news/bulletin_110419_01/Elisabeth_Sladen>
BBC Worldwide Press Office. "BBC Worldwide to Stage First Official Doctor Who Convention." 11 Nov. 2011. Web. 11 Nov. 2011. <http://dwconvention.com/news>
BBC Worldwide Press Release. "Annual Review 2010/11." 12 July 2011. Web. 11 Mar. 2012.

<http://www.bbc.co.uk/pressoffice/bbcworldwide/worldwidestories/pressreleases/2011/07_july/annual_review.shtml>

Bendoris, Matt. "Matt Meets ... John Barrowman." *The Scottish Sun.* 21 Dec. 2010. Web. 21 Dec. 2012. <http://www.thescottishsun.co.uk/scotsol/homepage/news/mattmeets/3312024/Matt-Meets-John-Barrowman.html>

Berriman, Ian. "Torchwood: Miracle Day — Russell T Davies Interview." *SFX.* 1 June 2011. Web. 1 June 2011. <http://www.sfx.co.uk/2011/06/01/torchwood-miracle-day-%E2%80%93-russell-t-davies-interview/>

Bettridge, Daniel. "Terra Nova and the Most Expensive TV Ever Made." *Radio Times.* 3 Oct. 2011. Web. 10 Mar. 2012. <http://www.radiotimes.com/news/2011-10-03/terra-nova-and-the-most-expensive-tv-ever-made>

Big Finish. Sarah Jane Smith page. 8 Apr. 2012. Web. <http://www.bigfinish.com/Sarah-Jane-Smith>

Blair, Andrew. "What Fandom Did for Doctor Who." Den of Geek. 26 Apr. 2012. Web. 27 Apr. 2012. <http://www.denofgeek.com/television/1339028/what_fandom_did_for_doctor_who.html>

Block, Alex Ben. "California Film Commission Reveals 2011 Tax Subsidy Recipients." *Hollywood Reporter.* 6 June 2011. Web. 6 June 2011. <http://www.hollywoodreporter.com/news/california-film-commission-reveals-2011-194800>

Brew, Simon. "Russell T. Davies on Torchwood: Miracle Day." Den of Geek. 4 Feb., 2011. <http://www.denofgeek.com/television/756096/russell_t_davies_on_torchwood_miracle_day.html>

Brown, Maggie. "The BBC is Producing Great Drama — But Not Enough of It." *The Guardian.* 14 Feb. 2011. Web. 15 Feb. 2011.<http://www.guardian.co.uk/media/2011/feb/14/bbc-great-drama-quantity>

Brown, Pam. "Captain Jack is Back." *The West Australian.* 4 July 2011. Web. 4 July 2011. <http://au.news.yahoo.com/thewest/entertainment/a/-/entertainment/9778988/captain-jack-is-back/>

Brown, Sophie. "The Official Doctor Who Convention — Part One." GeekMom. *Wired.* 31 Mar. 2012. Web. 10 May 2012. <http://www.wired.com/geekmom/2012/03/the-official-doctor-who-convention-part-one/>

Bulkley, Kate. "The U.S. 'Torchwood' Series: Bigger Budget, Bigger Stunts, More Sex." Deadline. 4 Apr. 2011. Web. 4 Apr. 2011. <http://www.deadline.com/2011/04/the-u-s-torchwood-series-bigger-budget-bigger-stunts-more-sex/>

Byrne-Cristiano, Laura. "It's Up to Fans to Get Captain Jack Back on 'Doctor Who.'" 9 Sept. 2011. Web. 15 Apr. 2012. <http://www.hypable.com/2011/09/09/its-up-to-fans-to-get-captain-jack-back-on-doctor-who/>

_____. "Video: Steven Moffat Says 'The Doctor Traveling on His Own Faintly Depresses Me.'" Hypable.com. 7 Apr. 2012. Web. 5 May 2012. <http://www.hypable.com/2012/04/07/video-steven-moffat-says-the-doctor-travelling-on-his-own-faintly-depresses-me/>

Cable, Simon. "New Doctor Who Episode Billed as Scariest Yet Sees Ratings FALL by 1.5m (And Britain's Got Talent is Also on the Slide." *The Mail Online.* 25 Apr. 2011. Web. 27 Apr. 2011. <http://www.dailymail.co.uk/tvshowbiz/article-1380150/Doctor-Who-sees-ratings-FALL-1-5m-Britains-Got-Talent-slide.html>

Campbell, Mark. *Doctor Who: The Episode Guide.* Harpenden, Herts, UK: Pocket Essentials, 2007. Print.

"Captain Jack Harkness — Leading His Torchwood Team into the Unknown." Squidoo. Web. <http://www.squidoo.com/captain-jack-harkness-torchwood>

"Cardiff to Host 'Ultimate Doctor Who Fan Event.'" *Wales Online.* 11 Nov. 2011. Web. 11 Nov. 2011. <http://www.walesonline.co.uk/showbiz-and-lifestyle/showbiz/2011/11/11/cardiff-to-host-ultimate-doctor-who-fan-event-91466-29760218/>

Chicago TARDIS 2011. Memberships. Web. <http://www.chicagotardis.com/memberships. php>

"The Co-Ordinator of Rassilon. Gallifrey Base forum. Official BBC Doctor Who Convention 24th-25th March 2012. 11 Nov. 2011. Web. 11 Nov. 2011. <http://gallifreybase. com/forum/showthread.php?t=127912>

Collett-White, Mike. "David Tennant's Dr. Who Out to Conquer America." Reuters. 23 July 2009. Web. 5 May 2012. <http://www.reuters.com/article/2009/07/23/us-ten nant-drwho-idUSTRE56M41E20090723>

Collis, Clark. "'Doctor Who' Actress Elisabeth Sladen Dies at 63." *Entertainment Weekly.* 19 Apr. 2011. Web. 21 Apr. 2011. < http://news-briefs.ew.com/2011/04/19/doctor-who-elisabeth-sladen-dies/>

_____. "'Doctor Who' Cast Members Karen Gillan and Arthur Darvill Preview the New Season." *Entertainment Weekly.* EW.com. 22 Apr. 2011. Web. 10 Aug. 2012. <http:// insidetv.ew.com/2011/04/22/doctor-who-karen-gillan-arthur-darvill/>

Conor. "Doctor Who Films in Spain, New Monster on Set." Photos courtesy of Spoiler.TV. Tardis Base. 8 Mar. 2012. Web. 10 Mar. 2012. <http://tardis-base.blogspot.com/>

Cook, Benjamin. "Holding Back the Years." *Doctor Who Magazine.* 24 May 2006 (369): 12–18. Print.

Cooper, Christopher. "Somebody Else's Problem." *Torchwood Comic #5.* Artist Stephen Downey. Dec. 2010. Print.

Cooper, Jarrod. 1 May 2012. Email.

Coupe, Mark. "Torchwood: The Lost Files." Den of Geek. 9 Aug. 2011. Web. 10 Mar. 2012. <http://www.denofgeek.com/television/1009571/torchwood_the_lost_files. html>

"Craig Ferguson Late Late Show with Matt Smith." TARDIS Newsroom. 30 July 2011. Web. 5 May 2012. <http://tardisnewsroom.blogspot.com/2011/07/craig-ferguson-late-late-show-with-matt.html>

"Craig Ferguson — The Lost 'Dr. Who' Cold Open." YouTube. 1 Dec. 2010. Web. 8 May 2012. <http://www.youtube.com/watch?v=M9P4SxtphJ4>

Curtis, Richard. "Vincent and the Doctor." *Doctor Who.* BBC. Dir. Jonny Campbell. 5 June 2012. Television.

Danny. Gallifrey Base forum. Official BBC Doctor Who Convention 24th-25th March 2012. 11 Nov. 2011. Web. 11 Nov. 2011. <http://gallifreybase.com/forum/ showthread. php?t=127912>

Davies, Russell T. *The Christmas Invasion. Doctor Who.* BBC. Dir. James Hawes. 25 Dec. 2005. Television.

_____. "Day Five." *Torchwood: Children of Earth.* BBC. Dir. Euros Lyn. 10 July 2009. Television.

_____. "Day One." *Torchwood: Children of Earth.* BBC. Dir. Euros Lyn. 6 July 2011. Television.

_____. "The End of Time, Part 1." *Doctor Who.* BBC. Dir. Euros Lyn. 1 Jan. 2010. Television.

_____. "The End of Time, Part 2." *Doctor Who.* BBC. Dir. Euros Lyn. 2 Jan. 2010. Television.

_____. "Everything Changes." *Torchwood.* BBC. Dir. Brian Kelly. 22 Oct. 2006. Television.

_____. "I'm Dreaming of a Fright Christmas." *Radio Times.* 17–30 Dec. 2005. 38–39. Print.

_____. "Kiss Kiss, Bang Bang." *Torchwood.* BBC. Dir. Ashley Way. 26 Jan. 2008. Television.

_____. "The New World." *Torchwood: Miracle Day.* BBC/Starz. Dir. Bharat Nalluri. 8 July 2011. Television.

_____. "The Stolen Earth." *Doctor Who*. BBC. Dir. Graeme Harper. 28 June 2008. Television.
_____. "Utopia." *Doctor Who*. BBC. 16 Dir. Graeme Harper. June 2007. Television.
Davies, Russell T, and Chris Chibnall. "Adrift." *Torchwood*. BBC. Dir. Mark Everest. 19 Mar. 2008. Television.
_____. "End of Days." *Torchwood*. BBC. Dir. Ashley Way. 1 Jan. 2007. Television.
Davies, Russell T, and Peter Hammond. "Small Worlds." *Torchwood*. BBC. Dir. Alice Troughton. 12 Nov. 2006. Television.
Davies, Russell T, and James Moran. "Day Three." *Torchwood: Children of Earth*. BBC. Dir. Euros Lyn. 8 July 2009. Television.
Davies, Russell T, and Terry Nation. "Journey's End." *Doctor Who*. BBC. Dir. Graeme Harper. 5 July 2008. Television.
Davies, Russell T, and Gareth Roberts. *Planet of the Dead*. *Doctor Who*. BBC. Dir. James Strong. 26 July 2009. Television.
_____. "The Wedding of Sarah Jane Smith, Part 1." *The Sarah Jane Adventures*. CBBC. Dir. Joss Agnew. 29 Oct. 2009. Television.
_____. "The Wedding of Sarah Jane Smith, Part 2." *The Sarah Jane Adventures*. CBBC. Dir. Joss Agnew. 30 Oct. 2009. Television.
Davies, Russell T, and Catherine Tregenna. "Adam." *Torchwood*. BBC. Dir. Andy Goddard. 13 Feb. 2008. Television.
_____. "Captain Jack Harkness." *Torchwood*. BBC. Dir. Ashley Way. 1 Jan. 2007. Television.
Dawtry, Adam. "Yates to Direct Bigscreen 'Doctor Who.'" *Variety*. 14 Nov. 2011. Web. 14 Nov. 2011. <http://www.variety.com/article/VR1118046098>
Dickson, E Jane. "The New Face of David Tennant." *Radio Times*. Web. 19 Dec. 2009– 1 Jan. 2010. 27–28. Web. 5 May 2012. <http://www.team-tennant.com/interview/id174.html>
Digital Spy. "David Tennant's Advice to The Doctor's New Companion: 'Watch Your Back.'" 12 Mar. 2012. Video. 27 Mar. 2012.
Dobson, Nichola. "The Regeneration of Doctor Who: The Ninth Doctor and the Influence of the Slayer." Flow. 28 Apr. 2006. Web. 27 Mar. 2012. <http://flowtv.org/2006/04/doctor-who-buffy-the-vampire-slayer-british-tv/>
"Doctor Who Insider Magazine — Further Details." Doctor Who Online. 5 Feb. 2011. Web. 27 Feb. 2011. <http://news.drwho-online.co.uk/Doctor-Who-Insider-Magazine-Further-Details.aspx>
"Doctor Who Joins Top Hollywood TV Spinoffs." *The Telegraph*. 15 Nov. 2011. Web. 15 Nov. 2011. <http://www.telegraph.co.uk/culture/tvandradio/doctor-who/8890925/Doctor-Who-joins-top-Hollywood-TV-spin-offs.html>
Doctor Who Official Convention. FAQs. 11 Nov. 2011. Web. 11 Nov. 2011. <http://dwconvention.com/faqs>
"Doctor Who's Day Roundup: Matt Smith Chats Scream Awards on 'Craig Ferguson.'" BBCAmerica.com. 18 Oct. 2011. Web. 5 May 2012. <http://www.bbcamerica.com/anglophenia/2011/10/doctor-whos-day-roundup-matt-smith-chats-scream-awards-on-craig-ferguson-video/>
DoctorWhoTV forum. Official Doctor Who Convention 2012. 11 Nov. 2011. Web. 11 Nov. 2011. <http://doctorwhotv.co.uk/official-doctor-who-convention-2012-28076.htm#disqus_thread>
DragonCon. Past Guest List. Web. <http://www.dragoncon.org/dc_past_guests.php>
Droese, Jim. Wizard World. Chicago, IL. 12 Aug. 2012. Interview.
DrWhoGuide. "Doctor Who Books Checklist." DrWhoGuide.com. Web. <http://www.drwhoguide.com/books.htm>
Duralde, Alonso. "John Barrowman Talks Marriage, 'Miracle Day,' and Going Kilt Com-

mando." AfterElton.com. 27 June 2011. Web. 27 June 2011. <http://www.afterelton.com/people/2011/06/interview-with-john-barrowman-torchwood-miracle-day>
DW_Experience. Twitter. 11 Nov. 2011. Web. 11 Nov. 2011.
Egan, Doris, and Russell T Davies. "Rendition." *Torchwood: Miracle Day*. BBC/Starz. Dir. Bill Gierhart. 15 July 2011. Television.
Espenson, Jane. 23 May 2011. Web. 23 May 2011. <http://twitter.com/#!/janeespenson>
_____, and Russell T Davies. "Bloodline." *Torchwood: Miracle Day*. Dir. Bill Gierhart. BBC/Starz. 9 Sep. 2011. Television.
_____. "Dead of Night." *Torchwood: Miracle Day*. BBC/Starz. Dir. Bill Gierhart. 22 July 2011. Television.
f!5h f!ng£r$ & cu$t@rd. "Doctor Who Insider Magazine Cancelled." The Doctor Who Site. 27 Jan. 2012. Web. 5 May 2012. Forum post. <http://merchandise.thedoctorwhosite.co.uk /doctor-who-insider-magazine-cancelled/>
Ferguson, Acquanetta. "Torchwood: Miracle Day: Eve Myles to UK Fans: 'Please hold on tight.'" *The Examiner*. 30 June 2011. Web. 30 June 2011. <http://www.examiner.com/torchwood-in-national/torchwood-miracle-day-eve-myles-to-uk-fans-please-hold-on-tight>
Firesnap. "Torchwood: Red Skies Review." 4 May 2012. Blog. <http://firesnap.livejournal.com/ 122233.html>
Ford, Phil. *Torchwood: The Dead Line*. BBC Radio. Dir. Kate McAll. 3 July 2009. Radio.
Foster, Chuck. "Doctor Who Insider Ceases Publication." Doctor Who News. 27 Jan. 2012. Web. 27 Jan. 2012. <http://www.doctorwhonews.net/2012/01/dwn260112 210008-doctor-who-insider.html>
_____. "Torchwood: Week Three Filming." Doctor Who News. 30 Jan. 2011. Web. 11 Mar. 2012. <http://www.doctorwhonews.net/2011/01/dwn3001112330-torchwood-week-three.html>
Franks, Dana. "Talking Telly: Dear Torchwood Fans, Give the New Series a Chance." Anglotopia. 8 Jan. 2011. Web. 8 Jan. 2011. <http://www.anglotopia.net/brit-tv/bbc/talking-telly-dear-torchwood-fans-give-the-new-series-a-chance-spoilers/>
Frost, Vicky. "Interview: Russell T Davies." *The Guardian*. 26 June 2011. Web. 26 June 2011. <http://www.guardian.co.uk/media/2011/jun/26/interview-russell-t-davies>
Gallifrey One. First-timer session. 17 Feb. 2012. Los Angeles. Recording.
_____. Hotel reservation notification. 2 May 2012. Email.
Gallifrey One's Network 23. Web. <http://www.gallifreyone.com/>
Golder, Dave. "Official BBC Doctor Who Convention Announced." *SFX*. 11 Nov. 2011. Web. 11 Nov. 2011. <http://www.sfx.co.uk/2011/11/11/official-bbc-doctor-who-convention-announced/>
_____. "Why Doctor Who's Falling Overnight Ratings are a Good Thing." *SFX*. 3 May 2011. Web. 3 May 2011. <http://www.sfx.co.uk/2011/05/03/pure-golder-why-doctor-who%E2%80%99s-falling-overnight-ratings-are-a-good-thing/>
Goss, James. *Torchwood: Almost Perfect*. London: Random House UK, 2008. Print.
_____. *Torchwood: The Lost Files. The House of the Dead*. BBC Radio 4. Dir. Kate McAll. 13 July 2011. Radio.
Gray, Ellen. "Some of Your Favorites May End up on Pay Channels." *The Inquirer*. Philly.com. 7 July 2011. Web. 7 July 2011. <http://articles.philly.com/2011-07-07/entertainment/29747341_1_starz-torchwood-eve-myles>
Hale-Stern, Kaila. "Benedict Cumberbatch and Steven Moffat Share Secrets of *Sherlock* Season 2!" io9. 4 May 2012. Web. 5 May 2012. <http://io9.com/5907824/benedict-cumberbatch-and-steven-moffat-share-secrets-of-sherlock-season-2>
Hanhart, Gillian. London. 2 June 2011. Interview.
Hardbarger, Bryan. "'Torchwood'—A Chance for Fans to Speak Out About a Possible Return." Sciencefiction.com. 29 Mar. 2012. Web. 29 Mar. 2012. <http://sciencefic

tion.com/ 2012/03/29/torchwood-a-chance-for-fans-to-speak-out-about-a-possible-return/>

Hibberd, James. "'Torchwood' Scoop: How Starz Handles Capt. Jack's Sexuality." *Entertainment Weekly*. 27 May 2011. Web. 27 May 2011. <http://insidetv.ew.com/2011/05/27/torchwood-captain-jack/>

Hills, Matt. *Triumph of a Time Lord: Regenerating* Doctor Who *in the 21st Century*. London: I.B. Tauris, 2010. Print.

Hinman, Michael. "Starz Leaves Door Open for 'Torchwood' Return." Airlock Alpha. 28 Mar. 2012. Web. 29 Mar. 2012. <http://www.airlockalpha.com/node/9032/starz-leaves-door-open-for-torchwood-return.html>

Hoscik, Martin. "Meet Doctor Who? That'll Be £120." SeenIt. Blog. 11 Nov. 2011. Web. 11 Nov. 2011. <http://www.seenit.co.uk/meet-doctor-who-thatll-be-120/1116327/>

Humphries, Mark. Gallifrey Base forum. Official BBC Doctor Who Convention 24th–25th March 2012. 11 Nov. 2011. Web. 11 Nov. 2011. <http://gallifreybase.com/forum/showthread.php?t=127912>

James. MIBTV Blog. "Interview: John Barrowman & Bill Pullman on Torchwood: Miracle Day." Video interview. 6 Apr. 2011. Web. 8 Apr. 2011. <http://blog.mipworld.com/2011/04/interview-john-barrowman-bill-pullman-on-torchwood-miracle-day/>

Jeffery, Morgan. "'Doctor Who': Jenna-Louise Coleman — The Press Conference in Full." Digital Spy. 12 Mar. 2012. Web. 27 Mar. 2012. <http://www.digitalspy.com/british-tv/s7/doctor-who/news/a372323/doctor-who-jenna-louise-coleman-the-press-conference-in-full.html>

_____. "John Barrowman: 'New Torchwood Worth Paying For.'" Digital Spy. 7 July 2011. Web. 7 July 2011. <http://www.digitalspy.com/tv/s8/torchwood/news/ a328744/john-barrowman-new-torchwood-worth-paying-for.html>

"Jenna-Louise Coleman: Titanic Role has Prepared Me for 'Doctor Who.'" Metro. 27 Mar. 2012. Web. 27 Mar. 2012. <http://www.metro.co.uk/tv/894345-jenna-louise-coleman-titanic-role-has-prepared-me-for-doctor-who>

Jensen, Michael. "Torchwood Casting One Night Stand for Captain Jack." AfterElton. 12 Dec. 2010. Web. 12 Dec. 2010. <http://www.afterelton.com/TV/2010/12/torchwood-casting-captain-jack-john-barrowman>

Jones, Paul. "Steven Moffat: The Companion is the Main Character in Doctor Who, not the Doctor." *Radio Times*. 19 Apr. 2012. Web. 1 May 2012. <http://www.radiotimes.com/ news/2012-04-19/steven-moffat-the-companion-is-the-main-character-in-doctor-who,-not-the-doctor>

Kasperowicz, Leslie. "Russell T Davies Bringing Gay Men Back to Showtime?" CinemaBlend.com. 7 July 2011. Web. 7 July 2011. <http://www.cinemablend.com/television/Russell-T-Davies-Bringing-Gay-Men-Back-Showtime-33321.html>

Kay, Janice. "New Details on John Barrowman's 'Torchwood' Novel." ScienceFiction.com. 2 May 2012. Web. 8 May 2012. <http://sciencefiction.com/2012/05/02/new-details-on-john-barrowmans-torchwood-novel/>

Kelley, Jennifer Adams. 13 Apr. 2012. Email.

Kennedy, Ed. "Weekend Meme: John Barrowman's Twitter Scavenger Hunt, 'Wilfred' Gets Renewed, and John Krasinski in a Bikini." After Elton.com. 7 Aug. 2011. Web. 7 Aug. 2011. <http://www.afterelton.com/meme-08–06–2011?page=0,1>

Kiernan, Jim. "Captain Jack Discusses 'Housewives' and New U.S. 'Torchwood.'" AccessHollywood. 7 Apr. 2010. Web. 7 Apr. 2010. <http://www.accesshollywood.com/torchwood/john-barrowman-discusses-housewives-and-possible-new-us-version-of-torchwood_article_30935>

Knight, Dominic. "No More Doctor Who Spinoffs Planned." ATV Today. 26 Mar. 2012. Web. 27 Mar. 2012. <http://www.atvtoday.co.uk/index.php?option= com_content&

view=article&id=4203:no-more-doctor-who-spin-offs-planned&catid=2:cult-sci-fi&Itemid=5>
Laight, Rupert. *Torchwood: The Lost Files. The Devil and Miss Carew*. BBC Radio 4. Dir. Kate McAll. 11 July 2011. Radio.
Levine, Stuart. "'Torchwood' Bow Draws 1.5 Million." *Variety*. 11 July 2011. Web. 11 July 2011. <http://www.variety.com/article/VR1118039702>
Lewin, Russell. "*The Sarah Jane Adventures*." *SFX*. Doctor Who the Fanzine. Spring 2012: 108–111. Print.
Lloyd, Robert. "Timeout with Doctor Who's David Tennant." 19 Dec. 2009. Web. 5 May 2012. <http://articles.latimes.com/2009/dec/19/entertainment/la-et-david-tennant19-2009dec19>
Martin, Will. "Eve Myles (Torchwood) Interview." 26 Jan. 2012. Web. 10 Mar. 2012. <http://www.cultbox.co.uk/interviews/exclusives/2870-eve-myles-torchwood-interview>
McAlpine, Fraser. "20 Stars of 'Doctor Who' on Twitter." Anglophenia. BBC America. 8 Feb. 2012. Web. 11 Mar. 2012. <http://www.bbcamerica.com/anglophenia/2012/02/20-stars-of-doctor-who-on-twitter/>
McCabe, Joanne. "Doctor Who Confidential Axed from BBC Three by Budget-cutting BBC." Metro. 28 Sept. 2011. Web. 11 Mar. 2012. <http://www.metro.co.uk/tv/876897-doctor-who-confidential-axed-by-budget-cutting-bbc>
McGann Is the Doctor. "**Doctor Who Insider Magazine Cancelled.**" The Doctor Who Site. 8 Feb. 2012. Web. 5 May 2012. Forum post. <http://merchandise.thedoctorwhosite.co.uk/ doctor-who-insider-magazine-cancelled/>
McLean, Craig. "Captain America." *Radio Times*. 9–15 July 2011, p. 18. Print.
Mels. "**Doctor Who Insider Magazine Cancelled.**" The Doctor Who Site. 30 Jan. 2012. Web. 5 May 2012. Forum post. <http://merchandise.thedoctorwhosite.co.uk/doctor-who-insider-magazine-cancelled/>
"*Merlin*: Cancelled by NBC but Season Two is Still Coming to U.S." TV Series Finale. 27 Jan. 2010. Web. 8 Apr 2012. <http://tvseriesfinale.com/tv-show/merlin-cancelled-season-two-coming/>
Millard, Rosie. "Best Job in the Universe." *Radio Times*. June 4–20, 2011, p. 17. Print.
Minchin, Brian. "Fated to Pretend." *Torchwood Comic #2*. Artist Steve Yeowell. Sept. 2010. Print.
MinkyKnights. Gallifrey Base forum. Official BBC Doctor Who Convention 24th–25th March 2012. 11 Nov. 2011. Web. 11 Nov. 2011. <http://gallifreybase.com/forum/showthread.php?t=127912>
Mr. BHT of Rassilon. Gallifrey Base forum. Official BBC Doctor Who Convention 24th–25th March 2012. 11 Nov. 2011. Web. 11 Nov. 2011. <http://gallifreybase.com/forum/showthread.php?t=127912>
Moffat, Steven. "The Beast Below." *Doctor Who*. BBC. Dir. Andrew Gunn. 10 Apr. 2012. Television.
_____. "The Doctor Dances." *Doctor Who*. BBC. Dir. James Hawes. 12 May 2006. Television.
_____. "The Empty Child." *Doctor Who*. BBC. Dir. James Hawes. 21 May 2005. Television.
Moran, James. Twitter. 14 July 2011.
_____. "Virus." *Torchwood: Consequences*. London: Random House UK, 2010. Print.
Morethanatimelord of Rassilon. Gallifrey Base forum. Official BBC Doctor Who Convention 24th–25th March 2012. 11 Nov. 2011. Web. 11 Nov. 2011. <http://gallifreybase.com/forum/showthread.php?t=127912>
Mutster101. "Torchwood: Fandom of Earth." The Annals of Fuckwittage. 13 July 2009. Web. 13 July 2009. <http://mutster101.livejournal.com/448886.html>

Naughton, John. "Is There Life After Doctor Who?" *Radio Times*. 9–15 Oct. 2010. Print. 16–17, 19.
"New Torchwood Series Shows Off Swansea and Gower." VisitSwanseaBay.com. 2 Mar. 2011. Web. 2 Mar. 2011. <http://visitswanseabay.com/index.cfm?articleid=42610>
"The New World: Canadian Ratings." Doctor Who News. 12 July 2011. Web. 12 July 2011. <http://www.doctorwhonews.net/2011/07/new-world-canadian-ratings.html>
Newman, Kim. *Doctor Who. BFI TV Classics series*. London: British Film Institute, 2005. Print.
Nishi, Dennis. "John Barrowman Promises New 'Torchwood' Will Still Have Plenty of 'Man-Love.'" *The Wall Street Journal*. 21 June 2011. Web. 21 June 2011. <http://blogs.wsj.com/speakeasy/2011/06/21/john-barrowman-promises-new-torchwood-will-still-have-plenty-of-man-love/>
"No One Gets You Closer." Doctor Who Official Convention. 11 Nov. 2011. Web. 11 Nov. 2011. <http://dwconvention.com/>
Owen, Kai. Wizard World. Chicago, IL. 6 Aug. 2011. Interview.
Paddon, Ben. "On Death, Television, and Ianto Jones." 27 Feb. 2011. Web. 27 Feb. 2–11. <http://www.benpaddon.com/tag/torchwood/>
Pascoe, Thomas. "Can the Very British Doctor Who Become a Hollywood Blockbuster?" *Wales Online*. 19 Nov. 2011. Web. 19 Nov. 2011. <http://www.walesonline.co.uk/news/need-to-read/2011/11/19/can-the-very-british-doctor-who-become-a-hollywood-blockbuster-91466-29805477/>
PBS. "A Look at the Sherlock New York Event." 2 May 2012. Web. 5 May 2012. <http://video.pbs.org/video/2230755130/>
Peat, Calvin. "Wizards vs Aliens Starts Filming." Shadowlocked. 2 Apr. 2012. Web. 8 Apr. 2012. <http://www.shadowlocked.com/201204022490/news/wizards-vs-aliens-starts-filming.html>
Porter, Lynnette. "Doctor Who and the Cultural Divide: Fandom in America." 20 Jan. 2011. Web. 20 Jan. 2011. <http://www.popmatters.com/pm/feature/135627-doctor-who-and-the-cultural-divide-fandom-in-america>
_____. "Yet Another British Invasion: Doctor Who in America." PopMatters. 13 Jan. 2011. Web. 13 Jan. 2011. <http://www.popmatters.com/pm/feature/135580-yet-another-british-invasion-doctor-who-in-america>
Potter, Alison. "Doctor Who's Steven Moffat: 'The Companion is the Main Character.'" Entertainmentwise.com. 20 Apr. 2012. Web. 4 May 2012. <http://www.entertainmentwise.com/news/73998/Doctor-Whos-Steven-Moffat-The-Companion-Is-The-Main-Character>
"Premiere of *Torchwood: Miracle Day* Smashes Series Record on Space and Space HD." Channel Canada. 11 July 2011. Web. 11 July 2011. <http://www.channelcanada.com/Article5858.html>
Radio Free Skaro. "Radio Free Skaro #280—The Devil in the Dark." Podcast. 13 Nov. 2011. Web. 13 Nov. 2011. <http://www.radiofreeskaro.com/>
Radio Times. Television listings. 21 Nov. 1963. 7. Print.
Roberts, Gareth. *Doctor Who: Only Human*. London: BBC Books, 2006. Print.
_____. "The Man Who Never Was." *The Sarah Jane Adventures*. CBBC. Dir. Joss Agnew. 18 Oct. 2011. Television.
Roco. "John Barrowman Issues Series 5 Update." Seriable. 5 Nov. 2011. Web. 11 Nov. 2011. <http://seriable.com/torchwood-john-barrowman-issues-series-5-update/>
Russell, Gary. "Elisabeth Sladen." *Doctor Who Magazine*. Holiday Special, 1991: 10–17, 51. Print.
_____, and Phil Ford. Gallifrey One: Network 23 Convention. Recording. 18 Feb. 2012. Los Angeles, CA.
"Russell T Davies Announces New Show 'Aliens vs Wizards' for CBBC." *NME*. 23 Jan.

2012. Web. 23 Jan. 2012. <http://www.nme.com/filmandtv/news/russell-t-davies-announces-new-show-aliens-vs-wizards/258039>

Ryan, Maureen. "Exclusive First Look: Captain Jack's 'Torchwood: Miracle Day' Makeover." AOL TV. 25 May 2011. Web. 25 May 2011. <http://www.aoltv.com/2011/05/25/captain-jack-torchwood-miracle-day-ma/>

Ryan, Tim. "New Series Gives Hawaii 3 TV Shows in Production." *Honolulu Star Bulletin.* 17 May 2004. Web. 27 Feb. 2012. <http://archives.starbulletin.com/2004/05/17/news/story7.html>

Schwarze, Kelly. "The Nerdist Hops the Airwaves to BBC America." GeekSugar. 21 Sept. 2011. Web. 5 May 2012. <http://www.geeksugar.com/Nerdist-BBC-Craig-Ferguson-Matt-Smith-19150874>

Scott, Darren. "Mad Man with a Box." *Doctor Who Insider,* 1 (May 2011), 6–11. Print.

Scott, Ryan. *Torchwood: The Lost Files. Submission.* BBC Radio 4. Dir. Kate McAll. 12 July 2011. Television.

Seitz, Mark Zoller. "The Problem of American Remakes of British Shows." *Salon.* 9 Feb. 2012. Web. 9 Feb. 2012. <http://www.salon.com/2011/02/09/prime_suspect_remake/>

SFX Weekender Boarding Pass. Web. <https://www.sfxweekender.com/tickets/>

Shearman, Robert, and Terry Nation. "Dalek." *Doctor Who.* BBC. Dir. Joe Ahearne. 14 Apr. 2006. Television.

"Sherlock Wins South Bank Sky Award for TV Drama." YouTube. 1 May 2012. Web. 5 May 2012. <http://www.youtube.com/watch?v=OS8IW0cqLSc>

63rd Primetime Emmy Awards. Fox. 18 Sept. 2011. Television.

Sladen, Elisabeth. *Elisabeth Sladen: The Autobiography.* London: Aurum, 2011.

Smith, John. "Doctor Who: Report from The Official Doctor Who Convention in Cardiff." 24 Mar. 2012. Web. 24 Mar. 2012. <http://www.anglotopia.net/doctor-who/doctor-who-report-from-the-official-doctor-convention-in-cardiff/>

Starz. *Torchwood.* Facebook page. Web. <https://www.facebook.com/torchwood.starz>

_____. Torchwood: The New World Character Descriptions. July 2010. Web. 21 July 2010. <http://www.starz.com/pressroomstatic/tcasummer2010/pdf/CHARACTER%20DESCRIPTIONS_TORCHWOOD%20The%20New%20World_August2010.pdf>

Swan, Lewis. Brit Movie Tours. 27 May 2011. Email.

Sweeney, Mark. "Virgin Media Pulls 'Doctor Who' Advert." *The Guardian.* 17 Apr. 2012. Web. 17 Apr. 2012. <http://www.guardian.co.uk/media/2012/apr/17/virgin-media-pulls-david-tennant-ads>

Thomas, Helen. Brit Movie Tours. 29 May 2011. Email.

Torch_wood Live Journal community. <http://torch-wood.livejournal.com/6958774.html>

Torchwood: Miracle Day. Gallifrey One. Los Angeles, CA. 17 Feb. 2012. Recording.

"Torchwood: Miracle Day Opener Ratings." Doctor Who TV. 15 July 2011. Web. 10 Mar. 2012. <http://doctorwhotv.co.uk/torchwood-miracle-day-opener-ratings-22722.htm>

"Torchwood: Web of Lies Part 1." Doctor Who News Page. 7 July 2011. Web. 7 July 2011. <http://www.doctorwhonews.net/2011/07/dwn070711195116-torchwood-web-of-lies.html>

"Torchwood: Week Three Filming." Doctor Who News. 30 Jan. 2011. Web. 11 Mar. 2012. <http://www.doctorwhonews.net/2011/01/dwn3001112330-torchwood-week-three.html>

"Torchwood Budget Triples for America." *SFX.* 5 Apr. 2011. Web. 6 Apr. 2011. <http://www.sfx.co.uk/2011/04/05/torchwood-budget-triples-for-america/>

"Torchwood Writer Russell T Davies on New Thriller." BBC News. 2 Feb. 2011. Web. 2 Feb. 2011. <http://www.bbc.co.uk/news/uk-wales-12338396>

Torchwood_Three Live Journal community. <http://torchwood-three.livejournal.com/>

Turner, Robin. "Dramatic Torchwood Scenes Filmed in Wales." *Wales Online*. 2 Feb. 2011. Web. 2 Feb. 2011. <http://www.walesonline.co.uk/news/wales-news/2011/02/02/dramatic-torchwood-scenes-filmed-in-wales-91466-28098239/http://www.walesonline.co.uk/news/wales-news/2011/02/02/dramatic-torchwood-scenes-filmed-in-wales-91466-28098239/>

_____. "Torchwood Touches Down in Gower." *Wales Online*. 30 Jan. 2011. Web. 1 Feb. 2011. <http://www.walesonline.co.uk/showbiz-and-lifestyle/showbiz/2011/01/30/torchwood-touches-down-on-gower-91466-28079797/>

tw_classic Live Journal community. <http://tw-classic.livejournal.com/149548.html>

Verhoeven, Paul. "Jenna-Louise Coleman is the Newest Doctor Who Companion." The Vine. 27 Mar. 2012. Web. 27 Mar. 2012. <http://www.thevine.com.au/entertainment/tv/jenna_louise-coleman-is-the-newest-doctor-who-companion!20120327.aspx>

Vieira, Meredith. *Today*. NBC. 9 May 2011. Television.

Walker, Kirsty. "Torchwood: Children of Earth: The Aftermath." End of Show. 12 July 2009. Web. 12 July 2009. <http://www.endofshow.com/2009/07/12/torchwood-childrenof-earth-the-aftermath/>

Web of Lies. Forum. Web. <http://www.torchwoodforum.com/showthread.php?15659-Torchwood-Web-of-Lies-question>

Westbrook, Logan. "*Doctor Who* Ratings Rise in U.S., Fall in U.K." The Escapist. 26 Apr. 2011. Web. 11 Mar. 2012. <http://www.escapistmagazine.com/news/view/109547-Doctor-Who-Ratings-Rise-in-the-US-Fall-in-the-UK>

Whithouse, Toby, and Bob Baker. "School Reunion." *Doctor Who*. BBC. Dir. James Hawes. 13 Oct. 2006. Television.

Wicks, Kevin. "'Today Host Meredith Vieira Visits Set of 'Doctor Who.'" Anglophenia. BBC America. 9 May 2011. Web. 10 May 2011. <http://blogs.bbcamerica.com/anglophenia/ 2011/05/09/watch-today-co-anchor-meredith-vieira-visits-set-of-doctor-who/>

Wilkes, Neil. "Gareth David-Lloyd Talks 'Torchwood' Exit." Digital Spy. 17 July 2009. Web. 17 July 2009. <http://www.digitalspy.com/british-tv/s8/torchwood/tubetalk/a165637/gareth-david-lloyd-talks-torchwood>

Wizards Vs Aliens blog. 8 Apr. 2012. Web. <http://aliensvswizards.blogspot.com/>

Zalben, Alex. "Doctor Who Recap: 'The Doctor's Wife.'" MTV Geek. 16 May 2011. Web. 11 Mar. 2012. <http://geek-news.mtv.com/2011/05/16/doctor-who-recap-the-doctors-wife/>

Index

ABC 38, 45
The Abominable Snowman 79
Ace 86
action figures 34, 56, 78, 124
advance screenings 18, 19, 49, 70, 109, 162
advertisements 5, 13, 22, 24, 39, 40, 49, 69, 70, 140
Agyeman, Freema 80
Ainsworth, John 11, 12
Almeria 43
Almost Perfect 107
American Idol 43
American influence 31, 50, 55, 60, 166, 167, 169, 171, 173
American personality 1, 31, 86
American West 25, 75, 169, 170
Americanization 28, 35, 36, 43, 51, 59–78, 114, 173
Angel 124
Army of One 57
astronaut 25, 75; *see also* Doctor Who, "The Impossible Astronaut"
Atlanta 70, 149
audio stories 9, 82, 88, 116, 117, 125
audiobook 20, 34, 56, 85
AudioGo 116
Australia 13, 31, 32, 33, 37, 56, 74, 134, 164

Baker, Tom 28, 120, 127, 176
Barker, Gavin 136
Barrowman, Carole 134–135
Barrowman, John 3, 4, 5, 47, 48, 52, 55, 56, 57, 61, 64, 65, 66, 67, 70, 74, 90, 92, 93, 95, 98, 102, 109, 113, 114, 132, 134, 135, 136–137, 138, 139, 141, 146, 154
Barrowman, Trevor 134
Battlestar Galactica 81, 109
BBC 2, 5, 6, 9, 14, 15, 20, 21, 22, 23, 24, 25, 32, 36, 37, 38, 39, 40, 61, 62, 64, 65, 66, 68, 69, 71, 74, 75, 76, 77, 78, 79, 80, 81, 82, 93, 96, 98, 105, 107, 113, 115, 116, 122, 123, 124, 125, 129, 130, 134, 135, 137, 139, 142, 143, 144, 145, 146, 151, 164, 167, 173, 175, 177;

Official Doctor Who Convention 152–163; partnership with HBO and VRT 3, 166; partnership with Starz 3, 4, 43, 46–49, 52–58, 63, 70, 83, 84, 85, 114, 133, 140, 176; programming supply and demand 41–45
BBC America 9, 12, 14, 18, 20, 32, 36, 40, 64, 75, 77, 85, 122, 130, 133, 134, 150, 162, 164, 167, 170, 171, 172; marketing strategies 3, 11, 39; programming 2, 16, 23–24, 38, 41; ratings 37–38; shop 11
BBC Books 78, 79, 84
BBC Radio 55, 78, 82, 84, 85, 108, 118, 146
BBC Wales 10, 18, 39–40, 44, 146, 148, 166
BBC Worldwide 6, 12, 13, 36, 49, 52, 60, 75, 152, 153, 155, 156, 160, 166, 167, 169, 172, 173, 175, 176; marketing strategies 3, 11, 37–40, 41, 45, 81, 133, 163, 171; production 2, 42–43, 58
Beach, Andrew 3
beauty 60, 65–66
Bedlam 2, 38, 77
Being Human 2, 38, 61, 77
Bewitched 176
Big Ben 68
Big Finish 9, 79, 81, 88, 124, 125, 126, 165
billboards 6, 39, 40, 49, 69, 71
bisexuality 66, 106
Blackpool 127
Blessing 100, 110, 111–112
Boeshane Peninsula 72
Bond, James 27
Boston 61, 70
brand 20, 37, 78, 81, 108–109, 145, 147
Branson, Richard 21–22
Brigadier *see* Stewart, Brigadier Lethbridge
Brit Movie Tours 26, 166
British Broadcasting Corporation *see* BBC
British Film Institute 49, 70, 165
British Idol 43
"Broken" 108
budget 13, 18, 35, 41, 43–44, 48, 49, 53, 57, 58, 59, 62, 63, 74, 81, 151, 161
Buffy the Vampire Slayer 124

189

Cabin Pressure 55
California 5, 59, 60, 64, 141, 142
California Film Commission 64
Camelot 53
Canada 11, 29, 30, 32, 33, 54, 58, 164
Cannes 49, 63, 71, 92, 145
canon 55, 71–72, 79, 84–85, 90, 92, 93, 94, 96, 97, 98, 100, 101, 102, 103, 105, 106, 107, 108, 117, 118, 165, 175
Cardiff 2, 18, 26, 31, 39, 44, 46, 47, 48, 50, 51, 52, 55, 57, 64, 68, 69, 80, 104, 116, 118, 152–153, 154–155, 156, 157, 158, 173
Cardiff Bay 44, 46, 47
Carter, Stephen 99, 117
casting 3, 47, 49, 61, 70, 95, 132, 171, 175
CBBC 23, 123, 129, 131, 168
CBC 54
CBS 38, 174
Central Park 19, 170
Character Options 124
Chicago 27, 70, 127, 148, 149, 150, 151, 153, 154, 163
Chicago TARDIS 150, 151, 153, 154, 163
Children in Need special 80, 120
Children of Earth 3, 42, 43, 46, 47, 49, 50, 51, 52, 53, 54, 55, 56, 57, 63, 64, 68, 74, 83, 85, 90, 91, 92, 93, 94, 96, 97, 98, 99, 100, 101, 102–104, 105, 106, 107, 108, 111, 114, 115, 134, 137, 138, 146, 147, 168, 175; *see also Torchwood*
Christie, Agatha 20, 164
Christmas episodes 6, 37, 168, 172; *see also Doctor Who*
The Christmas Invasion 166
Churchill, Winston 86
CIA 57, 72, 73, 110
cinematic tourism 26
Clarke, Noel 132
Coal Exchange 48
Coburn, Anthony 164
Cocoa Beach 25
Colasanto, Angelo 91
Coleman, Jenna-Louise 168, 171–172
comic books 11, 30, 78, 79, 82
Comic-Con *see* San Diego Comic-Con
commercials 21–22, 23–24, 60, 159
companions 14, 15, 16, 18, 38, 40, 76, 79, 80, 82, 86–87, 93, 99, 106, 111, 112, 119, 125, 126, 127, 128–129, 154, 162, 165, 168, 171; *see also* names of individual companions (e.g., Pond, Amy; Smith, Sarah Jane)
complaints 16, 23, 32, 88, 109, 142–143, 154–155, 158, 167, 175
Consequences 106–107, 138
conventions 5, 9–10, 19, 26–27, 31–32, 34, 40, 56, 75, 81, 88, 114, 119, 123, 125, 127–128, 138, 141, 148–163, 172
convertible 25, 86, 170
Cooper, Gwen 3, 46, 47, 49, 50, 51, 57, 61, 65, 67, 68–69, 72, 84, 93, 94, 95, 96, 97, 98, 99, 101, 103, 106–107, 108, 109, 110, 111, 116, 135
Cooper, Jarrod 149, 151
cosplay 34, 80, 82, 150, 170
Costello, Suzie 57
costumes 34, 148, 161
Courtney, Nicholas 6
Creation Entertainment 148, 155
CSI 111, 136
CTV 54
Cucumber 4, 169
Cumberbatch, Benedict 3, 55
Cushing, Peter 168, 175

daffodil 69
Daleks 1, 85–86, 161, 165, 175
Dancing with the Stars 2, 6, 38, 43
Danes, Oswald 5, 100, 102
Darksmith Legacy 79
Darvill, Arthur 18, 19, 132, 153, 154, 161, 162
David-Lloyd, Gareth 47, 55, 115, 138, 146, 149
Davidson, Andy 46, 48, 57, 69, 116, 137
Davies, Russell T 2–4, 5, 20, 24, 42, 47–49, 50, 52–53, 56–58, 61, 62–63, 65–66, 68, 69, 70, 72, 74, 76, 81, 90, 92, 93, 94, 95, 96, 98, 99, 100, 102, 103, 108, 113, 116, 120, 129, 130–131, 146, 165, 166, 168–169, 173, 175, 176
Davison, Peter 149
The Dead Line 96, 98, 107
de Lancie, John 70
Denver 64
de Souza, Lady Christina 87
Desperate Housewives 28
The Devil and Miss Carew 55, 97
Doctor: Eighth 9, 79, 124, 165; Eleventh 4, 11, 35, 79, 81, 85, 86, 87, 88, 113, 128, 148, 154, 177; First 11; Fourth 120, 128; Second 76; Seventh 79; Tenth 5, 79, 86, 87, 88, 90, 94, 128, 166; Third 127
Doctor Who 1–7, 9–36, 37–45, 49, 50, 53, 57, 58, 60–61, 63, 65, 71–73, 74, 75–77, 78–88, 89–90, 93, 94, 96, 99, 101, 105, 106, 108, 109, 110–111, 113–114, 115, 118, 120, 121, 122–131, 132–133, 144, 148–163, 164–177; "classic" series 9–10, 24, 75, 76, 81, 82, 85, 86, 120–121, 127, 151, 168, 169, 171, 173, 177; episodes: "Blink" 31; "Dalek" 85, 86; "Day of the Moon" 18, 44; "The Doctor Dances" 1, 83, 86, 96, 165; "The Empty Child" 1, 73; "The End of Time" 94, 120, 127; "The Five Doctors" 120, 128; "The Girl Who Waited" 43; "A Good Man Goes to War" 86; "The Hand of Fear" 120; "The Impossible Astronaut" 4, 18, 37, 43, 44, 130, 169; "Journey's End" 120, 127; "Rose" 45; "School Reunion" 31, 120, 121, 123, 125, 126, 128, 162, 166; "The Stolen Earth" 120, 127; "The Time Warrior" 120, 126; "Utopia" 99; "Vincent and the Doctor" 60; introductory narration 16–18; "new" series 9, 10, 82, 85, 87, 151

Doctor Who Confidential 44, 80, 120
Doctor Who Experience 3, 44, 80, 151–152, 156
Doctor Who Insider 11–13, 80
Doctor Who Magazine 11, 13, 30, 79, 126, 143
Doctor Who News 47
Downton Abbey 43, 164, 166, 167
DragonCon 149
Dreamland 125
Dreamwidth 39
Drummond, Esther 5, 68, 98, 110, 115, 117
Dushku, Eliza 109

Eaton, Rebecca 166–167
Eccleston, Christopher 1, 85, 165
Elementary 174
Emmerdale 172
England 33, 61, 68, 138, 174
Entertainment Weekly 18, 40, 49, 130
Espenson, Jane 5, 58, 68, 71, 72, 74–75, 99, 100, 108, 112, 132, 134, 135–136, 138, 139, 141, 142–145, 147, 173

Face of Boe 72, 101
Facebook 29, 33, 39, 51, 90, 133, 142, 144, 145, 146, 159
The Fades 2, 38, 77
fan videos 34, 82, 100, 148
fandom 7, 9–10, 11, 12–13, 21, 26, 17, 28–36, 38–39, 49, 78, 79, 94, 117, 123, 127, 128, 129–130, 131, 146–147, 148–151, 156–163, 172, 173, 177; cult 6, 10, 12, 15, 28, 31, 39, 42, 56, 78, 109, 124, 161, 164, 167, 173
fanfiction 39, 107, 117
fanon 79, 84, 100, 101
"Fated to Pretend" 108
FBI 72
Ferguson, Craig 4–5, 13–16, 17, 40
50th anniversary 6, 44, 57, 113, 114, 150, 151–152, 156, 158, 168, 169, 177
First Born 57
A Fistful of Dollars 43
Ford, Phil 4, 96, 119, 123, 128, 130, 131, 137, 139
4-5-6 91, 98, 99, 104
Four Square 133
Fox 3, 42, 45, 46, 63, 66, 165, 166, 176
Frame, Alonso 94
France 33, 40, 63
franchise 2–3, 6–7, 26, 32, 33, 35, 36, 42, 45, 46, 56, 58, 59, 61, 76, 77, 81, 82, 90, 93, 97, 105, 112, 113, 115, 118, 121, 131, 148, 149, 151, 156, 160–161, 163, 166, 167–171, 175, 176
Fright Night 20

Gallifrey 128, 173
Gallifrey Base 32, 33, 155, 159, 160
Gallifrey One 9, 10, 75, 119, 120, 123–124, 128, 148, 149–150, 153, 162, 163, 165, 174
Gardner, Julie 2, 3, 4, 20, 74, 81
Gatiss, Mark 132

Ghostbusters 70
Gill, Scott 67, 137
Gillan, Karen 4, 5, 14, 17, 18, 19, 23, 33, 38, 87, 153, 154, 161, 162, 171
Glasgow 135
Glee 66
Glue 133, 140
Gold, Murray 132
Gorman, Burn 115
Gower coast 3, 46, 48
The Graduate 25
Grant, Jo 121, 129
Guerrier, Simon 9, 10, 27, 81
guns 25, 110
Gwack 94

Hamlet 20
Hanhart, Gillian 73, 121–122, 166
Hardwicke, Chris 14
Harkness, Captain Jack 1–2, 3, 5, 7, 32, 46, 47, 50–52, 55, 57, 61, 62, 65, 66–67, 69, 71–73, 79, 82, 83, 84–85, 89–118, 125, 126, 128, 132, 135, 136, 138, 140, 142, 143, 146, 168; typical roles in stories: hero 90, 91, 93, 94, 102, 104, 105, 110, 112, 115; leader 2, 90, 91, 92, 93, 95, 101, 110, 111, 112; lover 90, 97, 101, 104, 107, 117; martyr 90, 112; redeemed 94, 100–101, 112; redeemer 94, 100–101; sacrifice 57, 90, 99–100, 101, 103, 110, 111–112; savior 90, 100, 104; sex object 90, 91–91, 94–99, 101, 105, 106, 107, 108
Harper, Owen 95, 100, 115
Harris, Neil Patrick 66
Harry Potter franchise 59, 175, 176
Hart, Captain John 66, 124
Hartnell, William 11, 164
Hartswood Films 166
Havins, Alexa 5, 98, 115
HBO 3, 53, 166
Head, Anthony 162
hero 5, 85, 87, 90–92, 93, 94, 102, 104, 105, 110, 112, 115, 129, 165–166
Heroes 109
hiatus 6, 43, 47, 50, 61, 75, 79, 81, 83, 85, 98, 120, 125, 161
Hills, Matt 9, 78
Hollywood 4, 20–21, 58, 59, 60
Holmes, Sherlock 27, 38, 174
homosexuality 66, 67, 95, 143
The House of the Dead 55, 104
The House That Jack Built 107
How to Train Your Dragon 20
Hub 51, 68
Hudson, Ernie 70
Hurricane Who 148, 149, 150, 151, 162, 163

icons 7, 12, 22, 25, 38, 46, 86, 170, 171, 173, 174
immortality 50, 57, 72, 73, 84, 89, 94, 96, 100–101, 107, 110, 111, 112, 113, 115; curse of 110, 111, 112

Independence Day 62, 70
intertextuality 7, 10, 56, 57, 78–88, 89–118, 124–125
iPlayer 37, 41, 55
iTunes 109, 139, 170

Jammie Dodgers 25
Janto 94, 96, 97, 98, 104, 105, 107, 117, 138, 146
Jones, Ianto 47, 52, 55, 67, 91, 94, 95, 96–97, 98, 99, 100, 101, 104, 106–108, 113, 115, 117, 137, 138, 146
Jones, Martha 79, 80, 87
Juarez, Vera 115

K9 and Company 6, 168
Kelley, Jennifer Adams 27, 149–150, 151
Kingston, Alex 4, 14, 39, 40
Knight, Tommy 127–128

Laight, Rupert 97
language differences (British or American English) 30, 61, 62, 63, 68, 69, 73
The Late Late Show 4, 13–15, 17, 40
Law & Order 61
Law & Order U.K. 61, 62
Leela 86
LGBTQ characters 62, 66
license fee 23, 42, 64, 84, 155
Live Journal 39, 145, 146
London 2, 21, 25, 26, 31, 42, 44, 46, 49, 50, 57, 62, 68, 70, 80, 86, 121, 155, 156, 166, 171, 173
Long Time Dead 57
The Lord of the Rings 10
Los Angeles 2, 3, 4, 14, 20, 21, 46, 47, 48, 51, 52, 55, 64, 65, 70, 75, 81, 125, 127, 134, 135, 148, 153, 154, 166, 169, 175
Los Angeles City Hall 47
LOST 56, 63, 109
The Lost Files 55, 97, 101, 108, 117

Mad Men 28
magazines 11–13, 30, 34, 78, 80, 82, 88, 90, 126, 138, 143; *see also* individual magazine titles
The Magnificent Seven 43
Manning, Katy 121, 129
marketing 2, 3, 5, 6, 7, 11, 37, 38, 39, 40, 41, 49, 70, 77, 80, 115, 132, 133, 145, 147, 155, 160, 161, 163, 171, 173, 175; *see also* BBC Worldwide
Marsters, James 66, 124
Master 101, 132, 165
Masterpiece Mystery! 166
Masterpiece Theatre 166
Matheson, Rex 5, 57, 67, 68, 70, 72, 73, 83, 84, 92, 95, 110–112, 113, 114
McCoy, Sylvester 149
McGann, Paul 13, 124, 165
The Men Who Sold the World 57

merchandise 34, 56, 78, 79, 80–81, 84, 124–126, 127, 155, 156, 159, 160, 173
Merlin 122, 123, 162
Millennium Centre 118, 153, 161
MIPTV 49, 63, 71, 92
Miracle Day 2, 3, 4, 5, 6, 32, 35, 42, 43, 46, 48, 49–52, 53–58, 61–73, 74–75, 83, 85, 90, 91–95, 98–99, 100–103, 105, 108, 109, 110–115, 117, 118, 132, 133, 134–138, 139–145, 146–147, 166, 167, 168, 169, 172, 174–176; *see also Torchwood*
Miss Marple 20
Mr. Invincible 118
Modern Family 66
Moffat, Steven 3, 16, 19, 24, 27, 35, 38, 42, 43, 50, 59, 75, 76–77, 86–87, 96, 113, 126, 129, 132, 152, 153, 156, 161, 166, 167–171, 175, 176, 177
Mokri, Holly 109
Monroe, Marilyn 86
Monument Valley 25
Moran, James 22, 98, 99, 106, 132, 136, 137–138, 139
Mori, Naoko 115, 162
Mrs. Robinson 22, 25
Much Ado About Nothing 20
Myles, Eve 3, 5, 47, 48, 49, 57, 61, 65, 70, 74, 109, 116, 149

NBC 21, 38, 39, 122, 174
NBC Universal 122
Nekross 130
The Nerdist 14
Netflix 109
The New World 3, 5; *see also Miracle Day; Torchwood*
New York 4, 18, 19, 24, 43, 62, 70, 86, 154, 169, 170
New Zealand 1, 33, 51
Nixon, Richard 25, 86
Noble, Donna 79, 87
Norton, Graham 77
novelizations 78–80, 82–83, 108, 124
novels 29, 30, 56, 57, 79, 82, 84, 85, 90, 93, 105, 106, 107, 116, 118, 138, 145, 160
nudity 66, 91

Official Doctor Who Convention 152–163
omnisexuality 67, 108
Only Human 105, 106
Orlando 3, 64, 148, 149, 162
otherness 111, 112, 174
Outcasts 77
Oval Office 25
Owen, Kai 48, 108, 127, 132, 135, 137, 139, 141, 142, 149

Panini Magazines 11, 12
Parade's End 3, 166
Paradise of Death 79

1. The Culture of Doctor Who 193

partnerships 43, 46, 52–53, 63, 70, 114, 133, 147, 176
Paul 39
PBS 9, 19, 23, 28, 32, 38, 40, 41, 42, 120, 127, 164, 166, 167, 173, 176
Pegg, Simon 39
Penguin 82, 124
Pertwee, Jon 120, 127
Peth, Astrid 87
Phifer, Mekhi 5, 65, 70, 114
Piper, Billie 87, 132, 165
Planet of the Dead 166
Poirot 164
Pond, Amy 4, 5, 14, 15, 16, 17, 22, 23, 26, 32, 38, 75, 76, 77, 79, 87, 88, 154, 169, 171, 174
Popular Culture Association 29, 130
Price, Tom 48, 132, 135, 137, 139, 141–142
Prime Suspect 164, 174
Primeval 38
proms 80
publicity 23, 33, 40, 47, 49, 50, 54, 63, 67, 70, 71, 76, 91, 94, 95, 129, 132, 142, 146, 147, 169, 171, 172
Pullman, Bill 5, 47, 65, 70

Quantum Leap 27
Queer as Folk 65, 168

Radio Free Skaro 153
radio plays 30, 55, 80, 82, 84, 85, 90, 96, 97, 98, 101, 102, 104, 117, 118, 145, 146
Radio Times 20, 21, 62, 65, 76, 164, 165
ratings 37–38, 40, 42, 44–45, 50, 52, 53–54, 55–57, 64, 75, 76, 77, 114, 122, 131, 133, 147, 167, 168, 172
Red Skies 116, 117–118
regeneration 7, 22, 76, 79, 86, 87, 88, 94, 118, 166
Rex Is Not Your Lawyer 21
Rhossili Bay 48, 64
Ritchie, Derek 131
Roald Dahl Plass 47, 68
Roker, Al 39
role model 21, 66, 106
role play 76, 80, 82, 148
Romana 86
RTS Award 129
Russell, Gary 119, 120, 123, 124, 128

San Diego Comic-Con 5, 14, 19, 33, 39, 40, 49, 139, 149, 150, 161–162
sanctioned texts 9, 12, 78, 79, 80, 82, 83, 84–85, 90, 94, 105, 106, 107, 108, 117, 118, 125
The Sarah Jane Adventures 2, 6, 23, 27, 28, 32, 33, 38, 82, 83, 97, 119–123, 127, 130–131, 151, 167, 168, 172; episodes: "Death of the Doctor" 129; "The Man Who Never Was" 119; "The Wedding of Sarah Jane Smith" 128, 129
The Sarah Jane Adventures Comic Relief Special 120

Sato, Toshiko 95, 108, 115, 162
Sci-Fi 9, 32, 38, 85, 122; *see also* Syfy
Scream Award 14
serials 75, 120, 164, 169
Severn bridge 68
Sex and the City 176
sex scenes 32, 62, 66–67, 95, 98, 99, 142, 143
SFX 44, 45, 121, 152, 155
SFX Weekender 153
Sherlock 3, 19, 38, 41, 42, 43, 55, 59, 60, 132, 156, 164, 166, 167
showrunners 2–3, 16, 19, 20, 35, 42, 48, 49, 52, 60, 62, 74, 75, 77, 81, 86, 120, 124, 126, 129, 132, 144, 149, 153, 166, 167, 169, 177; *see also* Davies, Russell T; Moffat, Steven
Showtime 4, 53, 169
Silurians 113
Simm, John 132
Single Father 21
Sladen, Elisabeth 6, 23, 24, 82, 119–131
Smith, John (BBC Worldwide) 37
Smith, Luke 112, 127, 128
Smith, Matt 4–5, 11, 12, 13–14, 15, 17, 19, 33, 38, 39, 40, 43, 76, 81, 85, 113, 129, 130, 152, 153, 154, 161, 162, 169
Smith, Mickey 132
Smith, Sarah Jane 6, 23, 82, 86, 119–131
So You Think You Can Dance 2
social media 22, 28, 32, 36, 39, 127, 132–134, 142, 144, 145, 147, 150, 167
"Somebody Else's Problem" 108
Song, River 4, 14, 22, 39, 40, 75, 88, 171
Space 11, 54, 56
space whale 174
Spain 43, 86, 169
special effects 62, 63, 64, 80, 140, 160, 161
Spike TV 14
spinoffs 2, 6, 7, 35, 46, 53, 57, 80, 82, 83, 84, 108, 109, 111, 118, 120, 122, 123, 124, 126, 127, 128, 151, 158, 160, 165, 168, 169
Star Trek 25, 27, 51, 70, 160–161
Star Wars 160–161
Starz 42, 61, 64, 65, 66, 67, 69, 71, 75, 93, 94, 95, 98, 109, 113, 115, 116, 134, 137, 139, 140–141, 143, 144, 145, 159, 166, 175; partnership with BBC 3, 4, 43, 46–49, 52–58, 63, 70, 83, 84, 85, 114, 133, 140, 176
Stewart, Brigadier Lethbridge 6
Stormageddon 88
Strictly Come Dancing 43
Submission 55, 96, 97, 101, 102
Supernatural Saturday 38, 77
surveys 28–36, 90–92, 170
Susan 86, 164
Swansea 48, 49, 70
Syfy 9, 32, 38, 61, 85, 122–123; *see also* Sci-Fi

talk shows 5, 19, 70
TARDIS 12, 16, 17, 27, 39, 40, 53, 82, 86, 96,

105, 106, 120, 124, 126, 127, 148, 149, 150, 151, 153, 154, 163, 165, 171
Target 78, 82
tea 27, 166
Tegan 86
Television Critics Association 50
Tennant, David 5, 20–22, 28, 76, 85, 120, 128, 129, 154, 165, 169, 172
Terra Nova 63
Thatcher, Margaret 86
Thomas, Helen 26–27, 166
Time Agent 1, 72, 93, 95, 112
Time Lord 1, 85, 86, 165, 166, 177
Titanic 172
Today 39–40
Tonight's the Night 55, 70, 139
Top Gear 2, 38, 39
Torchwood 2, 62, 68, 69, 73, 82, 83, 84, 85, 91, 92, 93, 95, 97, 98, 100, 110, 111, 112, 118
Torchwood 2, 3, 4, 5, 6, 7, 26, 27, 28, 29, 30, 32, 33, 34, 35, 36, 38, 40, 41, 42, 43, 46–58, 60, 62–77, 80, 83, 84–85, 89–118, 121, 122, 124, 127, 130, 131, 132, 133, 134–147, 149, 151, 153, 159, 162, 165, 166, 167, 168, 169, 172, 174, 175, 176; episodes: "Adrift" 66, 96; "Bloodline" 111, 113, 114; "Captain Jack Harkness" 108; "Day Five" 99; "Day One" 43, 68, 96, 98; "Day Three" 98, 99; "Dead of Night" 66, 95, 99; "Everything Changes" 95, 98, 103; "Exit Wounds" 43, 124; "Fragments" 124; "Immortal Sins" 66, 115, 142–144; "Kiss Kiss, Bang Bang" 66, 95, 96, 124; "The New World" 53, 54, 56, 68, 72, 98, 103, 114, 137; "Small Worlds" 108; *see also Children of Earth; Miracle Day; The New World*
Torchwood magazine 30, 90, 138
Tovey, Russell 94
trailers 5, 18, 39, 40, 49, 69, 71, 140, 145, 161, 169
transmedia 78
Tranter, Jane 52, 175, 176
Trcpic, Shawna 65
Troughton, Patrick 76, 169
Tumblr 12, 39
Tur, Arlene 115
TV Guide 5, 40, 49, 62
Twitter 12, 22–25, 29, 33, 36, 74, 75, 114, 131, 132–145, 156, 159, 176

Tyler, Jackie 27
Tyler, Rose 2, 79, 83, 85, 86, 87, 96, 105, 106, 122, 125, 132, 168, 170

UNIT 113
Upstairs, Downstairs 164
Utah 4, 18, 25, 86

Van Gogh, Vincent 174
van Statten, Henry 86
videogames 78, 160
Vieira, Meredith 39–40
Virgin Books 79
Virgin Media 21–22
"Virus" 106
The Voyage of the Damned 94
VRT 3, 166

Wales 3, 10, 18, 33, 40, 44, 47, 48, 49, 51, 57, 64, 68, 69, 70, 73, 116, 118, 122, 132, 134, 136, 137, 138, 153, 156, 158, 166, 163
wardrobe 72, 73, 95, 105; coat 65, 72, 93, 94, 106, 115; fez 5, 10, 148, 170; Stetson 5, 25, 86, 170
Washington, D.C. 25, 57, 64, 68, 69, 84, 95, 116
Washington monument 68
Web of Lies 108, 109, 110, 139, 140, 147
webisodes 78, 109
The West Wing 31
Whithouse, Toby 43
Williams, Anwen 94, 99
Williams, Rhys 46, 48, 57, 108, 135
Williams, Rory 17, 18, 76, 79, 132, 154, 162, 168, 169
Wizard World 27, 148, 150
Wizards vs. Aliens 130–131, 169
World War II 2, 72, 86, 93, 108
writers 5, 7, 9, 22, 27, 31, 58, 67, 71, 75, 79, 81, 86, 97, 108, 112, 113, 114, 119, 129, 131, 132, 134, 136, 137, 139, 142, 144, 146, 148, 152, 172, 173, 176

X Factor 2, 6, 43, 63

Yates, David 175–177
Young, Mal 81
YouTube 5, 14, 15, 19, 24, 39

www.ingramcontent.com/pod-product-compliance
Ingram Content Group UK Ltd.
Pitfield, Milton Keynes, MK11 3LW, UK
UKHW042011140426
5217IPUK00015B/1100